GROWING UP?

To Diana,

With affection,

[signature]

Aug '15

GROWING UP?
A Journey with Laughter

Patrick Casement

KARNAC

First published in 2015 by
Karnac Books Ltd
118 Finchley Road
London NW3 5HT

British Library Cataloguing in Publication Data

A C.I.P. for this book is available from the British Library

ISBN-13: 978-1-78220-315-5

Typeset by V Publishing Solutions Pvt Ltd., Chennai, India

Printed in Great Britain by TJ International Ltd, Padstow, Cornwall

www.karnacbooks.com

To Margaret

My brother is getting it all right. I am getting it all wrong.
And I'm not quite *in the frame* which became the story of my life.

CONTENTS

ACKNOWLEDGEMENTS

I particularly wish to thank my wife, Margaret, who had already put up with me writing four books and then, on top of all that, she had to put up with me writing this one as well.

I much appreciate my family for allowing me to include those episodes that involved them.

My brother Michael and his wife Christina have also been most helpful in checking the text for things needing to be corrected, and for their ongoing encouragement for me to get this book completed. Michael also contributed a further description of some incidents which involved him, that I have been keen to include here too.

I am also indebted to Doris Lomax and her daughter Laraine for permission to publish poems written by Doris.

FOREWORD

Suzie Hayman

Beginnings are always fascinating. We often want to know "What happens?"—stories are all about resolutions and solutions. But they are also about beginnings and that's the first thing children demand—where did I come from, how did I begin? You may like to know Patrick resolved into (I won't say ended up as—he's got some way to go still in his life's journey) a psychoanalyst. You'll be entirely entertained to find out how he got there, with various digressions from his own journey into those of family—his parents entertaining the Duke of Edinburgh and being guests of Mountbatten, his brother being taken under the wing of wildlife photographer Eric Hosking, his father's award of Commander of the Order of Orange Nassau, and his court martial.

Patrick's life has been full of variety. He was brought up with the story that he was so impossible as a child he drove away all the nannies employed to look after him, until at four Tucky arrived to use a strong hand until he went to boarding school. At prep school he avoided rugger by going down with flu—he remembers being so ill that while the rest of the school were sent home for Christmas early, he and another boy were kept until a few days afterwards. And, given lines as a punishment for talking in class so often, he hit on the wheeze of building up a cache, written in advance. That worked until he decided to be clever by writing out a whole sheaf of "I must not ..." to be filled in later as appropriate, and stymied by having a different pen nib to work with.

At Winchester College he sang the *Messiah* in Winchester Cathedral, when the carefully rehearsed lighting effects succeeded in fusing the entire cathedral and plunging it into darkness—no *lux aeterna* there! And he was taught to eat oysters by his tutor at Cambridge, swallowed whole and washed down with beer, "Something I managed to do on that occasion but I've never brought myself to do since." Perhaps if it had been with champagne he might have tried again ... He did National Service in the Navy, taught in a prep school, read anthropology at Cambridge (because he found it was "the study of man embracing women" and thought that sounded promising), worked as a brickie's mate as part of a course while deciding whether to be ordained or not, before training to be a probation officer. Eventually he became a case-worker for Family Welfare Association, and thence trained as a psycho-therapist and finally a psychoanalyst. We're all familiar with authors claiming to have been samurai warriors, bottle washers, and hobos on their way to writing the Great American Novel—none of them have anything on Patrick.

Once asked "What is Patrick doing now?" his mother replied "Well, I know that Patrick was a social worker. He is now working as a physi-otherapist. I now understand he is training all over again, to be a psy-chotic." Patrick thinks his mother could not get her head round those psycho words, but knowing him I'm not so sure—mothers do know more than we think. I've always known Patrick as a psych—whether o or analyst I'll reserve judgement. That might have been only a way station on the journey of his life; it's fascinating to read this book and see at least how he got there.

His memoir is full of fascinating details of a period so many people would find "another country". An earnest lecture in school on space flight that "proved" it would be impossible to fly to the moon; receiv-ing a teacher's salary of £3 10 shillings a week, with board and lodg-ing; ordering a grey suit that cost the grand sum of £30—most of a term's salary; and the time he drove his evening partner home from a formal dinner having consumed sherry, a bottle of wine, and an entire bottle of exceedingly good port. Shocking in retrospect but at the time, it was the gentlemanly thing to do. His account of the "first eighty years" is engrossing and lively. I can't wait for the next eighty …

Suzie Hayman is trustee of the charities Family Lives and The Who Cares? Trust, patron of Unique Kidz & Co, counsellor, accredited parenting practitioner, agony aunt for Woman magazine, author, and broadcaster.

INTRODUCTION

For nearly forty years I had no settled idea of what I wished to do with my life. This book is mostly an account of that journey.

Having read anthropology and theology, I worked as a bricklayer's mate before training to become a probation officer, and then a family caseworker (working in the East End of London).

I then trained again to become a psychotherapist, and subsequently undertook yet another training to become a psychoanalyst. It was only then that I began writing, having subsequently published four books on the themes of *learning from*: from the patient, from our mistakes, and from life. As that last book, from a quite different perspective, was partly autobiographical, I have chosen to include some passages from it here. This account would not be complete without them.

A major theme in this process of my eventually "growing up" was to be found in my fierce resistance to anything imposed upon me: in particular, my family's expectation that I would join the Royal Navy like my father and all the men in his family.

I include here a photo taken of me at the age of four, my brother then being six, when we were dressed as little sailor boys. My brother can be seen saluting very correctly. I am getting it all wrong, as I did in most things. I am also "not quite in the frame", which was to become the story of my life: never being quite where I was expected to be.

I was not inclined to accept other people's ideas of what I should do or how I should be. My journey of growing up, of trying to find my own way in life, took decades rather than years—often I think to the despair of my parents. Some of that journey is recorded here. Frequently, I sought diversion and often I turned routine tasks, like exams, into a challenge of my own making: probably to the despair of my teachers.

This is by no means meant to be a systematic autobiography. I have therefore allowed myself to digress, and sometimes to leap ahead to other times that came to mind as I was writing. When funny things happened to me, which often they did, I have felt no need to "write beyond the truth". Life was often funny enough just as it was. I have therefore refrained from exaggeration in what I tell here.

My moving from one place to another in this account reflects the many changes in my life, from one home to another and from one school to another.

I do not discuss girlfriends, and I mention little about married life and the children, except for a few special incidents. The rest is just as it happened, warts and all. I hope the reader has as much fun in reading this as I did in writing it.

CHAPTER ONE

I am born into a passing age

Prince Otto von Bismark has to be rescued (by the butler) from a rusty shower

Preamble

I was brought up being told that I had always been very strong willed; also that I had been "so difficult" as a child I had apparently "driven away" all the nannies who had been employed to deal with me. There was only one who stayed, from when I was four. She came to be called "Tucky" (her full name being Miss Powell-Tuck).

Tucky stayed until I was ten. Years after she had left, when I met her again, she told me that she too had left because she had found me "impossible". But I don't think that was the only reason she left as I had been at boarding school from the age of eight, and mother told me that Tucky didn't really want to be looking after my two sisters, born when I was seven and when I was nine. So, Tucky might have been teasing me, even though there is often a grain of truth in jest.

An aunt has memories that might help to explain Tucky's problem with me. One was when Tucky had been getting impatient with me, as I (aged seven) wasn't concentrating on what she wanted me to do. "Put your mind behind it," she demanded. I had apparently replied: "Put my mind *behind* it? Where do I put it? Do I put it *here*? Do I put it *there*? Where do I put it?"

1

My mother's family, until the war, lived in an amazing house called "Marden" where I was born. I have no early memories of that house, though I visited it years later when it had become the "Convent School of the Sacred Heart".

My mother was one of six children, she having four sisters and a brother. She used to recall that her parents, before the war, had fifteen "indoor staff".

My father's family was entirely dedicated to the Royal Navy. My grandfather was an admiral, my father and one of his brothers both became captains, and their younger brother became a lieutenant-commander. My own brother (Michael) eventually became a commander, RN.

I was expected to follow suit. But I was made of different stuff. For many years, my own life followed a zigzag course with no obvious sense of direction except for my enduring avoidance of being sucked into the family "business": the Royal Navy.

When I was in my thirties, someone asked my mother: "What is Patrick doing now?" I was told that she didn't have a clue. Her reply, as reported to me, had been: "Well, I know that Patrick was a social worker. He is now working as a *physio*therapist" (she could not get her head around my then being a *psycho*therapist). She had, apparently, continued: "I now understand that he is training all over again: I don't know why, but I gather that he is *training to be a psychotic*." Such was my mother's flimsy acquaintance with those "*psycho*" words! I was actually beginning my further training to become a psychoanalyst, which then continued to be my full-time profession. I subsequently wrote four books on the clinical work of psychotherapy and psychoanalysis, challenging a lot of what I had been taught during my various trainings. The first book was published in twenty languages, so it seems to have found a ready readership. My journey, by that time, seemed to have been fulfilled.

"Where was I born?"

When I was seventeen (it was early summer 1953) I went to Salzburg for the Music Festival. On the way we had to go through the frontier between Germany and Austria. Being not so many years since the war, the train had to stop at the border while the conductor got us to fill in entry forms before we could be allowed to cross the frontier.

2

This required us to enter "place of birth". But I could not remember where this was, and I didn't know then that I could have found this information in my passport; nor did the conductor suggest I looked there.

The conductor left me trying to remember while he did the rest of the train. Sometime later he returned and it was fortunate he could speak English. "Well, have you remembered?" he asked. I replied: "I'm very sorry, I really can't remember. You see, I was really *very little* at the time, but I know it ended with '*ham*'." The conductor could now see a way through the impasse. "Could it have been Birmingham?" he asked. Not wanting to lose this way around the problem I replied that maybe it could have been. "Well, that will do," he said, and he filled in the form stating that I was (allegedly) born in Birmingham. I later learned that it was Woldingham.

Marden Park (near Woldingham)

My mother's family had lived in a huge house, known in the family as "Marden". I have no significant memories of this, even though I was born there, as my parents kept moving and by the time I was only a bit over two we moved to Malta where my father was serving in the navy.

A sense of my mother's home

An older cousin (Christopher), who had been visiting Marden while it was still the main family home, told me of a time when Prince Otto von Bismark had been staying as a house guest there. According to Christopher, the butler had been summoned to von Bismark's room as the shower, which had not been used for ages, was coming through with water that was red with rust. The butler had to flush this out before running down to the drawing room to announce to the family gathered there that their guest would be a little late. The butler had then gone into the details of washing the rust off the naked von Bismark, to the amusement of all the assembled family.

Other tales of Marden remembered

In about 1960 I met someone who had known my family at Marden before the war. He told me two of his memories from that time. The

3

first was after there had been a ball there, and he explained the custom in those days. One had to visit the house after a party, during the following morning, to present one's visiting card. This was officially just a matter of courtesy, but he thought it might also have been a test to see if you were sober enough to turn up for that ritual the next morning.

This man then told me that, when he went with his visiting card, the front door was opened by two footmen. Then, striding between them, the butler came forward with a silver salver upon which he had to place his visiting card. He found this very daunting.

This man's other memory of Marden was that he had later been promoted to being a member of a house party held there. This meant he was allowed to stay over the weekend. On the Monday morning he had turned up for breakfast at eight o'clock. This was the time he'd been told breakfast started, but there was no one there except for my grandfather (to him, Sir Bernard Greenwell) who was sitting silently at the head of the large table. On the sideboard were various hot dishes, all under large silver covers, from which you were expected to help yourself. Having eaten his choice of cooked food, this man had started on the toast, which was in a rack behind the spread copy of *The Times* which my grandfather was reading.

As my grandfather had not been speaking a single word beyond saying "Good morning", this man had nervously eaten through the entire rack of toast. Sir Bernard had then reached around his paper, feeling along the rack for toast, but there was not a single piece left! The butler had to be summoned for more to be made. Then the chauffeur was called to drive my grandfather to the station, by which time he'd missed the train—all because this man had finished the toast. The chauffeur had to drive him the entire way to London so that he would not miss a meeting he was due to attend. This man said he had never been able to forget his embarrassment on that morning.

My earliest memories

The one memory I do have of being in Marden (aged two) is of running down a long carpeted passage, not seeing that there was a step somewhere along it and falling head over heels down the step. I can remember crying until someone came to pick me up.

My next and most vivid early memory is that of arriving in Valletta harbour (Malta, Grand Harbour) some time while I was about two and a half. What I can still see, in my mind's eye, is what I saw from the deck of the ship in which we had travelled out to Malta. It was night-time and I had become entranced by the dancing lights on the water, reflecting the white, red, and green lights of the "dhaisas" (the Maltese gondola-type boats) that were there to take people ashore. What I do not remember is what had been happening just before that. I am told that I'd been woken up, as the ship had berthed and we were soon to disembark, and I had been screaming my head off in protest. Apparently nothing would calm me, so our mother had suggested to whoever was helping her (with us children) that she take me up on deck. I was then awed into silence.

When I went back to Malta during my National Service, I was able to place that memory with the silhouette of Bighi Hospital in the background, across the water of Grand Harbour.

Where we lived

As our father was in the Royal Navy, being stationed here and there, we had many changes of home. Our mother used to tell us she had lived in seventeen different houses in the first seventeen years she'd been married. I have only vague memories of the early places we lived at. But what I do remember is that I would frequently wake up wondering where I would be when I opened my eyes, and would I know where I was? I am sure this contributed to the subsequent importance of the continuing sameness of my two boarding schools: the only places that didn't keep changing during my childhood.

"Orchards" at Pulborough (East Sussex)

I have only a few memories of my paternal grandparents' home, "Orchards". One memory, from the early days of the war, was being in a cot that was set up on the ground floor, apparently so that it would be safer than upstairs if we were bombed. I can remember having a kind of dartboard at the end of the cot, which had hooks with numbers, and I had flat rubber rings I would throw onto these hooks.

I think it must have been at some later time we went to visit these grandparents at Pulborough when some German planes flew over. I believe I was with my brother Michael at the time, in the garden, and we had been taught to lie face down if planes came over. I did that, but Michael had lain on his back and he told me he could actually see the

German pilot in his cockpit. Shortly afterwards we heard the explosion of bombs dropped a little further on.

Michael also remembers that this was at the height of the Battle of Britain, and he told me that we regularly used to watch the twirling contrails of aircraft high in the sky. He also remembers a Spitfire crashing and landing upside down in the field near the house. The pilot had successfully bailed out, and he remembers being with a crowd of others looking at the wreckage. He says he can still visualise the instrument panel in the cockpit, looking at this until someone came to shoo onlookers away.

"North Park" near Godstone

We quite often went to stay at "North Park" with our mother's eldest sister (our aunt Joyce) and my uncle, with their children: Christopher, Philip, and Rosemary. While there I came to think of Rosemary (we were of similar ages) as absolutely wonderful. She was the first girl I can remember knowing. In fact (aged four) I asked her to marry me.

However, I soon turned out to be fickle as I later asked Tucky (called my new "governess") if *she* would marry me. I think I was wanting to make sure she stayed for ever, all other nannies having left rather quickly.

The times tables

I don't know how old I was at the time, but one afternoon I can remember playing with numbers on a big sheet of paper. I discovered that if you add 2 and 2, and then go on adding 2's, you end up with a 2 and 0, making it twenty. I thought this was perhaps a fluke, so I tried it with 3's and then 4's, and all the way to 9's. Every time, the number after the last adding came to the original number with a 0 on it.

I thought I'd discovered something amazing so I took this to Tucky to show her. I don't know if she was impressed or not. The only response I remember (from her) was that she told me this was called *times* tables and she suggested I went off to learn them all by heart.

Going out to tea

My brother Michael has reminded me that we used to be made to eat "doorsteps" of bread before going out to tea. Mother's assumption had been that we'd bring shame on the family by eating too much of the delicate offerings, and biscuits, during the rationing at that time. So, filling us up with bread beforehand was to dampen our appetites before we set off for tea.

"Stokehill Wood" (Yelverton, Devonshire)

I can remember (aged five) being driven in a car to another of the houses where we lived, known as "Stokehill Wood". I can remember the car being so filled up with things we were taking with us that I had to squeeze in on top of the stuff on the back seat, with my head virtually touching the roof.

What I don't fully remember is a story that has often been told since. We'd just arrived at Stokehill Wood and were being taken for a walk with Tucky. Typically, I was being bolshie and was not keeping up, which is what I was being told to do. Instead, and I do remember this bit, I was kicking leaves along with my boots, stumping along and taking no notice of anything else except for the rustling noise I could make with my feet.

In the meantime, Michael and Tucky had arrived back at the house; but I was nowhere to be seen. I had apparently gone on past the gate to the house, not yet knowing it was to be our home, and I'd disappeared. Somehow I was found and brought back, but it must have been an alarming time for Tucky who would have felt very responsible for not having kept me in sight.

Making it snow

While we were at Stokehill, I can vividly remember a time when we'd been just too much for mother and she had, in desperation, suggested we go into the garden to see if we could make it snow. "Why don't you go and sing Pooh's song for snowy weather, and then maybe it will snow?" So Michael and I had gone round the garden chanting in loud voices Pooh's snowing song, which (from memory) goes like this:

Nobody knows, tiddly-pom, how cold my toes, tiddly-pom, how cold my toes, tiddly-pom, are growing.
The more it snows, tiddly-pom, the more it goes, tiddly-pom, the more it goes, tiddly-pom, on snowing. (A. A. Milne)

We sang this over and over and then a miracle happened. It really did begin to snow, and it snowed and snowed and kept on snowing.

"Chargot Cottage" near Luxborough

Our next home was to be in this little cottage which was magical. It was actually just half of a cottage, the other half being lived in by a local man called Tarr and his sister. Outside there was a tiny garden, and across the road was the last of a series of (I believe) seven small lakes, all interconnected, ending with a stream flowing down the side of the road. All around were flowers and birds, and there was the possibility of fishing in a lake near the cottage. Sometimes we would see a blue flash of colour as a kingfisher flew by.

I am told that, about the first day we'd been at "Chargot", I'd spent all day at the gate telling everyone who went by: "Tomorrow is my birthday." That was my sixth birthday.

At the birthday tea party, I can remember being made to stand on my chair to make a speech, but I don't personally remember what I'd said. However, I've been told my speech went like this:

> "Thank you for coming to my party, and thank you for my presents. I hope you will all be able to come to my next birthday party, when the war might be over and you can all give me bigger and better presents."

Doing arithmetic

One day, when Tucky was teaching us arithmetic, Michael was having some difficulty with his sums. Tucky tried showing Michael up, saying: "Patrick has done his sums so why can't you do yours?" She eventually lost her temper and made Michael get out of his chair, so that she could sit down to show him how to do it. This was a folding chair with rather thin metal legs. I can remember the chair subsiding under her weight (and she was quite heavy) squashing right down to the ground. Tucky's face was a treat, particularly as she would go bright red on occasions like that. So, instead of doing more sums, we went down to the village blacksmith with Michael and me both triumphant at this fresh turn of events.

Sawing logs

Michael and I each took our turn in cutting logs at a sawhorse, and we proudly built up piles of logs. One day, I was told off for not stacking my logs as neatly as Michael did. He, of course, had a beautiful pile and my logs were all in a heap. I was told to make my logs *neat and tidy like Michael's*.

Instead of making my logs into a tidy heap like Michael's, I thought it would be much easier to make his pile like mine. All I had to do was to knock his pile over so that it became a messy heap *just like mine!* He, of course, was furious and took to immediate retaliation, and I don't blame him. He pushed me violently into a huge bed of nettles near to the logpiles. There I lay screaming, unable to get out and unable to move without getting stung in lots of fresh places. Eventually my mother, or Tucky, came and rescued me.

I can remember that I was so badly stung, all over, I was like one huge nettle sting which blinked red and white with my pulse. I believe I was then covered from head to toe with calamine lotion.

Mother beginning to cook

Until we got to Chargot, mother had always had someone to cook for her, as had always been the case in her parents' home. At Chargot, however—it then being the start of the war—mother had to discover how to cook for herself. In particular, I remember her first attempt at fairy cakes. These turned out to be as hard as concrete and Michael made the point by repeatedly dropping one of these stone-like cakes onto a plate, saying: "Are these really meant to be *fairy* cakes?"

Tarr

The man next door, Arthur Tarr, was a great character. He had picked up half of the casing from a mine that had been dropped by a German plane. The story was that the pilot might have mistaken a cloud-filled valley for the Bristol channel, dropping the mine (or mines) on land rather than in the sea. "Tarr" (as we called him) had taken this casing home and turned it into a water butt in his back garden.

Another thing Tarr did was keep bees. Each year he would take the honeycombs out of the hives and spin these in a special spinner, which went round so fast the honey came out of the combs. The honey would drip down the inside walls of this machine, eventually coming out of a little tap at the bottom. Sometimes Michael and I were invited to help. Our job was to provide a finger to catch the drips, between filling one honey pot and the next. We would then lick our fingers which was the best bit.

One day Tucky was making pancakes for Shrove Tuesday, tossing these in the kitchen. Tarr came through the gap in the fence, which divided his back garden from ours, and asked to take part. I can remember Tarr trying to toss his pancake, but with no success. In the end he tossed it up in the air and stepped back, while Tucky stood by with a plate in each hand to catch his pancake before it hit the ground.

Tarr was in the Home Guard, like in *Dad's Army*. He came home one day to say that a German aircraft had been shot down quite near to where we were living, the pilot having bailed out. This pilot had been going along the roads near where he had landed, asking to be taken prisoner, but no one wanted to do anything about it. "I've got the cows to milk," or "I haven't got time for all that," was what the farmers were saying to this pilot who was trying to give himself up.

Visiting Tarr (years later)

When our daughters, Hanna and Bella, were quite young, we took them with us to meet Tarr and his sister. As we were going on holiday in Somerset, we planned to call in for tea.

Having arranged the date for this, we later realised we hadn't allowed ourselves enough time to get there from London, to be in time for tea. So we arranged instead to spend a night at a hotel on the way. At rather the last moment before leaving London, we'd written to Tarr to say we would not be arriving until teatime the day after we had first suggested. We didn't have any phone number for him.

When we arrived, we were greeted with great smiles and laughter, Tarr remembering all kinds of things and going through some of the things I have recalled above. We were then taken to a table spread with fine things, including a lot of Devonshire cream and home-made cake, and some whortleberry jam for old time's sake. He then said he'd wondered what had happened the day before, as they had tea all ready for us, but we hadn't turned up. "Anyway, you are here now so it doesn't matter." We explained about our letter, which they hadn't received.

While we were having tea, there was a knock at the door. "That will be the postman," said Tarr, and so it was. He came back with a mischievous grin on his face. "Oh, look," he said, "there's a letter from you. It says you won't be here until today; and so you are."

Coley

We had a cleaning lady we knew as "Coley". I think her name was really Miss Coles. I seem to remember her wearing an old fashioned cap, with elastic round the edges and a frill standing out, like a Mrs. Bridges' cap (from *Upstairs, Downstairs*). My main memory of her was when I was not being allowed to go out to play, Tucky having insisted I spell my full name properly before being allowed out. I'd been crying about this when Coley asked me what was the matter. "Oh," she said, "*I'll* tell you how to spell Casement," and she proceeded to dictate the spelling while I wrote it down. Then, triumphant, I went out to play.

Learning to ride a bicycle

My brother decided to help me learn to ride a bicycle. (I must have been about seven.) I clearly remember him holding onto the back of the saddle, while I was wobbling around trying to steer, and we made our way down the road alongside the stream by Chargot cottage. He then let go without me realising. I continued down the hill, gradually gaining pace as I wobbled off the road towards the stream.

Michael ran behind me shouting: "Lean to the right, lean to the right." I did this and, miraculously, the bicycle stopped going towards the stream and began to mount the grassy slope back towards the road. I believe there was some kind of gate across the road and there I fell off. I hadn't yet learned about using brakes, but from that day on I could ride a bicycle.

Going to see Bambi

Father seemed to spend most of the war in America. One time father came back having just seen the film *Bambi*, which he was determined to take us to see when it was around in England. He'd looked everywhere to find out where the film was showing, and the nearest he could find was in Bristol, a considerable distance from Chargot. Nevertheless, he

11

was determined we were to go, even though it meant booking us into a hotel in Bristol for the night.

At the station, while father was buying our tickets, I was trying to read a notice over the ticket office. As it was wartime, all stations had a notice to warn people only to travel when this was essential. It read: *Is your journey really necessary?* I got stuck on the last word, so I said to my mother: "What is that long word there?" She told me the word was *necessary* and quickly tried to shut me up. I answered her back, in an embarrassingly loud voice: "Well, is *our* journey really necessary?" I was quickly rushed onto the platform, and we continued on this totally unnecessary journey to Bristol. It was of course a wonderful film, even though it had a very sad bit where Bambi's mother had died and Bambi goes around the forest calling for her.

The next day we went to the Bristol zoo. It just so happened that, the same week as I was initially writing this, I found a letter in *The Times* in which someone had been asking if elephants can sneeze. Well, I could tell this person that elephants certainly can sneeze. The only memory I have of that zoo visit, in Bristol, was being in front of an elephant when suddenly it did a really *enormous* sneeze, and a load of elephant "snot" went all over my face and glasses. That was certainly one way of finding out whether they sneeze!

Getting me ready to go to prep school

Mother got it into her head that I might be teased at school for having sticking-out ears, which I did when I was young. She therefore set about trying to put this right, not having checked with any medical person to see if this might help. If she'd asked a doctor she would have learned that her method of trying to correct my sticking-out ears was not going to achieve anything except, probably, to give me a complex about how I looked, which it did. She made me wear a rugger scrum-cap, or something like it that she'd made, putting this over my head every night and making me wear it throughout the night. Each morning she would take this off, and out would pop my ears, sticking out just as much as they always did.

When I eventually got to prep school (Maidwell, near Northampton) aged eight, as mother had anticipated, I *was* teased about my ears. On one occasion, two boys held onto my ears, one boy on each, while they ran round me. I was afraid my ears might be torn away from my head. Fortunately I seemed to grow into my ears over time.

Wartime food

During the war, our mother introduced us to kinds of food we'd never tried before. One thing was carrot cake, which was soggy but wonderful. Another thing, which was not so wonderful, was nettle soup. We went around picking young nettles, mother doing the picking, and then she boiled this up into a dark green mush. It was even worse than spinach. *Much worse.*

One day we had boiled marrow. For some reason I took against that too. I *knew* I hated it, probably without even trying it. I never ate marrow for years after that until, one day, someone served marrow with white sauce. I thought this was delicious. What was it? I could hardly believe it was that much hated slimy food called marrow, which I had shunned for all those years. I've loved it ever since.

Tucky's bed

I remember Tucky had a room at the top of the cottage, with a large bouncy bed. One evening, when we should have been going to sleep, Michael and I had gone up to explore this. We discovered it was more bouncy than any bed we'd met before, so we were bouncing up and down with great excitement. Then we saw Tucky's face appearing over the top step of the stairs. She'd been creeping up on all fours to catch us in the act. The most memorable thing about this was (again) how red her face had gone, from being angry with us. We loved that.

Being beaten with a hairbrush

There was a time when I was being beaten with a hairbrush in mother's bedroom. I am not sure whether it was she or Tucky doing the beating. What I do remember is catching sight of my own screaming face in a mirror, which was beside the chair where this punishment was taking place. I think it was seeing my own face like that which shocked me at least as much as the hairbrush.

Back at North Park

As we moved several times between Chargot and North Park, some of what I recall will be out of order. But it won't matter.

Erika and Eva

Quite near to the beginning of the war, two refugees had turned up at Marden asking if they could be given shelter. Christopher said they'd first gone there because they could see it was big enough for there to be a room for two homeless people. (Big enough indeed!)

These refugees, Erika and her daughter Eva, were from Czechoslovakia. From Marden they were sent on to North Park, where my aunt Joyce and uncle David took them in. They asked if they could stay "for a few days or weeks". In the end they stayed for years, at least until the end of the war. Erika was a very strange woman. According to Christopher she claimed to be an army psychologist, but was probably no such thing.

My first sister being born

My sister Elisabeth was born while we were again living at North Park. I was then seven. I later learned that mother had a theory about having a nanny to look after the baby: "It helps to lessen the problem of the first child's jealousy, because when the next baby is born the older child gets *more* of the mother's attention, *not less*. That's because the nanny takes on the baby and the mother has to spend more time with the older child." I always thought that sounded fine for the first child, to have more of mother's attention, but I don't ever recall noticing that this system was working for me when my sister was born! By then (wartime), mothers were doing more of the mothering of a new baby anyway. The next change of care came for me when I was sent off to boarding school.

I have an entry in *Learning from Life* about Elisabeth, from that time. I wrote:

> When I was seven, I was travelling by train with my mother who was holding my baby sister. In the railway carriage we met a friendly lady who, as a way of making conversation, asked me if this was my sister. I am told I had proudly replied that she was, whereupon this lady asked (as it was wartime) if my father had seen my sister yet. My mother remembered, with embarrassment, that I replied: "Oh, no. He's been away for years and years and years." (*Learning from Life*, p. 25)

14

Green fried bread

My cousins Christopher and Philip were quite a few years older than me. One day, they had been melting a green candle in a coal shovel over an open fire. Then one of them thought it would be fun to see if they could fry some bread in the melted wax, so they proceeded to try. Having achieved that, frying it in a coal shovel that they'd vaguely wiped clean, they insisted I eat it. Not to be outdone, I agreed. On the whole, it was OK except for some gritty bits of coal that had got into it too.

Christmas at North Park

One year we were at North Park for Christmas and it had been decided we should put on a concert show, all the children taking part. What I remember in particular is that I was in bed with colitis, something that seemed to flare up when we had richer food for Christmas, as I was not meant to eat anything other than very bland food.

On this occasion I was brought from my sickbed to take part in this concert. I was to play the King in one of A. A. Milne's poems. From memory it goes roughly as follows:

> The King asked the Queen and the Queen asked the dairy maid, could we have some butter for the royal slice of bread. The dairy maid said certainly, I'll go and ask the cow now before she goes to bed.

I forget who played which other parts, but I think Rosemary was the queen and Eva was the cow. I know that I was the king, with an absurd white wig made out of cotton wool underneath a crown.

"Byways" (near Petersfield, Hants.)

For a time (when I was aged eight to nine) we lived at a house called "Byways", in Steep. That is where my sister Susan was born.

Tucky was still with us at Byways. We once found her at the piano, accompanying herself while she was singing. She had quite a good voice but, being little boys, we didn't appreciate that nearly as much as we enjoyed seeing how red her face went when we laughed at her. Sadly, I don't think she ever again took the risk of playing, or singing, while we were around.

Picking mushrooms

There was a time when it was suggested that Michael and I might go out to pick mushrooms, one early morning. There were fields nearby where there were lots of mushrooms to be found. I said I didn't want to go, so Michael set off on his own. When he'd been gone for a while, I thought it would be fun if I went out too. Perhaps I could surprise everyone by picking up even more mushrooms than he could find.

I got to a field where there should have been plenty of mushrooms, but I could only find stalks. There were no mushrooms at all. It was foggy that morning so it was some time before I realised that, through the fog, I could just make out someone else picking mushrooms in this field. It was only when I got nearer that I could see it was Michael. He'd got all of the mushrooms and I, as far as I know, had found none.

Sunburn

During one summer, while we were at Byways, we went to Hayling Island for the day. Michael and I wore our bathing costumes, which in those days had a front that covered our chest—our nipples—to be decent, with straps that crossed at the back.

It was a sunny day with quite a breeze. Even though the sun was out, it didn't feel at all hot. We therefore played on the sand and in the sea for almost the whole day, in our bathing things. No one had given a thought to the possibility of us needing protection from the sun. But when we got home, my back was bright red and blazing hot, burning terribly. It hurt so much that, for two or three nights, I was completely unable to lie down.

My whole back formed blisters full of liquid, and it was as if my skin had been lifted right away from me with a layer of water underneath. It took ages for this to heal, and even then I was left with a white "X" across my back where the straps had been. That white X, in contrast to the brown from the sunburn, lasted for almost a whole year.

Susan (my second sister) being born

Susan arrived very soon after Michael and I had come home for the summer holidays, she being born on 30th July which was also our father's birthday. Michael and I were placed for the night with people down the road. I can remember being in a bedroom with him and, for whatever reason I cannot think, we were using deaf and dumb signing. One of us had come across the signing alphabet which we had learned, and which I still know.

I recall that mother was worried about Susan ("Sue" from then on) being so small when she was born. Sue also seemed to be rather slow in putting on weight. Each day mother weighed her and the weight was written down. Once, Sue was on the weighing scales when she did a poo, and mother turned to me saying she thought it wouldn't really be cheating if she weighed Sue with her poo. It might help to make it look as if she had put on a bit of weight.

After Sue's birth, mother used to do "recovery exercises" on the floor, lifting her legs up and down, and she invited me to do them with her. Quite why she suggested this I don't know. Perhaps she was trying to help me feel involved in things to do with this latest baby.

We later heard that, shortly before Sue was born, there had been a drama when my sister Elisabeth went walkabout with a doll's pram, disappearing from the garden. This was a few weeks before D-Day (6th June 1944) which was when British and American forces landed in France to counter-attack the Germans.

The roads had been filled with convoys of lorries and tanks, all making their way towards the coast in preparation. We had only been at Byways a short while, so it was remarkable that someone had recognised Elisabeth, still pushing her pram on the *other* side of the main road going up Stoner Hill. This was about a mile from the house. How she had crossed the road, with all the lorries on it, nobody was ever able to find out.

Don't stare at cripples[1]

We were brought up with lots of *do's* and *don'ts*, such as: *Don't point* and *Don't stare at cripples.* I suppose that this was prompted by the fact that, at that time of the war, there were quite a lot of men around who had lost an arm or a leg.

When my first sister (Elisabeth) was born, there was plenty to stare at, but there were some things that could not be put into words. I think I resolved this by deciding that Elisabeth had been born a cripple: something clearly missing.

When my other sister Susan was born it seemed to be just too much of a coincidence to think that our mother had given birth to *two* cripples.

17

Perhaps that was what made them sisters rather than brothers. But I don't think that any of this was ever mentioned or talked about.

It seems I had remained in ignorance from an early age. An aunt told me of a time when I (aged four) had come back from a tea party, after which we had all bathed in the family swimming bath. My mother was rather shocked to hear this as I had not taken any bathing costume to that party: "Were you all little boys, or boys and girls together?" asked my mother. I'm told that I replied: "I don't know, you see we weren't wearing any clothes."

Christmas

While at Byways I can remember being ill again with my colitis, another Christmas time. I was brought a delicious glass of something to drink in bed. Afterwards I said how good it was: it was "the best lemonade I've ever had". I was then told it was champagne.

Unfortunately, mother was keen to have another Christmas show, to which neighbouring children and their parents were invited. This included singing and dancing, and it may have included Tucky playing something on the piano and/or singing. I forget the details. But there are two things I do not forget: the dance I had to do, and the little pageant of *Moses in the Bulrushes*.

For my dance, mother had made a crêpe tutu dress for me. She played the piano while I danced around like a complete "prat", with little steps and going on tip-toe towards each corner, bowing and skipping and whatever, all of this choreographed by mother. I blush to think of it. What can she have been thinking, to put a boy of nine through that?

Moses in the Bulrushes involved all of us. I believe Michael was dressed with a beard, and perhaps on this occasion I may have been allowed to be "manly" with a beard too. We were probably Moses and Pharaoh. I think Elisabeth was the mother of Moses, and Sue was in the dog basket as the baby Moses. The basket had bulrushes sticking up all around it, inserted into the wickerwork sides. This was not the only family show such as this that we did (see later under "Haben House", our next home).

Buying clothes to last

Sue was christened at "Whale Island", or *HMS Excellent* as it was properly known, which was the Royal Navy gunnery school. Father was based there more often than anywhere else, he having trained as a gunnery officer. He ultimately ended up there as the captain.

There is a photo somewhere of us all after that christening, Michael wearing his first ever long trousers. As this was in 1944, and the war was still on, mother was very conscious of the shortage of clothes. In fact there was a rationing of clothes at that time, so she'd bought the longest trousers she could fit onto Michael, with the waist raised as high as it would go—almost to his armpits.

This was not the only saving on clothes I remember. While I was still at Maidwell (our prep school), mother had bought a man's full-size dressing gown for me because she'd seen it in a shop window at half price. I suspect the reason for it going so cheaply was that it was in the most hideous colours. It was maroon and red. She then took up a *huge* hem on this. So huge was the hem it reached right up to my armpits. This meant that the whole body of the dressing gown was double thickness, and it looked utterly ridiculous. But I was not going to have any other dressing gown, so this was what I had to wear at school.

By the time I went to Winchester, the hem of this dressing gown had been let down somewhat, and repeatedly the hem was let down until I had grown into the fullsize for which it had been made.

Strangely, even though I still thought it was so awful, I kept this dressing gown right through my time at Cambridge and Oxford, and I still had it when I got married. It was my wife (Margaret) who eventually persuaded me to get rid of it.

Note

1. In speaking of "cripples" here I am quoting from the shocking non-pc language of that time. We would of course speak quite differently now of those who suffer from disability.

CHAPTER TWO

Prep school years

"All the teachers have given up on you"

Maidwell hall

My brother Michael and I went to a very fine prep school we called Maidwell (near Northampton). I went there in 1943, aged eight.

I remember quite a few boys crying a lot, feeling homesick, but I didn't. This was probably because I had my brother Michael there, a bit of home having come with me. He was called by everyone else "Casement One" and I was "Casement Two", but I was allowed to call him "Bro".

My first form teacher was Miss Hardwicke. I don't remember much of that first term except for Bill Rogers, the teacher who was very keen on rugby football.

The first year

I should perhaps explain that I had never been to any school before this: I'd always been taught at home by my governess, Tucky. So this, when I was aged eight, was my first-ever experience of real school—of any kind.

One of the things for which I was especially grateful to Michael while we were both at Maidwell, was that he taught me to *"peewit"*, which was calling like a peewit (bird). This is a very high note that dips and then goes up again. Michael said that, when we were out playing in the grounds around the school, I could always find him by using this call. He would then "peewit" back and we could run towards each other. For me as a new boy this was very reassuring. I'm not sure how long this went on, but it was a brilliant idea.

A best friend

For most of my time at Maidwell I was a rather isolated child. I didn't easily make friends. However, in an early letter home (kept by mother) I wrote: "Don't tell anyone but my best friend is Roberts-West." We'd made a "hut", under some bushes near the gate to the front drive. I have no idea what we did there other than sit and talk, and maybe eat sweets if we ever had any. Nor do I have any idea why this news had to be kept secret. But that friendship did not last long.

My memories of my five years at Maidwell are curiously sparse, except for my so often getting into trouble and a strange focus on the times that I was ill.

Getting flu

Towards the end of my first term at Maidwell there was a flu epidemic. This had an interesting knock-on effect, especially in relation to the first game, which played rugby football (or "rugger" as we called it). The second game would only play football, except for rugger once a week to introduce boys to the rules and how to play it. The third game, which was for first-year boys, would only play football. I, of course, was in the third game so I had never seen rugger played nor did I know what the rules were.

A major problem about the school being struck by this flu epidemic was that more and more boys were falling ill. An increasing number of "dorms" were being designated as sickrooms, still trying to keep the infection from spreading to the remaining boys. But the sports master, Bill Rogers, would not allow his rugger game to be interrupted by any shortage of players. He insisted that younger boys be recruited to the first game, in order to keep up the numbers.

I was eventually one of those recruited, I not knowing one single thing about rugger; what it was about, what it was for, what the aim of the game was, or anything about how it was played. I was placed at the back of the pitch, near the great big goal posts, wondering what I had to do.

I soon found out something about this. At one moment, a terrifying moment that has remained etched in my memory, one of the biggest boys in the school came lumbering towards me with the ball under his arm. What was I meant to do? I had no idea. I imagined I was somehow meant to stop him, but how could I do that? He was twice my size. The only thing I was determined to do was somehow to run away, without it being too obvious. But I could not just turn round and run, which was really what I wanted to do. So I stood, frozen to the ground, trying to guess which way I should go in order to get out of this big boy's way at the last minute. He too was clearly wondering how he would get around me. Unfortunately, just as I darted to my right he darted to his left, which meant that he tripped over me, dropping the ball which went into touch.

The game came to a stop anyway, because of the ball being in touch, but Bill Rogers chose that moment to give a pep talk to the entire game. He said: "That is what I like to see. That boy showed real courage. He brought down this great big boy, even though Casement Two is only half his size. He is obviously made for playing rugger." He then turned to me saying: "You are wasted back there, boy. Come up here and play *wing*," whatever that was.

The game went on. Only a few minutes later, with me running up and down like everyone else (but still having no idea what I was meant to be doing), the ball was passed to me. I somehow caught it and stood transfixed to the spot. What to do now? Half the other side then ran at me. I panicked, throwing the ball away from me, hoping to stop them running at me, but I threw the ball *forwards* into touch. I learned later that was something you must never, ever, do in rugger.

Bill Rogers stopped the game again and gave another speech. "I was obviously wrong about Casement Two. He clearly has *no idea* what he's doing. Go back to where you were before." Thus ended my rugger career, until my very last term in the school (see later).

That night I developed a high temperature, going down with the flu, and I no longer had to face the ordeal of being made to play more rugger, or more *anything*.

23

As I remember it, this flu epidemic was so severe the headmaster decided there was really no point going on with the school that term, especially as it was getting close to the holidays. So all the boys who were well enough to travel were sent home early. I, and one other boy, were kept at the school, too ill to travel.

I may have remembered the next bit wrongly, but my recollection is that neither the other boy nor I was able to get home in time for Christmas. I believe we both had Christmas at Maidwell, going home a day or so afterwards. At least that is how it felt, as if I was missing everything to do with Christmas at home.

Chickenpox

One term we had only been at the school for a few days when I developed some spots. These were quickly diagnosed as chickenpox, I being the first boy in the school to get it.

As a result of having the pox I was isolated in the usual sickroom until I was no longer infectious. This meant that I was completely on my own, while all the other boys were carrying on in the school without me. The time eventually came when I was no longer infectious, but then a huge number of other boys also went down with the pox. It seemed as if I had exchanged places, from being the only boy in the sickroom to being almost the only boy up and having to do lessons. But I'm sure it wasn't really quite as black and white as that, as there were at least two waves of other boys getting the pox.

Mumps

When it came to mumps, I went down with this in the second wave of the school epidemic, finding myself in what was known as "tower dorm", which by then had been taken over as one of the sickrooms. I found Michael was already there, overlapping with me for just one or two nights.

This dormitory had windows that faced in two directions, because of being under one of the towers. When we began to get better, one other boy and I started to count the stars as they began to appear, beginning with the evening star. Gradually, other stars could be seen, which we counted between us, running between the two windows to make sure we didn't miss any. After a while (great surprise) the stars became too many for us to keep up with our counting.

24

I think it may have been while we were out of bed, still trying to count the stars, that the headmaster came round. When he asked what we were doing out of bed, I explained we were trying to count the stars. Instead of being cross with us, he went down to his study and returned with a book about the sun, the planets, and the stars. I read this from cover to cover in the following days, and I became absolutely fascinated by it; and I've continued to follow the advances in astronomy, and later cosmology, ever since.

My thumbnail

A day or two before going back to Maidwell for my first summer term, I was watching mother making reed baskets. She had an extremely sharp knife, with which she was cutting lengths of reed.

I tried this knife and found it was so sharp I could take a swipe at a reed with the knife and it went through it like butter. I could even do several reeds at a time. "Look, see how many reeds I can cut through all at once," I said proudly as I prepared to show her. I took a great big swipe at these reeds and, as I had predicted, the knife went through them all. But it also went through almost all of my left thumbnail too!

I can vividly remember seeing my thumb with no nail at all and, for a moment, also with no blood. Then the blood began to spurt out of it. Mother immediately put my thumb into her mouth, believing this to be the best thing to do to prevent it becoming infected. Then, while Tucky was attending to my thumb, mother went out to the garden to see if she could find my thumbnail. She thought that the hospital might be able to graft it back on! However, it was cherry blossom time and she could not find my nail anywhere, the lawn being strewn all over with blossom that looked similar to my thumbnail.

The doctors bound up my thumb with sterile gauze and bandage, and that is how it was when I went back to Maidwell. For many weeks of that term I had to go, every day after lunch, to see Matron who would re-dress my thumb. Unfortunately, she had the mistaken notion that she had to remove the gauze each time, which always made it bleed, so it was many weeks before we got the gauze off without more bleeding. Only then did it begin to heal. Alas, as I had to carry my thumb with my left hand stuck into the neck of my jumper, like in a sling, the band-aged thumb was always sticking out. This was too much for one boy who banged it on the end with a book, setting off the bleeding again

25

and another whole time of trying to get it to start healing. I have often wondered why Matron didn't let the scab grow around the gauze, for the gauze to stay there until the scab had done its stuff. Surely it would have come away in the end without any of the trouble we went through.

One side-effect of this thumb was that I missed weeks and weeks of sport. That was wonderful as I had no wish at all to play cricket. However, when I did start playing, I had to take off my glasses in case a ball broke them. In those days there was no safety glass for spectacles, so it could have been dangerous with the risk of getting splinters of glass in an eye. The main effect of not wearing my glasses was that I could barely *see* the ball. I could, however, see someone running towards me, about to bowl. If I didn't hit the ball, and I hardly ever did, it might hit me; so I was tempted to run away from the wicket in order not to be hit. I don't think I ever got any runs.

Cut eye

I used to enjoy gym, but one day I tripped and cut my eyebrow quite deeply against the smooth edge of a bench. It seems that my eyebrow was cut through by the bone underneath. As I have since been told, cuts to the head often bleed dramatically and this was no exception. I can remember running from the gym, which was some way up the back drive, to find Matron. I had blood pouring down my face. The matron decided not to have it stitched. Somehow, plaster was used to stick the sides together until it healed. I still have a scar but by now it is almost invisible.

"Radio malt" and other trips to Matron

Some of us were lucky enough to be given, as a tonic, what was known as "radio malt". I think it was called this because of someone known as the radio doctor, who would be giving health tips on what, in those days, was known as the *wireless*. This malt stuff was thick and delicious. We would be given a long spoon and told to help ourselves. We soon learned how to make a spoonful become quite a big affair. It was possible to keep on twisting the spoon so that the malt would build up into a great big "golluptious" ball around the end of the spoon. On such a day I could hardly get it into my mouth because it had sometimes become almost too big.

26

Not so nice were the penicillin injections, and I had to have a whole series of them. For this there would be a needle that looked, and felt like, a sharpened knitting needle. It had to be fat because the penicillin in those days was too thick to go through any finer needle. I can remember hating this as it hurt so much.

Appendicitis

During my second summer term (1945) I got appendicitis. The treatment for this, again in the sickroom, was to put me on a starvation diet. I can remember the doctor coming to see me after about a week of this diet, slapping me on the stomach and saying that I could get up and go back to class. I looked and felt like a Belsen victim by then. As I recall, my tummy seemed to have collapsed onto my back bone. I even thought I could see my backbone sticking up into the surface of my tummy, which of course was impossible but that was my impression at the time.

Back home

After that summer term we went back home, which by then was at "Haben House" (Rogate, West Sussex). Mother had booked me into the hospital in Petersfield to have my appendix out. The surgeon was going to be Surgeon Rear-Admiral Wakeling, obviously someone known to my father.

Years later, I was being examined by a consultant at Middlesex Hospital. He had a team of junior doctors with him, who were also invited to examine me. When the consultant came to my appendix scar, he asked: "Who on earth took out your appendix?" When I told him it had been a surgeon admiral in the Royal Navy, he said: "Of course. I can see it now. Out with the cutlass and *POW!*" He explained that, for years since then, the procedure for appendectomy had been to separate the muscles, so as to create a small window through which to operate. This makes it unnecessary to cut through the muscles, making recovery afterwards much quicker. I clearly didn't have that kind of procedure used for my appendix.

In hospital

I was taken to Petersfield hospital where I was put into a private room, this being the first time mother had a child go through an operation, and she clearly wanted to have me treated as well as possible. The problem then was that I was utterly alone in this room.

On the day of my operation, I was meant to stay in this private room but I needed to go to the loo, which I knew from the evening before was just down the corridor. I slipped out of bed and started down the corridor, only to be caught and told to go back to bed. When I said I needed to go to the loo, I was told that a nurse would bring me what I needed.

The nurse then brought in a strange glass object, a sort of vase with a long neck sticking out on one side. "Use that," she said, before disappearing. I wondered how on earth I was going to get a poo into this glass thing! Having decided it would be well nigh impossible, I had another shot at getting to the loo down the corridor, and that time I wasn't caught. It was only the next day that I discovered what the glass thing was for.

On the day after my operation, the sister came in and said to me, "Have you had your bowels open yet?" I had no idea what she was on about. "Have you had a bowel motion?" I still had no idea. "Well, you better try using this," and she lifted me onto what I later learned was a bedpan.

On that first morning I had been lying on my back, unable to sit up without help, when a nurse came in with a cup of tea. I can't imagine what she was thinking, as she handed me this steaming cup of tea and left me holding the cup and saucer above my face. I tried swinging it sideways to put it onto the bedside table, but I couldn't reach it, so I was left for about half an hour holding this cup of tea above my face. After that I knew to ask for any subsequent cups of tea to be put on the table by my bed.

After my operation, because my tummy had been cut through (as described above) I was not allowed out of bed at all. In fact, it was a whole week before I was told I could begin to get up, by which time I had almost lost the use of my legs. I can clearly remember that my legs could hardly take my weight, so that I was barely able to walk.

The day that I came home from having this experience in the hospital, my brother Michael also began to complain of a tummy ache. Our mother thought he might be playing up, perhaps trying to get the attention I'd been having. It was only after some time that a doctor was called, who diagnosed that Michael had a burst appendix and needed to be operated on immediately. He was rushed to the same hospital

28

where I'd been, but there was no time to arrange for a private room. He had to be in a public ward, which was probably a lot more interesting than being in solitary confinement. But he didn't get the five star treatment I'd been having.

Back at Maidwell

The headmaster

The head (Oliver Wyatt) was very much loved by all the boys. He was a bachelor. (I learned later that he'd lost his first love and had never married.) He was a man of great integrity, a JP, and a lay preacher. It was he who had bought Maidwell, together with its fantastic grounds— many acres of which were spread around the school. In one part there was what was known as the wilderness, which was thick with trees and shrubs. There we would build huts and chase each other around.

The school grounds

There were many wonderful beds of flowers in the school grounds and, in the spring, the place was a mass of daffodils. Many of these, Oliver told us, had been given to him in exchange for some of his orchids and lilies, for which he had become famous. He sometimes used to say it was the flowers that made it possible for him to run the school, without it running at a loss. He was a member of the Royal Horticultural Society and there are now some flowers named after him. There is also a clematis called "Maidwell", which Oliver introduced into this country.

There were fine grounds for games, the main football pitch having been extended and sown with grass while we were there. When this had been laid, we used to do stone picking, long lines of us walking across the pitch, picking up whatever we could find of the thousands of flints and other stones that had been dug up when the pitch was levelled. Then there was the huge roller, which a team of us would push.

There was a lake, with all manner of birds nesting around it, and stepping stones across it which, I believe, only prefects were allowed to use. Or was it only Michael, when he was head boy? Throughout the garden there were birds of every kind, nesting and singing. I can clearly remember goldfinches and goldcrests, which I have hardly seen since then. There were also innumerable butterflies, many of which I used to know by name.

The winter of 1947

When we went back to school for the beginning of the 1947 spring term, on the very first day it began to snow. It then snowed more than I have ever known, before or since. The morning after the first storm, we couldn't get out of the doors. Someone had to climb out of a ground floor window to get a shovel in order to clear the snow away from the door, so that it could eventually be opened.

The snow of that winter stayed for the whole of that term. There was still some snow showing in the fields when we went home, and I believe that it was a record cold winter for the whole of that century. Michael was at Winchester by then, and I later heard of the ice that used to form during the night in the basins between the beds in the dormitories.

The windows of the dorms would ice up with wonderful shapes of ferns spread across them. This was where the condensation from a dozen or so sleeping boys would collect on the windows and, when it was as cold as it was then, it would freeze.

Another problem that came with this snow was that the roads were completely impassable, and they remained so for days if not weeks. We had to build a sledge to get provisions from the local railway station, Lamport. It was something like two miles away.

One of the masters designed and oversaw the making of a sledge. It had a frame and a huge piece of plywood bent over the frame, which was used to hold the provisions collected at the station. What was missing was to have runners on the bottom, so that it could slide more easily. I think these were added later. Certainly, on the first day it was almost impossible to push.

Teams of boys were allocated each day to take this monstrous sledge down to Lamport station. The day I was in the team, the very first day, I remember the snow had drifted across the road to such an extent that the road was only discernable by following the hedges. We dragged the sledge along the top of the hedge, all the way down to the station and back. At one point a boy fell off the hedge and sort of disappeared into a snow drift, having to be hauled out by the rest of us. It was all most exciting.

Miss Douglas

The piano teacher was Miss Douglas, known by all as "Duggie". She was a tiny little lady, with a mass of black curly hair, who would travel in from Northampton most days of the week to teach boys the piano. I think I was her most nightmarish pupil, as I never really co-operated with her well-meant teaching. She had been taught by a famous teacher, Tobias Matthay.

When Duggie had been trying to get me to play with a relaxed wrist, she used to flick my wrist up from underneath saying: "Nice floppy wrist." My wrist and arm were meant to fly up in the air in response to this flick. However, I got very irritated by her doing this so repeatedly. One day, when I saw her flick coming once more I made my wrist and arm as stiff as I could. The result was dramatic. As she had really lost her temper with me this time, she'd made to hit my wrist really hard from beneath, but her hand met with an equally hard resistance. She ended up with a broken wrist, and she had her arm in plaster for several weeks, not able to play at all. She must have hated me. She got the headmaster to give me a beating.

Another time, she had taken the trouble to write out a music theory exam paper for me to fill in, but I didn't fancy doing this. I just felt bored with it, and started messing around. When I came to the bottom of the first page, I saw she'd written "Turn Over". I knew the abbreviation (p.t.o.) used to indicate turning a page, so I added "Please" before what she'd written. She was magnificently furious, and again she sent me to the head. But I never minded being beaten. I always felt I deserved it, and it was always administered fairly as well as sternly.

The boys were sometimes quite cruel about Duggie, as she was such a character. She once fell into the cattle grid that guarded the drive entrance to the school. She hadn't been able to open the side gate, so she'd tried to walk across the bars. She had slipped and got her ankle stuck between them. I don't know how long she was there before some passer-by helped her out, but she was quite seriously hurt. The boys of course went around chanting "The cow-catcher's caught a cow," not that she ever deserved to be called a cow. It was just irresistible to small boys.

I would have learned much more from Duggie if I'd taken notice of her frequent commands not to look at my hands. For decades afterwards, I remained unable to sight read as I always refused to do what she'd been telling me to do, imagining that I would never be able to find the notes unless I looked for them.

31

It was only years later that I made myself learn how to play without looking at my hands. Then, and quite quickly, I found I became able to sight read. Alas, I had lost all those many years of pleasure from sight reading, by refusing to learn the simple skill she was trying to get me to learn.

Going to church

At the local church there was an organ that had to be kept going by someone pumping a long lever at one side of it. A boy would usually be doing this but, if the boy got behind or stopped pumping, the organ notes would begin to subside until they stopped. The organist would then be slapping on the side of the organ to wake up the organ pumper.

We used to be given pennies to put in the collection. I can remember one day, when I and another boy were sitting near the back, we began playing with our pennies—putting them in our eyes like dark glasses. When I was doing this, one of the pennies dropped and rolled across the aisle. I got beaten for that too.

Visits from home

Mother would come to visit us once a term, travelling by train. She used to stay in the village, in a café that rented out rooms, and we would go there to have tea with her. Strangely, that is all I remember about her visits, except for the occasion when Oliver invited her to have tea with him in the Oak Room, the old library, along with Michael and me.

That was when Michael was head boy, which he was for two terms. As part of that privilege, Michael would have a room of his own in the headmaster's wing of the school, and he would have access to a bathroom there which was shared with the two other prefects who were in an adjoining room. Oliver was telling our mother that it was left to Michael to decide how often he had a bath, to which she replied: "So, Michael, how many baths have you had this term?" I think he replied that it had been only three so far!

Peter Scott's visit

While Michael was still at Maidwell, Oliver invited Peter Scott to come to the school to give us a talk about birds. He drew a wonderful picture of a special kind of goose, using coloured crayons on one of the blackboards, and signing this too. Michael remembers that this was a red-breasted goose. This picture remained on that blackboard for about a year, until one of the teachers (Miss Hawkins) wanted more blackboard space than she had on the side she'd been using. She turned the board over and found Peter Scott's picture. She just rubbed it off to make space for whatever she was about to write. There was then a "mutiny" in the school about this. It was too late to recover the signed picture, but not too late to make a protest. The whole school marched around the place with a placard on a stick, which had some ominous message about Miss Hawkins, such as: *Miss Hawkins should go*. Of course she didn't "go", but at least she knew we were not pleased with her that day.

Being taught by the headmaster

I have a particular memory of being taught by the head that I recorded in my last book:

> I vividly recall a time when I was being taught by the headmaster, when I was called up to his desk to have my Latin sentences corrected. Trying to complete just one more sentence before going up, I half stood while continuing to work out the verb to complete the sentence. He said: "Don't hurry," so I sat down to finish it properly. He then yelled at me for being insolent. I suspect that I was often insolent but on this occasion I was simply taking him at his word. (*Learning from Life*, p. 26)

Fire drill

One really important thing we learned at Maidwell was through the regular fire drills that we used to have. I think we had these every term, or at least every year.

We all had to go through the exercise of being led from our dormitories, in an orderly fashion, to rope ladders down which we had to climb, being supervised in this by the prefect of each dormitory. But, in addition, we learned some important safety procedures, such as placing a damp sheet or towel across the bottom of doors, to limit the smoke that could get into a room, while waiting to be rescued if we could not get out any other way.

We also learned that we should keep close to the floor, where there would be less smoke. And, if we found someone who was unconscious, we should tie their wrists together with a handkerchief or something similar, so that we could put the tied wrists over our head, then crawling along with the unconscious person sliding along beneath us. I don't think I've ever heard of these precautions from anywhere else. Fortunately I have never had to make use of them, but knowing these things could save a life.

Gas masks

Another drill, each term until the end of the war in 1945, was putting on our gas masks. This was in case there was a gas attack from Germany. We each had one of these strange things that we had to put over our heads, with goggling eye pieces and an odd filter thing on the front. We had to breathe in and out strongly, as a test to see that the rubber around our faces was fitting well. Trying to talk with a gas mask on made our voices sound very peculiar.

Being told to write out 100 lines

I was quite frequently given a punishment for talking in class. For this I would be told to write out 100 times *I must not talk in class*. I sometimes built up for myself a cache of these, written in advance. For other offences, I also wrote: "I must not ..." to be filled in later with whatever it was that I must not, but I think I got rumbled when my pen nib was not working the same when I completed these.

"Altus" and "latus"

One of the other things I repeatedly had to write out 100 times was the meaning of the Latin words *altus* and *latus*, having to write: "*Altus* means high and *latus* means broad." But very often, when I again had to remember which was which, I continued to get it wrong, and again it would be 100 lines. What struck me as extraordinary was that at no time were we encouraged to recognise the link between Latin and English. Or, if we were taught this, I missed it—which is quite possible.

I didn't see this connection until I found myself teaching Latin at a prep school (see later). There, whenever a boy asked me the same

34

question as I had kept on asking at Maidwell, "Sir, what does *altus* mean?" or "Sir, what does *latus* mean?" I would never give the direct answer. Instead, I would say: "Think of altitude" or "Think of latitude." Those boys would then have a way of remembering the difference, probably for ever, without having to write it out hundreds of times as I had to.

Another complaint I have about the teaching of Latin at Maidwell was that I don't think it was ever explained to us *why* we were learning Latin. It has only been in later years that it became clear to me that Latin gives us such an excellent grounding in grammar, much of which we also need to understand in English. But, learning English as our mothertongue, we take in such grammar as we do without knowing it. Or we don't take it in at all, hence the common mistakes we hear, or see in print, when people say things like "with Tom and I" rather than "with Tom and me". People today often fail to recognise the essential grammar here, that prepositions are followed by the accusative "me", whereas "I" is always used as the subject of a sentence, followed by a verb. Such basic things are much more easily overlooked when people haven't had to work at the grammar, as in Latin and then also in English. Too often people just pick up speaking as others speak, thus picking up the common grammatical mistakes that so many people make nowadays.

Potato picking

A lot of these memories are in random order, but it probably won't matter to the reader.

As part of the war effort, Oliver offered a local farmer help from the boys at Maidwell, to do the potato picking. This was a back-breaking job, bending over the furrows and picking the potatoes into buckets, then unloading the buckets into the trailer behind a tractor. But it was different from playing games and quite good fun. I certainly preferred it to playing games.

Reading about science

I became fascinated in how things worked and I was greatly encouraged in this by two books in particular: *Lively Things for Lively Youngsters*, and *How It Works and How It Is Done*. Years later, my first therapist claimed that my reason for being so interested in the second of these books was really that I'd been wanting to find out about how babies were made. I still think that was a load of psychoanalytic *bollocks*. I was just hugely curious about the world around me.

Another book, which I had asked to be given, went into explaining how a radio worked. I learned about how a signal was tuned, using a coil and a thing called a condenser, and how this signal was amplified by using a valve. There was also a cunning way by which a volume control could be made, which meant feeding part of the amplified signal back into the circuit before the amplifying stage. The result was that, if this was carefully managed, the output could be made louder by stages. However, if too much of the signal was fed back (in this feed-back loop) it would get out of control and whistle—as sometimes happens at a public lecture (see later).

My invention

While I was still at Maidwell I came to realise that it must be possible to record on tape the signals that go into making a television picture. Even though these would be much more complex than sound signals, recorded on tape for music, it would surely be possible to put the picture signals also on tape. That would mean that programmes for TV could be recorded and played back whenever these were wanted, rather than always having TV going out live. No such thing as a video recorder had ever been made at that time, and this was in 1947 when I was twelve.

True to all the greatest discoveries, my discovery had come to me when I was in the bath. I duly leaped from the bath, just as Archimedes did, shouting *Eureka*, and rushed to tell my parents.

The result was that they found a man called Mr. Porter, who worked in a radio and electrical shop in Petersfield. He agreed to take me under his wing, and I would go there one morning a week to learn about things in his shop. Alas, he had to tell me that I wasn't the first person on earth to think of a "video recorder": "They are already working on it." But it was some years before such a thing was actually produced.

Making a radio

With the help of Mr. Porter, I made a one valve radio (I was still at Maidwell at the time). This worked with two batteries. One was called an "HT" (high tension) battery, which fed the main circuit of the radio, and the other was called an accumulator (low voltage) which fed the valve. The accumulator had to be charged, like a car battery, and Mr. Porter used to keep this on charge for me during term-time, so that it would be in good condition for when I came home for holidays.

Food

On the whole, the food at Maidwell was good. One of the favourite things we had was what we called "submarines". These were a kind of Cornish pasty with the pastry pulled up to a peak, rather like the conning tower on a "sub". Every day, for anyone who was still hungry, after whichever pudding we'd already had, there was always a supply of rice pudding.

At teatime we each had a large glass of milk from the local dairy, with nearly half an inch of cream on the top. This was delicious—except when the weather was hot. This milk was always put out immediately after lunch had been cleared, and quite often it would go sour. But we were still expected to drink it, even when sour.

Sweet rations

As it was wartime for my first three years at Maidwell, lots of things were rationed, including sugar. I think it was only after the war that some sweets became more available but they were still rationed. For some reason the headmaster never used sugar. He may have been diabetic or he may have just chosen to go without his sugar ration. The cook would therefore put his sugar on one side each week "for a rainy day".

Once a week there would be a sweet-time, when we could queue up for our choice of sweets—as long as we kept within the rationed limit. I recall a ration book for sweets with E's and D's in it, which represented different quantities. A teacher would cut out an E or a D from our ration books, and allow us to have what we chose. Some boys would get a lot of sweets at the beginning of term, and then find they had none towards the end. Others would save up and have a binge with sweets later on.

It turned out that there was a problem with this system. Unknown to anyone, the teachers had been giving sweets out at double the rate determined by the ration books. This meant that the full amount of sweets allowed had been used up before we got halfway through the term.

There could have been a big crisis over this as the hoarders, those saving for later, might have had to go without their sweets because the greedy ones had been having double rations already.

However, the cook came up with a splendid idea. With the agreement of the headmaster, or it may have been his suggestion in the first place, she used up the sugar he'd been saving, and she made huge quantities of home-made sweets such as peppermint creams. These were much more delicious than shop sweets, and I'd been one of the ones who had been saving up to have sweets later. So the *E's* and the *D's* were still used, but for the rest of that term they were still allowed to count for double the proper ration. It was a great day for some of us when the teachers had been giving out the wrong ration of sweets.

Pocket money

At the beginning of each term we would hand in the pocket money we'd brought with us. I recall that I was usually given twenty-five shillings. Whenever we wished to use some of this, we would ask Miss Hardwicke or some other teacher to buy us a modelling kit, or something similar, from the town. We would then have to complete a cheque, from a little chequebook that each boy had. We had to make this out to the headmaster "O. E. P. Wyatt, Esq" and fill in the amount in words and figures. This would be duly deducted from the amount we'd handed in, and the balance would be returned to us at the end of the term. It was a good way to teach us how to write cheques, for later life.

I remember that I usually brought back over half of my pocket money each term, which I would give to mother. But at the end of one term, shortly before I went on to Winchester, she decided I could keep this. I had after all saved it by not spending it all, so I could spend it on whatever I chose.

I'd never before had an opportunity to spend money like this, so I had no idea what to spend it on. In the end I went to a hardware shop and bought stacks of nails, and screws of every imaginable size. *You can never tell what sizes you might need one day*, was my reasoning at the time. For years after that father had these nails and screws in the garage, and they did come to be useful, eventually. But they were never all used.

The first biro

I recall one of the masters boasting over a *Biro* he'd just bought. It had cost him *three guineas* (probably £60 today). He showed us how it worked, with a little ball at the end and ink inside that would, according to the advertisement, write something like three miles before running out. It is incredible to think of the cost of that first biro, in money of that time, compared to the biros one can now buy for about *5p*.

Smoking

Mr. Brierley (the new games master) used to smoke some revoltingly strong tobacco in a pipe. One day he had dropped his tobacco pouch, but he'd failed to pick up quite all of the tobacco. Another boy and I swept this up and rolled it into some classroom paper, which we proceeded to smoke in one of the toilets. By the time we came to tea I was looking green in the face and feeling extremely ill. I felt so ill, and looked it, that the matron let me go to bed immediately after tea. I know I'd been unable to eat any of it. I was so put off smoking by that experience I never smoked again until I was at Oxford. It was such a mistake starting then as it took me about twenty years to come off it. But it had helped that I had already been put off for a lot of other years that I might have been smoking.

Being called, yet again, to the headmaster's study

I wasn't sure what I had done wrong this time so I went with some curiosity to see the head yet again. But, instead of telling me off for something he gave me a short lecture (also reported in *Learning from Life*). He said:

> I have news for you. All the staff have now given up on you. Everything has been tried and nothing has worked. At least, everything has been tried except for one thing. No one has thought to put you in a position of responsibility because no one has seen you as capable of being responsible. So I am going to take a risk with you.

I am going to give you the responsibility of being a school prefect. Please don't let me down. (*Learning from Life*, p. 11)

Winchester entrance exam

Oliver never told me that I was due to take the Winchester entrance until the day of the exams. For these I had to go over to the vicarage where the local vicar was to invigilate me. The only exam I remember is the Greek exam. For this, for the first time ever, I was given a large Greek lexicon. It was part of the rules of the Greek exam that a lexicon could be used for the translation. As I had never used one before, and this was so large, I could not find the section for words beginning with the Greek letter *Xsi*. As there are not so many words that begin with this letter, that section in the lexicon was much smaller than those for any of the other letters. I never found the *Xsi* section.

As a result, when I could not find the meaning for the main verb (beginning with *Xsi*) in a sentence near to the beginning of the translation piece, I guessed the meaning. Unfortunately I had guessed wrongly, which threw out the meaning of most other verbs that followed. However, not to be defeated, I looked up almost all the verbs which didn't fit in with the meaning I'd guessed, so that I was able to find way-out meanings for some otherwise quite straightforward words. The result must have been an extraordinarily bizarre scrambled egg of unusual meanings. I've no idea what the examiners may have thought of this, but it didn't prevent me getting into Winchester.

Playing rugger

In my very last term I began to know what the rules of rugger were. Father had given me an illustrated book of rules called *Why the Whistle Went*, illustrated by a cartoonist called Fugasse. The front page had a picture of a referee looking very alarmed, clutching at his throat, having swallowed the whistle. Anyway, this was very useful and I learned all sorts of basic things like having always to pass the ball backwards, not throwing it into touch as in my first attempt at playing rugger.

I also noticed that, in the second game which still only played rugger once a week, I was actually head and shoulders taller than any of the other boys. So one day I decided I would play the game for earnest. This was very easy in that second game, among all those midgets. When I got the ball I could hold it above their heads, and I could use my weight to drag whichever boys were trying to hang onto me, until I got to the line where I could score a try. In fact I scored so often that day I was removed from the second game and made to play among boys of my own size.

Playing in the first game was quite a challenge, but to my amazement, never having been the slightest bit keen on any sport, I began to enjoy this. Within three weeks I was promoted to be in the team.

In the first match I played in, I scored a try. I was a wing three-quarter and was able to outrun most other boys, which was a big advantage. There was, however, a disaster in one game we played, just before another match. The games master, by then Mr. Brierley, set the team members to play opposite their matching partners. This meant that I was playing right wing three-quarter, having to mark the left wing three-quarter who was John Innes. At one moment I was speeding down the wing when Innes tackled me. Unfortunately for him, he got one arm between my legs which were pumping their way so fiercely that my legs scissored his arm and broke it in two places. I remember seeing his arm with a pronounced zigzag break. The last I ever saw of Innes was the day I left the school, he with his arm still in plaster. I hope his arm made a good recovery.

Leaving Maidwell

Like most other boys I wept when I left Maidwell. It had been a truly wonderful school to be at and a great privilege. It had also provided a stability in my life that had not been possible to find elsewhere, as our home kept on moving. At Maidwell, for all of those five years, at least the school stayed the same. It was one of the best decisions our parents made, in my opinion, to give us the chance to be at that school.

CHAPTER THREE

Life at our first settled home

Dreaded parties and seeing double at a Hunt Ball (aged 14)

Rogate (West Sussex)

We went to Rogate shortly after my younger sister (Sue) was born, so that was probably in 1944 or early 1945, to a house we knew as "Haben".

At some stage, but I cannot remember when, mother enrolled as something like an air raid warden in the village. For this she was supplied with uniform and boots. Her function, or so we were told, was to stand at the crossroads directing people to a decontamination centre in the event of a gas attack. She was meant to instruct people to strip off their clothes immediately, and to be decontaminated in a shower that would be provided.

Clothes also had to be decontaminated. I don't know how people were going to be supplied with new clothes. Also, what was mother going to be wearing at the crossroads? Did she have to set an example by standing there entirely naked? We never quite worked that out.

The village was an extraordinary place and we formed a strong attachment to it: the people, the village shop, the church on the hill, and the little church about two miles away; that was Terwick church, which was in a field set back from the road. In the spring there used to be lupines in the field, set apart from the farming of the field alongside it.

43

I believe it was protected by the National Trust, or something like that, but the lupines disappeared some years later. I don't know why. I think a farmer just ploughed them in.

One of the headstones on a grave at Terwick church was to commemorate a gypsy from the area. His widow had been asked what she would like to have engraved on this and she chose, as far as she could remember it, what she'd read on a gravestone just inside the church gate. That reads: "Never, never more to part." What was engraved on her husband's headstone, which happens also to be by far the largest in the whole graveyard, is: "Never, *never no more* to part". I love the gypsy grammar in that.

This reminds me of a gravestone I was shown in Sheffield. The inscription on that was in Arabic and in English. The English reads: "*In peace at last from wife and daughters*". I think that is really funny. It might also be more true than it was meant to be.

The village telephone exchange in Rogate was a special institution, while it was still manned by a real person, before these things became automated. For instance, when mother telephoned to speak to someone in the village (for example Mrs. Bodkin) the woman in the exchange would ask her if she wanted to speak to Mrs. Bodkin herself or did she want to be connected to the house? When she enquired why she asked this, the woman in the exchange replied: "Well, I've just seen Mrs. Bodkin go into the village shop. I could connect you to the shop if you like."

While our father's parents were living in the New Forest, mother would telephone to speak to them every Sunday afternoon. On one occasion she was trying to remember the number and said to herself, but aloud: "What is the number I want?" The woman in the exchange offered her the New Forest number, as it was her usual time to ring there, and she was right. Another time, mother asked for New Forest 274, giving the number she thought it was. The exchange woman interrupted and said: "I think you've got that number wrong. I think you mean 374," and, again, she was right. All of that disappeared when the telephone exchanges became automatic.

This brings to mind the time when self-dialling began to be introduced. I was visiting my sister Elisabeth in her Gloucester Road flat, which she shared with several other girls. Their telephone had just been changed to self-dialling, no longer needing to go through a telephone exchange manned by a person. For this they had a very slim book of codes that could be used for self-dialling (STD): all the big cities like

London, Birmingham, Edinburgh, and a few smaller places. Probably the smallest was Little Budsworth.

A man visiting one of the girls in the flat was studying this list of dialling codes and was amazed to find Little Budsworth among the places that could be self-dialled: "Perhaps a managing director of the telephone company lives there." He then thought it would be fun to ring someone in Little Budsworth. "How many people living there would be on the phone? Would the numbers be less than 100 or more?" He tried a few double figure numbers but couldn't get through. Then he tried a few three figure numbers until someone answered. (This was just about fifteen years after George Orwell's book 1984 had been published, in which he introduced the idea of *Big Brother is watching you*). Inspired by that, this man said to the lady who answered his dialled number: "Is that *Little Budsworth*?" When the lady answered that it was, he went on: "I have news for you. *Big Budsworth* is watching you," and he put the phone down on the poor lady.

Haben house (Rogate)

This house, like all the others before, was rented. It was only after some ten or more years at Haben that our parents lived in a house they actually owned: Terwick Old Rectory.

Haben belonged to the Carnegie family. It had a lawn, a garden, and an orchard. On the garden side was an extension to the original house that was covered in pebble-dash. I recall the drawing room in that extension being freezing cold every winter, and yet we were expected to practise the piano in there without any heat being provided.

Tucky was still with us when we first moved to Haben, but she was replaced fairly soon by a nanny for my sisters. She, Evelyn Duggan, was eventually teaching them at home, and creating a little home school for them with, I think, three other children. Our mother took on the task of teaching French. When someone asked her how she set about teaching "*le*" and "*la*", mother said that she just taught them to think of *he the's* and *she the's*.

The first Sunday at Haben

Michael and I had been at Maidwell when the family first moved into Haben. On our first Sunday we were taken to Terwick church and

I was encouraged to wear my new school cap on the way to church. It was apparently the grown-up thing to do. This cap had wide navy blue and white circles, from the crown to its peak, and was very visible.

Unfortunately, having put this cap on my head, I'd forgotten I was still wearing it. Also, I hadn't yet learned that men (and of course boys) were expected to remove their headgear upon entering a church, as a sign of respect. So there I was, sitting in the front pew, with my cap still on throughout all of the first part of the service. When the vicar came out of the chancel, to read the first lesson, he came to me and kindly removed my cap. He then proceeded to read the lesson from the lectern, which was an eagle on a stand made of brass. I can remember sitting in that pew with the blush in my face spreading right to the tips of my ears, feeling hot all over with embarrassment.

Meeting strangers

After lunch on that Sunday, Michael and I were encouraged to go exploring in the neighbourhood, on our bicycles. There was a round trip that was described to us, which we followed. When pushing our bikes up a hill, we met a man and a woman who were out walking, the man in shorts with striking white hair and jet black eyebrows. I'd never met anyone with both black and white hair.

This man said to me: "You are the boy who was wearing his cap in church this morning." I nearly died. It felt as if the whole neighbourhood had heard of my *faux pas* in church. It turned out that the couple were John and Judy Hewick, he being known by most people as "the Brig" (brigadier).

We came to see a lot of John and Judy. One memory of Judy that I have often enjoyed recalling is when we were in church, saying the general confession: "We have done those things we ought not to have done and we have left undone those things we ought to have done ...." At that moment Judy leaped out of her pew and ran out of the church. It so happened that the Hewicks then lived in what was known as the Dower House, across the field from the church. We learned later that Judy had suddenly remembered she'd forgotten to put the Sunday joint in the oven. So, not to waste a moment, she had rushed back home to make up for her "thing left undone".

Ken Mathews (the local vicar)

One person who became hugely important to the family was the Rev Ken Mathews: only one "t" he would remind us. "I share it with Betsy" (his wife). He'd previously been a Royal Navy chaplain. I still remember his car number, GL 3414.

There were many stories about Ken Mathews in Terwick church. One was about a mousetrap placed under the altar. When Ken was standing at the altar, during the service, he stepped on the trap and we all heard the snap as it went off. Also, in the pulpit, Ken would sometimes hold onto the brass candlestick during his sermon. On one occasion he got so carried away that he lent on this and it bent alarmingly towards the congregation. He just yanked it back to its upright position and carried on.

Once Ken had forgotten to read the bans of marriage for a couple soon to be married in Terwick. He rushed out to the car park and read the bans there to whoever had not yet driven off home.

Each Christmas, Ken would preach a wonderful sermon on the Christmas story. These were known as his "I was there" sermons. He would give us an imagined memory from the position of a character in the Christmas story: one of the shepherds, one of the kings, etc., choosing a different character each year. They were most memorable.

Occasionally I would go for a walk on the Hampshire Downs with Ken, sharing with him my thoughts (then) of perhaps being ordained. He was very sensible and helpful, and he never in any way pushed me towards that end. One thing I also remember from those walks was Ken's interesting habit of smoking his pipe upside down, whenever it was raining, as this helped to keep it from going out.

Terwick church

This little church was the focus of many family memories.

From the time we first started going to this church we were placed in the front pew. I don't know how that came about, whether we had been shown to that pew by a churchwarden or whether mother had assumed that was to be our place. Anyway, that remained "our" pew for many years after.

It became quite handy to be in this pew when our mother took to playing the harmonium. We could help her by singing the *Te Deum* and the *Venite*. It was also a help when she was playing for a service that was broadcast from Terwick, while Ken Mathews was still there. In one hymn, which was *For All the Saints*, she began an extra verse by mistake. Father signalled frantically to her, so she quickly turned the opening phrase into a kind of "Amen". She was paid *three guineas* by the BBC for that service, the only money she ever earned in her whole life.

"Frog's hole"

On the way to Terwick church was a house, built down a slope from the road so that you could only see the roof and top windows. It was called "Frog's Hole", and this was where Peggy Tamplin lived. Her brother was there too when we first came to Rogate and it was he who made the wrought iron light brackets in the church.

Dancing lessons

Mother had the bright idea of hiring Peggy Tamplin to teach us to dance, she being a ballet teacher and a sometime ballet dancer herself.

I remember being taught how to waltz, being told to practise with a chair as my partner. I danced all around the flower beds at Haben, dancing with a dining room chair as instructed. However, Peggy soon cried off from continuing to teach me as I kept stepping on her toes. "My feet are far too valuable to me, for me to put them at risk by dancing with Patrick."

Another family concert

We were all learning the piano, and Michael was also learning to play the clarinet. I subsequently took up the viola and then the violin.

At Haben we had just one concert that I remember. Elisabeth and Susan played piano pieces, Susan's being called "Climbing". For this Sue had to end up playing *arpeggios* that went higher and higher up the piano, she sliding up the piano stool until she had to leave it, walking up the piano to reach the last few bits.

I played the *Solfeghietto* by C. P. E. Bach. I played this very fast, right through, with no slowing at all. After my race through this piece I came to an abrupt stop, and then I heard one of the audience say: "Is that all?"

It would have been much better if I'd ended with at least some bit of *rallentando.*

The high spot of this concert, for me at least, was when Michael played a piece on the clarinet, with mother accompanying. For this he needed a music stand, which we didn't have. Somebody's grandmother held the music for him, holding it up before her face so that he could see it. As he played, his clarinet began to dribble and I remember watching the drips collecting in the grandmother's lap, she being the only person unaware of this happening. I thought this very funny, but I remember nothing of the music itself.

Tawny (our cocker spaniel)

When we were first at Haben we had a golden cocker spaniel called Tawny. He was quite a character and he seemed to have an unfailing memory for when each lady dog in the village would next be on heat. He would then take up his position outside the house, waiting for a possible chance of meeting the lady in time to give her puppies. He even kept this up outside the vicarage for several years after the lady dog there had died, but he was always right about when it would have been her time, if she had still been alive.

There was another dog in the village that was called Porridge, very aptly named as she looked just like porridge. She too was one of the dogs Tawny fancied. She was owned by Lady Perth who had a big house in Fyning, near to Rogate. She knew of Tawny's reputation. Therefore, when Porridge had got out while she was on heat, Lady Perth rang mother to ask her to lock Tawny in until Porridge had been found, which she did. Some hours later Lady Perth rang again to say she was very worried as Porridge had still not come back. Was it possible she might be somewhere around our house or garden? Mother said she was sure not, but she went to look. She then found she'd locked Porridge in with Tawny, who had been having a wild old time. Porridge had to go to the vet to prevent her having Tawny's puppies.

Tawny used to get in the way of Mr. Davey, the gardener who came with the house when we rented it. He would be there about two days a week. On one occasion mother heard Tawny yelping and screaming around the garden, limping. "Davey" tried to reassure her: "It's all right, madam. He only put his foot under mine."

More about Davey

Old Davey was quite a character. He had earned a well deserved reputation for being one of the finest hedgers in the neighbourhood. He was paid to go along the hedgerows, trimming them and laying the tops down in a special way that kept them controlled and looking neat and tidy. He was clearly very good at it.

For us, he would do the vegetable garden and whatever else needed doing in our garden. Unfortunately he came in for some target practice when I'd been given an airgun. Michael had discovered we didn't need to waste pellets for target practice. We could remove the barrel from inside the gun, using this to stab into slices of potato we laid out in the garage. With one of these harmless potato pellets in the gun, I'd aimed at Davey's bottom as he was bending over to pick something up, a target too tempting to miss. He felt something hit him and reported this to mother. Father, probably not knowing that this was only a potato pellet and certainly wanting to make sure I never again pointed a gun at anyone, then confiscated the gun from me. All I ever wanted to do with it was to shoot potato pellets, but I never saw the gun again.

When Robin (the son of Mr. and Mrs. Carnegie) got married, the wedding was a very grand affair. I believe he married someone with a title. In fact he too got a title later on, when he became Lord Northesk. As the wedding was at some distance from Rogate, and there were many people in the village who might like to see Robin get married, the Carnegies laid on a coach to drive them to the wedding. This was largely filled with people like Mr. Davey, who worked for the Carnegies.

The next Monday morning Davey was very full of this experience. He'd never seen such a grand house and garden, and he spent a lot of time trying to get mother's interest in his description of it. As she was wanting to get on with other things, she was obviously not showing the degree of interest that Davey was hoping for. He then came out with his most arresting detail: "*And*, madam, do you know how many toilets they have in that house? They have *seventeen* toilets." At this mother *did* take notice.

I remember Mrs. Carnegie senior as a little and rather bent old lady with a deeply wrinkled face. She bred a special kind of spaniel that looked almost pink, and we would sometimes see her walking about ten of these at a time, with their leads spread out like a fan in front of her.

Tucky and some special soup

One lunch time, we were eating some soup that Tucky had made. It was so good mother asked her how she had made it. Tucky replied that it was very easy. She'd found some stock in the larder and just added a few things to it. Mother wasn't so sure about there having been any stock in the larder, so she enquired further. It turned out that the stock Tucky had found had been made from boiling up the dog meat that had been obtained from the butcher. As meat was still rationed then, the only meat that could be used for dogs was meat that had been deemed to be unfit for human consumption. To make it clear that this was not to be eaten by people, this unfit meat would be painted green. So the stock, from which this lovely soup had been made, had come from meat that had been painted green. Michael and I still thought the soup was wonderful. Tucky did not. She rushed out of the dining room to be sick.

More about Michael and me

We were often not getting on well together, particularly while we were both at Maidwell and again when we were both at Winchester. But there were times when we did. For instance, when Michael had started at Winchester he came back with all kinds of new things for me to hear about and to learn about. One thing that clearly caught my twelve-year-old interest was when Michael told me that our bodies make something called *methane* and this comes out when we *fart*. In fact, he went on to show me that it is possible to set light to farts with a match. When he demonstrated this to me I was most impressed.

Making explosions

This was another big thing. Michael showed me how to mix magnesium powder with concentrated iodine, producing something called magnesium iodide. This is the stuff that is put into crackers and pistol caps. Being an unstable compound, it will release a lot of energy—most of it as noise—when it is disturbed.

We used to be able to buy ingredients like these from a chemist in those days, and we had bought quite a lot. We first tried some reasonably small amounts, which we'd leave to dry on pieces of blotting paper,

51

and we would set these off the following day when they were fully dried. I remember that I then suggested we could use up all the ingredients we had, putting the mixture onto an array of blotting paper pieces, each bit with a pile of this damp black stuff put there to dry.

The following morning I woke up first and could not wait to try at least one of these piles, as they looked dry enough. I woke Michael so that we could enjoy this together. Rather gingerly, we touched one of these piles of stuff, but when it went off it disturbed all the other piles. This created what would be called a chain reaction. All this stuff went off simultaneously, with the most tremendous *BANG* I'd ever heard. Our father, who had been woken by the explosion, rushed in. I have no idea what he thought might have happened. (We didn't have terrorists in those days but it certainly sounded as if a bomb had gone off.) The bedroom was filled with purple smoke and he peered through this to check we were both still alive and well. It was a great moment.

Mole trapping

In a rare moment of co-operation, Michael and I agreed we would both trap moles, curing the skins so we could make moleskin waistcoats. I think the inspiration for this may have come from reading a book called *Little Grey Men*, in which the little men wore waistcoats made from moleskins.

Anyway, the idea was great even though the practicalities were rather different. We bought a pile of mole traps and used to go out early each morning, to check for moles and to set traps in the newest looking molehills. However, this enterprise came to a dramatic end.

One morning, I came across the biggest and freshest molehill I'd ever seen. I rushed to get one of my traps, to claim this as mine, only to get back to find that Michael had put one of his traps into *my* molehill. I became extremely cross and took Michael's trap out so that I could put in one of mine. He then came back and claimed this was *his* molehill, not mine. What transpired was a "fight to the death", with each of us pulling up the other's mole traps and throwing them at each other as hard as possible. That ended the mole trapping forever, and we never got our moleskin waistcoats. I think Michael did skin a few moles and cured the skins, but I don't know what became of them.

Flying our boxkites

Michael and I had been given boxkites for Christmas.

One day, when the wind was good for kite-flying, we flew one of them in the grounds of Fair Oak (the Carnegie's house). We had devised a way in which we could fly our sister's Teddy, on a parachute, up to the top of the string. We tied the teddy bear to a ring that slid up to the kite when the parachute was caught by the wind. We also fashioned a release mechanism, by sharpening the edges of the lid from a baked bean tin, through which the kite string was fed, fixing the lid near the top. The cotton between the teddy and the ring, once it got up to the kite, would be cut through by this lid—releasing the teddy to fly down by parachute. This was great fun. But it nearly ended in disaster when Teddy landed high up in an oak tree. If Michael hadn't been so adept at climbing trees we might never have rescued the teddy bear from that oak.

Playing tennis

On one occasion, but only one, Michael and I were invited to play tennis with the grandsons of Lady Perth. I don't know if there was a Lord Perth somewhere but I don't recall him ever being mentioned. I'm sure I played tennis very badly, as usual, which might have been why we were never invited back. After tennis we were asked to stay to tea, which we did.

However, when we got home, we found that mother had laid out a full tea for us in the dining room. So, not wanting this to go to waste, we sat down and ate *all* of that too. It was either then, or it may have been on another occasion, there was some item for tea that needed to be divided. Of course we were both keen to make sure the other didn't get the bigger bit. In the end Michael fetched the kitchen scales to weigh each piece.

Two methods of hitchhiking

On another occasion, Michael and I had been travelling somewhere (I forget where) and we were trying to get back home from Petersfield. We got as far as what was known as the "Adhurst turning", off the A3, where we set off to hitchhike the remaining few miles to Rogate. Here we had a difference of opinion as to the best way to do it. It was hardly likely, in those days, that we would have agreed on much.

Michael said that it was better to walk, and to thumb lifts as you went, as this showed good intention. It also meant that if you didn't get a lift you did at least make headway along your journey. I, on the other hand, said it was better to wait at a turning (like at the corner we were at) as cars would be slowing down anyway, and that would make it easier for them to stop. So, with this difference of plan, Michael set off walking and I stood at the corner trying to get a lift.

After nearly an hour, with no success whatever, a tramp shouted to me from his perch on the fence behind me. He called me over and explained that of course I hadn't got anyone to stop. I wasn't hitching properly. I had been doing it with my forefinger when I should have been doing it with my thumb. The point was that Michael and I had disagreed about this as well. He'd said *thumb* and I'd said *finger*, believing that a finger was more polite than using a thumb. So the tramp explained that when I'd been using my finger, this had *not* meant *I would like a lift*. Instead, it meant *Carry on. I'm not wanting a lift*. The result had been that any car that might have stopped to give me a lift had carried on, because that was what I seemed to be indicating with my finger.

After that I tried using my thumb, but still with no success. Later, when the bus for Rogate came along, I realised that Michael had the money which had been given us for our travels. I therefore had no money at all to pay for the bus. Here the tramp came to my rescue once more. He tossed me a sixpence to pay for my fare!

When I got back to Haben I found that I'd arrived just a few minutes after Michael, who had also had no success with the hitchhiking. He'd walked the whole way (about four miles) but at least he had got home first, proving the wisdom of walking as well as hitchhiking.

Some kitchen stories

For some time, mother used to cook porridge in a *haybox*. This was a wartime method for saving energy. You brought some porridge to the boil and then placed it in a box, with hay tightly packed around the pan and over the top of it, then leaving it overnight. In the morning it would still be piping hot and fully cooked. There was no such thing as instant porridge in those days.

Mother often used a pressure cooker. She was cooking vegetable soup one day when the safety valve had blown. This resulted in a fountain of soup that went right up to the ceiling before cascading down onto the kitchen surfaces. Most impressive.

Father was invited to spend an afternoon shooting, somewhere near Nyewood. He said they'd only seen one pheasant in the whole time they were there, which everyone shot at. The pheasant was not killed, but it seemed to have come down from the sheer weight of lead that had been pumped into it. I think they may have drawn lots, to see who would take this home, and father was the one to come back with it. Mother then spent ages plucking it, and even more ages picking lead shot out of the carcass. She had then left this on the kitchen table, ready to be cooked, but she hadn't allowed for Tawny (the cocker spaniel). She came back a bit later to find that he'd eaten the whole carcass, as if all the effort put into this had been just for him.

Even though mother had a few notable failures in cake-making, she nearly always made great cakes for the daily afternoon tea, which was a ritual never to be missed. One of the best bits of this process was when the mixing bowl had to be licked out. Michael and I used to take turns. It was just wonderful being allowed to scoop up the remains of the mixture on a finger which could then be sucked. But it was a really sad day when mother bought a rubber spatula which she then used for scooping out even the tiniest bits of mixture, leaving nothing at all for finger-licking afterwards. Her cake-making was never the same for us after that.

One day, when the rest of the family was out, I was in the kitchen alone. I put a kettle on, to make a cup of tea, but I did this too quickly. The Aga lid fell back onto my other hand which was holding the kettle. This left three knuckles of flesh burning on the lid. I now know what burning flesh smells like! I put some antiseptic on the knuckles and played the piano non-stop until mother got home, trying to distract myself from the pain. I still have funny knuckles where this happened.

Parties

One of the worst things about coming home from school was being introduced to the social diary, which was a list of invitations mother had accepted on our behalf. I dreaded these parties and I don't remember liking any of them.

The only party I really enjoyed was one in Petersfield. Michael and I had been sent off by bus for this party, which I don't think either of us wanted to go to. When we arrived at the house, we were greeted with the news that we were a day late. The party had already happened. Bliss! We set off home rejoicing, but mother was not quite as happy about this as we were.

The eight to eighties dance

When I was probably aged about twelve, there was a huge dance put on by the commander-in-chief, Portsmouth, and his wife. Michael thinks that this may have been Admiral Sir Algernon (Algie) Willis. The invitation was for people from the age of eight to eighty, to include a grandchild of eight and a granny of eighty.

Mother had bought a second-hand dinner jacket for me, specially for this dance. I believe she bought it for £3 (from a jumble sale) and it looked like it too. I'd never worn a dinner jacket before.

On the way to this dance, mother was driving while talking all the way to whoever was sitting in the seat beside her. Several times I tried to get her attention but I was told to wait. Couldn't I see that she was talking? So I never had a chance to put to her the essential question that was troubling me all the way to Portsmouth. *Which way round should I hold a girl when dancing, or trying to dance?* I didn't know whether I should have my left hand on a partner's shoulder or my right. This question was never asked and therefore never answered. As bad luck would have it, I got it wrong when I first tried dancing, but my partner somehow helped me to see that it should be the other way round.

I didn't do much better when Michael and I later went to a dance given by a certain Mrs. Orpen. She saw us there and said to her two daughters: "Come on girls, here are two boys." So I was again thrown straight into the ghastly business of trying to dance. Then, after we had been stumbling around the dance floor with our partners, Mrs. Orpen came up to Michael and me, snatching her daughters away from us with the words: "Come on girls, we'll find some boys who *can* dance. It really is just too bad we pay so much to send our daughters to a good school and then, when they have a chance to show their skills at dancing, they have to find themselves with boys who don't know the first thing about it." She was not my favourite person.

Tying a bowtie

One dinner party I went to was given by a Dr. Pope, whose son was Sam. It was a dinner jacket "do" but, on this occasion, neither Michael nor father were there to tie my bowtie. I think the only other times I'd worn a DJ had been to the dances mentioned above, so I had not yet seen the need to learn how to tie this. Mother also didn't know, so she rang up Brigadier Hewick who knew but could only tie it on himself. He tried tying a bowtie on the knob of his banisters, but he still couldn't describe over the phone how to do this. In the end I went to the dinner party carrying my bowtie, asking Dr. Pope if he could please tie this for me. It was so shaming, I made a point of learning to tie my own tie after that, a skill which later came in very useful for dinners in the wardroom during my National Service. There we would always change into evening dress for dinner, so I very soon became able to tie a bowtie with my eyes closed. But I had not learned this in time for that dinner party at the Popes.

A hunt ball

Another alarming occasion was when two local sisters were going to a hunt ball at Winchester, this being held in the Guildhall. The elder sister had a boyfriend who was an army officer, in the Guards or something like that. The younger sister had no partner, so her mother had got in touch with mother and it was all fixed up before I got home for those holidays. Another dreadful surprise.

I was picked up at Haben by the young officer, who drove us all to Winchester. Mother told me the tickets had been so expensive she was almost sure that drinks would be included. But, just in case they weren't, she gave me a half-crown (two shillings and sixpence) which she thought would cover any drinks I might need to buy.

When we got to the Guildhall, I shyly asked my partner if she would like a drink, having already discovered that drinks were definitely not included in the tickets. She conveniently chose an orange juice, which cost sixpence, and I had one too. That left me with enough money for just three more similar drinks, perhaps two for my partner and one for me. I felt I was about to be very embarrassed by this.

However, when we got to the table that the young officer had reserved for our little party, I found the table was already laden with drinks: four bottles of champagne (no less) and several bottles of wine, some beer and whatever else. "Don't worry, young man," he said. "The drinks are on me."

Somehow, and I never discovered how, we got through all of the champagne and quite a bit else as well. And what was most strange about it was that the girls hardly drank anything. I can't believe I drank nearly two bottles of champagne, but I must have drunk a great deal.

At about midnight I went to the gents and noticed that there seemed to be two of me in the mirror. I stared and stared at this strange sight until these two images settled back into one. Maybe, I thought, it was time to drink some orange juice instead of alcohol—at least some of the time—and surely we would be going home soon. I was aged fourteen at the time, and didn't know that these hunt balls went on long past midnight. In the end we didn't leave until 2.30 am, driving back to Rogate for me to be delivered back to Haben. The young officer said he hoped I knew the way, but I had no idea how to get there from Winchester. By this time, the white line in the road had also become double in my eyes, as in the mirror before, so I have no idea how we got back or how the young officer was able to drive as he must have consumed a huge amount of alcohol. Anyway, I woke up in my own bed the next morning so we must have got back somehow.

Christmas presents

Michael and I tended to be very reluctant over giving presents to each other at Christmas. One year (when we were probably about twelve and ten) we agreed that we would simplify matters and not give anything at all to each other. It seemed a really good idea.

All went well until we got to breakfast. Mother then said she thought it was just not on for us to give no presents.

At that moment I happened to have opened an envelope from one of my godfathers. (This godfather always gave me a generous present each year, until he met me for the first time when I was aged about eighteen. After that he never spoke to me or wrote to me again!) On this occasion his present to me was a ten shilling note (a lot in those days). I then told Michael I thought mother was right in saying we should give each other something, so I handed him the note I had just received. Michael thought I was being exceedingly generous, which I was compared to other years. He immediately put the note in his pocket and it looked as if I had really lost out in a big way. Then, at the end of the day, Michael said he'd forgotten his present to me. He put his hand in his pocket and pulled out the ten shilling note, which he handed back to me, wishing me a happy Christmas.

A very economical Christmas

One year I had a great idea. I bought a big packet of rubber bands, which I thought would do for lots of presents as I could put a few into different envelopes and send these to all the aunts. I suppose they got between ten and twelve bands each. I then wrote a note to each aunt saying I hoped the enclosed would prove to be useful.

I got a letter from mother's sister Ruth, saying that someone had given her a lovely present of elastic bands, but whoever it was had not put a name at the end of the note that came with them. Aunt Ruth added that she thought it was just possible that I had given them, as it seemed to be *the kind of present I might have given*. So, if this had been from me, she wanted to say how very useful these would be and she thanked me for them.

Another mean present from me

One year, when I was about fourteen, I had the good idea that Michael might like to have a record of Mozart's clarinet concerto, especially as he was learning the clarinet at Winchester. The only problem with this good idea was that the concerto came on two records (78 rpm records that took about seven to ten minutes to play each side). However, I really didn't think my budget for Christmas would stretch to giving *two* records to Michael for one Christmas. Perhaps I could give him the second record some other time. So, for that Christmas, Michael got only the first half of the Mozart clarinet concerto. He never got the other half!

Christmas dinners

We used to have quite a big Christmas (or Boxing Day) dinner each year, usually with friends invited. On one occasion we had Granny (father's mother) and her help (the very Irish Josephine) helping in the kitchen. We also asked John and Judy Hewick.

59

There were several problems that evening. The turkey, which had been put in the bottom oven (to keep it warm after it had been cooked) would not come out of the oven when the time came to start carving it. The dish it was on had expanded with the heat, and had become firmly stuck against the sides of the oven. Someone had to sit, with feet against the Aga, straining to pull the turkey out. Someone else was standing behind to catch the turkey in case it came out too suddenly. It did eventually come out, so all was well.

Later, when we came to the Christmas pudding, there was a problem with the brandy. Not enough had been put on the pudding, when the brandy was lit, and it had begun to go out as the pudding was being carried through to the dining room. At this point Josephine (the help) arrived with a pan that was most generously filled with more hot brandy, which she began to pour over the burning pudding.

This created a fresh problem as the brandy in the pan also caught light and the pan became too hot to hold. Josephine then dropped the burning brandy on the hall floor, and it spread out with eerie blue flames.

John Hewick came to the rescue, as any good brigadier would, trying to stamp out the burning brandy. But, all this did was to set his shoes alight, with burning brandy sticking to the soles. I can still see the Brig dancing like a dervish, kind of tap dancing, trying to make the brandy go out. It remained a story to tell in the family for many years after that.

Eric Ellington

Looking ahead a good few years, when I was at Cambridge we were encouraged by the college chaplains to seek out students from abroad who might have nowhere to go for Christmas. Perhaps some of us could invite these students into our homes.

One such student I'd got to know was someone from Jamaica called Eric Ellington. He was at Clare College, doing a PhD in chemistry. He was also a brilliant musician and organist, with an open invitation from Kings College for him to play the chapel organ whenever it was free. I asked Eric to join us at Haben which he did.

Rogate church and their nine lessons and carols

That year Rogate put on its own attempt at having a carol service, like the famous nine lessons and carols broadcast from King's College chapel each year. Eric and I went to hear the choir rehearsing. The vicar then was the Rev Lendon Bell. On that occasion he was doing his best to help out the tenors, and he was no tenor.

When we got back for supper, Eric (deeply read in Jane Austen and speaking naturally in her style) remarked on the choir rehearsal we'd just been to. He said: "If the vicar's life depended on his singing softly, I do not think he could save it."

At the eventual carol service, we had the first lesson read by a teacher at the local infants' school. She read the lesson from Genesis with her own quite different (and shocked) emphasis. She read out: "Adam and Eve were in the garden naked, and they were *NOT ASHAMED!*"

Eric played the harmonium for us at Terwick church, taking Elisabeth and me (and possibly Susan too) to sing while he practised the *Venite* and *Te Deum*. He did some amazing runs and descant passages high in the treble, as he would if he were playing in King's College chapel. He also had a wonderful broad grin and I remember him saying "Splendid" as we sang and he played. I don't know whether he was remarking on our singing or on the wonderful effects he was managing to bring out of that old harmonium. But, whichever it was, I don't think we ever again heard the harmonium played as well as he played it for that Christmas service.

On Boxing Day we went to watch the horses and hounds of the local hunt, with all the splendour of the red-coated huntsmen and the calling of the horn. Eric came too. Strangely, while the foxhounds were dashing across the fields, with the horses in full gallop behind them, a fox took shelter under our car. Eric saw it creep out, to run off in the opposite direction to the hounds. "Do you usually bring the fox with you?" he asked, as if we had been hiding the fox in the boot of the car.

When our parents had their golden wedding, I tried to get Eric to come over for it, writing to the address I last had for him in Jamaica. I was utterly shocked to receive my letter returned with a note on the back saying "Deceased". I wrote off again to the same address, adding on the envelope: "Please open this letter—anyone who knew Eric Ellington." I got a reply saying that he'd been murdered. I could hardly believe this. He was such a fine person. He was also brilliant. When he was at Cambridge, still studying for his PhD, he submitted another thesis to London University who gave him a PhD (London) before he'd finished at Cambridge. He was then immediately recalled to Jamaica University, as they only needed him to have one PhD and they wanted to have him on their teaching staff straight away. I was told that Eric was hugely liked at the university there and a chemistry laboratory was being built, to be dedicated to his memory. He was a very great loss.

Still at Rogate

Granny and her chamber pots

Granny (father's mother) used to come to stay from time to time, while we were at Haben. When she came, Josephine would usually bring a chamber pot with her so that Granny would not have to go to the loo in the night. But Josephine quite often forgot to take the pot back with them when they left. As a result, I once found at least four of Granny's pots under the bed in the spare room. Quite a collection!

Learning how to master bullocks

I'd read somewhere that the thing to do with bullocks, to show that you are not afraid and that you are the boss, is to stare at them, looking straight into their eyes. One day, when I was wanting to take a short cut across a field of bullocks, I decided this was a good opportunity to put that claim to the test. So I duly stared them all in the eyes and strode right through their ranks, until I reached the far side. I then found that they were all behind me, moving towards me in a rather menacing way. I therefore tried to deal with this by walking backwards, still staring at them. But this didn't work as they continued to push towards me, seeming then to be in control—with me walking backwards. I therefore had to walk towards them again, to reassert my dominance. However, this was no use as that just ended with me back at the wrong side of the herd, away from the stile I'd been trying to reach. I had to repeat this procedure a third time until I was within running distance of my exit. I then ran, with the bullocks running after me, until I could leap over the stile. I was certainly not going to try *that* again.

A second car

While we were still at Haben it was decided that we needed a second car, as father was driving each day to Whale Island and mother needed a car to take my sisters to school at Elsted. The car she found was a very old London taxi, complete with a klaxon (a big rubber bulb that you squashed to make it sound). The space to the left of the driver was still preserved, as for luggage, with no seat there, but it was also blocked up so you couldn't get in or out on that side.

Mother would drive this car around the village, but she couldn't always manage to open the door on the driver's side. It was stiff and could get stuck. When this happened, if she could not hail a passer-by to open it for her, she sometimes had to climb out through the window!

The back of the taxi still had little seats that faced backwards, as well as the long seat facing forwards. Sometimes mother would pick up so many children for the school run, or for a party, she could get a whole cricket team of children in the back, eleven all at once.

When we first collected this taxi from the previous owners (two nurses) we were told we had to keep the taxi's name. It had always been called Fred. So Fred it was.

We thought that Fred was a real treasure and there was certainly no other person in Rogate with a car to compare with it. All of us children thought it was marvellous fun having this taxi to go around in. But father didn't think we should be boasting of this: "It is only that we need a second car. It is not meant to be for fun!"

However, as soon as father saw Fred for the first time, he was equally thrilled with this ancient taxi. He found an old cap, from which he removed the naval crest, making it look like a taxi driver's cap. He then drove round Rogate, showing off this taxi to anyone who was known to him.

The taxi had an amazingly tight lock, so that it could be "turned around on a sixpence", as the saying goes. To show this off, father went to see some friends, who were then living at Terwick Old Rectory, driving round in front of the house and wheeling Fred in a tight circle. He did this so fast that he left deep ruts in the drive, where the wheels had dug in as he turned, but fortunately it was possible to rake these ruts out afterwards.

I once went with father through London, he driving Fred, when a taxi driver signalled for to us to stop. He jumped out of his cab to ask if we still called the taxi Fred. It turned out that Fred had been his taxi for years, and he was thrilled to hear that the name had followed the taxi right through to us. The name also went with the taxi when we sold it.

At some stage on the journey, we were going up a hill when Fred suddenly stopped. The engine petered out and would not start again. We had just passed a garage at the bottom of the hill, so I helped to push the taxi round until father could freewheel back to the garage. When we got there Fred started without any trouble, so we went back on our journey. But as soon as we went up the hill the same thing happened again. This time we stopped at the garage, back down the hill, where the garage man pointed out that an electric lead had worn through and it had swung against the engine when we reached a particular incline. This was why the engine had been stopping. After he put insulation tape round this bit of wire, there was then no further trouble.

Other cars

Another car we had was a Morris Minor with a number plate that had the letters MOO, which of course was then called "Moo". The next car (a blue one) had the letters POO, and mother definitely didn't want the car to be called "Poo" so she called this car "Blue Moo" on account of its colour. All these cars were bought second-hand.

The Mad Hatter's Tea Party

We as a family performed *The Mad Hatter's Tea Party* in the village hall. We did this twice, the first time having been such a success. Both times we were produced by Mary Knight, the daughter of Mr. and Mrs. Carnegie.

For the first time, the personae dramatis were Michael, *Mad Hatter*; a farmer's daughter, *Alice*; myself as *The March Hare* and Elisabeth, *The Dormouse*.

Elisabeth was so bright she knew everyone's lines as well as her own. So, when we were rehearsing, if any of us got stuck with our lines the dormouse would give us a whispered prompt.

The second time we put this on (a few years later) Elisabeth was Alice and Sue was *The Dormouse*. We loved shouting at her "The dormouse is asleep again."

That was my only acting ever (see later, under "Cambridge").

Keeping chickens

Our parents decided it would be nice to have chickens in the garden, using part of the orchard for the hen houses.

When mother went to a local farmer to order some young pullets, she said there was one thing in particular that was important to her. "What is that, madam?" asked the farmer. She said: "Can you guarantee that these hens will lay before breakfast?" The farmer said: "Madam, I really can't guarantee that; it all depends on what time you have your breakfast." It was only then that mother realised what she'd said. She had meant to ask if the hens would be laying before Christmas.

Mother quite often said things that were not quite what she'd meant to say. She used to tell us of another such occasion, soon after she'd married father. She had been invited to tea by an admiral's wife and, after tea, this lady (rather patronisingly) had been saying: "It can be quite an ordeal being married into the Navy. If ever you want some help, please don't hesitate to ask." Mother, not wanting to take up her time, had meant to say: "But I would not want to bother you." Unfortunately, she said instead: "*But I couldn't be bothered with you.*" Then, realising her mistake, she'd begun to apologise—trying to make it better but only making it worse. The admiral's wife had only heard what she had expected mother to say.

The Petersfield Music Festivals

One of the highlights each year, during our early years at Rogate, was the Petersfield Festival. The way this was set up involved choirs from lots of local villages, which took part in the annual competitions. There were different categories, allowing choirs to compete in sections—like all male choir, mixed choir, unaccompanied choir. These competitions took place over several days. Then, for the final day of the festival, all the choirs joined up to sing choruses for a major work such as the *St. Matthew Passion, Elijah*, or whatever.

The conductor for the Festival, during the time we attended those concerts, was Sydney Watson, who at some stage had been master of music at Winchester and (I believe) later at Eton.

Another concert in Petersfield

When Elisabeth was probably about five years old, at an age when she could still swing her legs while sitting in a chair, mother took her and me to a concert at which Antonia Butler was playing a cello concerto.

Throughout this concerto, Elisabeth had taken to swinging her legs and there was nothing we could do to prevent her doing this. She just carried on. To our horror we saw that Antonia Butler took to playing with her eyes closed, and we had a nasty feeling that it might have been in order not to be distracted by those swinging legs.

While I was at Cambridge I attended a recital given by this same Antonia Butler. I went backstage to speak to her afterwards, and I asked her if she remembered playing at Petersfield some years before. She replied: "Yes, indeed I do. In fact, I'll never forget it. There was a little girl in the front row who kept on swinging her legs while I was playing. In the end I had to play the rest of the concerto with my eyes closed." I felt I had to confess that this was my sister.

Taking up photography

When I was probably about fourteen I showed an interest in learning photography, especially as there was a darkroom at Winchester where boys could develop and print their own films. I begged to be allowed to buy a camera.

Mother eventually agreed that I could use some of the savings in my Post Office Savings Bank for a camera. So, when she was next going to London, I accompanied her and we went together to Dolland & Aitchison's camera shop, somewhere near Oxford Street.

I shall never forget that shopping expedition, largely because we had to walk a great distance and, as bad luck would have it, the elastic in my pants totally failed while we were walking. The result was that my pants slid down to my knees, while I continued to walk with my knees almost lassoed together by them. I remember it as really uncomfortable as well as quite embarrassing.

I recall that I paid £14, which in those days was a lot of money, for a second-hand camera, quite a good one. I was immensely proud to be the owner of such an expensive item, more expensive than anything I'd ever possessed.

When we got back to Haben, I got into a panic during the night whenever the house produced some of its quite usual creaking sounds. That night, those creaks seemed not to be the innocent noises of a house. Instead, I imagined they might be the creaks of a burglar who had some-how known I'd bought this camera, seemingly creeping upstairs to the darkroom in the loft, where I'd put it. I was greatly relieved, next day, to find my camera (of course) still sitting where I'd left it.

I was encouraged in this new interest by a naval photographer, to whom I was introduced by my father while he was the commander at Whale Island (*HMS Excellent*). This photographer gave me a reel of 35mm film, left over from some cine filming, and he showed me how I could use a "changing bag", which I had to buy, so that I could use lengths of this film to load into cassettes for my camera. The changing bag was made of black plastic, with sleeves on each side through which I could put my arms, with elastic over the sleeves to keep out the light. In the confines of this darkened space I became adept at feeling my way through the procedure of winding a film onto the spool of a reusable cassette that I could then fit into my camera. I could also load up the developing tank in this changing bag, for when I was about to develop a film, without having to resort to a darkroom.

Sometime later, this naval photographer sent a message to me at Winchester, saying that he was upgrading his enlarger and he would like to offer me his present enlarger at a special price. I knew how good this enlarger was, as this man had allowed me to borrow his enlarger for printing a photograph that I'd entered for a photo competition at Winchester. I believe I actually won a prize for it, or at least was commended for it, so I knew that his enlarger was tried and tested and that it was in very good shape.

Our parents were at that time in Krefeld, Germany, so I thought it proper to ask permission to spend the £20 that this man was asking for his enlarger. He was also offering to include with it a complete set of full size enamel dishes for developing and fixing photos. It was a bargain. However, I got no response from Krefeld for about ten days, by which time I was expected to give a reply to this naval photographer. He'd given me a date by which he needed to know. The date having come, and no advice having yet been given, I telephoned this man to say that I would like to accept his generous offer. I then received two telegrams on the same day. One was from the photography man, telling me that he'd be driving through Winchester the next day and would be bringing all the stuff for me. The other telegram was from mother saying: "Don't buy, writing." Well, she was just too late to stop me buying this photographic stuff.

Learning to drive

My first driving lesson ever was given by an aunt. She took Michael and me to an unused airfield where she put us through the paces of learning which pedal was which and how to change gear. We also did some steering, not that it mattered much as we had the whole airfield to ourselves, or so we thought. We were driving along the main runway when a small aeroplane overtook us, going over our heads and landing a short distance in front. We thought this most exciting. When the plane had come to a stop someone drove up to the pilot. We liked to imagine that this could be a spy returning in the plane or someone coming in with smuggled goods, then being driven away in the car that had been waiting for the plane to land. We never knew what it was. Anyway, we were not quite as alone on the airfield as we'd imagined.

Mother once took me up towards the Downs for a practice drive, and on the way back she decided it was time to get me to do an emergency stop. She knew that the driving examiner would tell me that when he slapped his hand on the front ledge of the car I would have to act as if there'd been an emergency, stopping as quickly as possible. So mother decided to do the same thing, but she'd forgotten to look behind to see that it would be safe to put me through this procedure. When she slapped I stopped, only to find that a huge lorry had been driving down the hill behind us, the driver having to do an enormous swerve to avoid driving straight into us, or over us. The driver was hooting like mad and was clearly not happy.

When the time came to take my test, which was in Cambridge, I was told I'd been too tentative. I should have another month's practice and come back for a repeat test. My driving instructor was not pleased with this. He said there was no way I needed more practice. I just needed to drive with more confidence, so he arranged for me to have one more practice with him just before the next test that I'd arranged.

At the time of that final practice my instructor told me he was very pleased that he had me for the first lesson that day, as he knew I could drive. He explained he'd been out partying the night before and had a terrible hangover, so he told me to drive wherever I liked as long as I got him back in time for the next lesson. He then went to sleep beside me.

The test, immediately after that so-called driving lesson, went smoothly. I was amused then to hear the examiner (who was the same one as I'd had before) saying: "You did fine. It all goes to show what a bit more practice can do, eh?" Little did he know that I hadn't had any practice apart from driving around with my hung over instructor asleep beside me.

CHAPTER FOUR

Winchester College

Having fun and I turn exams into a game

Being introduced to Winchester

Some time before Michael went to Winchester we were taken there by father, who showed us around.

Having been to see the house called Kenny's, where father had been, we were going down the road towards the college chapel when we met two old dons. They had both been at Winchester when father was there. One was called "the Bobber", who was huge and had enormous feet. The other, "Jacker", was really quite small. They were pushing wheelbarrows with pots of jam and marmalade, which they were about to exchange. They explained that they would, each year, share the jam/marmalade-making between them. They were two hugely single bachelors.

I later learned from my father's mother (Granny) that she'd met the Bobber on several occasions, but there was one time when she was introduced to him without being able to hear his name. As it was raining, with a strong wind, she'd been keeping her head down while she was holding onto her hat. Granny told me it was only when she saw those huge feet that she realised who it was she'd been introduced to. "*Oh, it's the Bobber*! I'd know you anywhere by your feet."

Another story that went around about the Bobber was that he'd once crashed his car. When he went to court, to give an account of how this had happened, it was reported that he'd said: "How can I distinguish between the accelerator and the brake when my shoes are so big they cover both at once?"

Going to Winchester

Michael went to Kenny's over two years before I did. (It may be of interest to know that the fees were then £400 p.a.)

As mother had noticed that there'd always been more friction between Michael and me when we'd been together at Maidwell, she thought it might be a good idea if I went into a different house at Winchester. (It was a wise perception.) However, when she went to see the housemaster, Freddie Goddard, he'd said to her: "If you don't like my house you don't have to send your second son here, and you can take your first son away too." Not to be forced into doing that, mother capitulated and I went to Kenny's too.

I was shocked by the prevalence of school rules which were sometimes quite cruel, even if not intended to be. One such rule was that boys (or "men" as they were called) should never be seen walking alone between their house and school, or to chapel. It could be said to be a safety matter, but the rule also stated that boys had to be either in pairs or threes. If a single boy was in danger of being alone he should go to a pair and ask to be allowed to "make a three". Or he should go to a three and ask to "make two pairs".

That might be no problem to most boys. But for me this was almost more than I could manage. Even though I would usually hide my shyness behind mucking around, or in being a bit of a clown, I actually felt almost unable to cope with the social demands of that rule. It seemed to put me into a begging position, having to ask to make a three or to make two pairs. Too often, the answer was "No." So I had to ask another pair, or another three, and so on. The result was that I soon got caught into a scapegoat dynamic, other boys in my house seeming to gang up against me, leaving me without the required permission to join whichever group I was asking to join.

In the end I sometimes found myself stuck at the house, unable to get to chapel unless I waited until everyone else had gone. Then, by running all the way, I might be able to get there without being seen. But that was a risky business as I would also be in trouble if I was late.

70

I quickly became phobic of the whole business of getting from my house to chapel. I therefore took to leaving very early, when there would be no one around to see me alone on the street. Every day, for most of my first two years, I would go up to chapel straight after breakfast, ages before anyone else would be leaving the house. I would then go to the school bookshop, Wells, where I would pretend to be looking for books. Finally, when the chapel bells were ringing, I would slip round from the bookshop, a distance so short that no one was expected to go through the *twos* or *threes* charade. It was only towards the end of my second year that I began to find enough confidence to follow the walking rule like everyone else.

Being beaten in my first week

I had only been at Winchester for a few days when I was summonsed to the prefect's study by one of the prefects. He may in fact have been the head prefect that term. I had no idea what I'd done wrong, but it seemed clear I was going to be beaten for it. "Bend over that chair," I was commanded, which I duly did. I then heard a terrifying "swish" of the cane and heard a terrific thud, but it was not on me. Raison, the prefect, then said to me: "That was for having the same names as me. I am John Patrick and you, I gather, are Patrick John." We both laughed and that was it.

Cold baths

In those days the school houses did not have any normal baths. They only had hip baths, made of galvanised steel, placed in a large wet room with pairs of taps around the walls, and a drain in the corner. These baths would be filled with warm water after sports, but in the mornings they would be used for cold baths. We were expected to plunge backwards into a cold bath, leaping out to get dry.

The hip baths would soon enough become encrusted with dirty "gunge", accumulated from soap and dirt. Boys used the same bath repeatedly, topping up the water to keep it more warm than cold. One chore, from time to time, was for a junior to scrape this gunge off with a razor blade. I know I had to do this several times, a task usually given as a punishment for something.

One boy was given the punishment of having a cold shower. I was amazed to see him standing under a shower, unobserved by the prefect

71

who'd set this punishment, this boy still wearing his pyjamas and dressing gown. He'd been told to stand under a cold shower for two minutes, which he was doing (watch in hand). But he'd discovered a way of setting the shower head so that it produced a clean funnel of spray that went neatly around the space where he stood, without any of it falling on him. I was impressed by his ingenuity.

Washing in the dormitories

Between the beds, in each dormitory, was a washstand with an old fashioned bowl on it, and a tooth mug. The juniors (boys during their first two years) would be given regular chores that they had to perform, keeping things going, and in the dormitories there would be one or two boys who had to fill the bowls at night. In the mornings they had to tip these into a bucket, which would be emptied into the nearest of the two bathrooms. We would sleep each night with this bowl of dirty water between the beds, made no more pleasant by the fact that we would also have cleaned our teeth into it.

The tinea inspection

At the beginning of each term we all had to be inspected by the house doctor, then someone who was already retired. He sat on a chair while we walked past him with our trousers and pants lowered, and he'd tell us: "Get *that thing* out of the way—this way, now that way," while he shone his torch on our privates, inspecting us for possible signs of *tinea cruris*. We also had to show between our toes for any signs of athlete's foot. Anyone with symptoms of either would have to report to Matron, who would dish out the required cream for either condition, all of this so that we did not pass these infections onto others.

The house Matron

Our Matron, known always and in each house as "the hag", was someone who almost lived up to that description. But she was a nice enough person, even though her knowledge of medicine was primitive to an extreme.

During my first year, it may even have been my first term, I cut my left forefinger quite deeply in the dining room. I was cutting a slice of bread and did so with such vigour I did not notice, until too late, that my finger was in the way of the bread knife. This sliced quite neatly into my finger, almost to the bone. Not deterred, I just pressed the cut tightly together until it stopped bleeding, and so it would have remained had the matron not insisted on giving me the once over with her favourite treatment for any cut. She insisted on opening up the wound, until then not bleeding at all, while she poured iodine over it. And, *Wow*, how did that hurt! It also delayed the healing of my finger for many days, she having set it bleeding all over again. I still have the scar.

Getting Matron into the dorm

Sometimes we would set a trap for the matron at bedtime by making a lot of noise, banging and shouting until we heard the door of the dorm opening. As agreed beforehand, everyone would immediately stop what they were doing, lying as if asleep in bed, with no one she could catch or blame for the noise. She once arrived to find us all "asleep" but some shoes were still in the air, midway across the dorm.

Prefects' tea: cutting sandwiches

One of the chores I was made to perform for the prefects was to prepare Sunday tea for them. We did it in pairs. The first time I did this, I was given the task of spreading butter onto the face of a loaf and cutting a slice very, very thinly. My partner in this was then given the task of spreading honey onto my wafer-thin slices. The result was that the honey broke up all of the bread, to the point where there was no sandwich left once I'd cut off the edges. So, instead of having a plate of dainty little sandwiches, the prefects had to use spoons to eat these bundles of sticky crumbs we'd served to them. We were told that next time we'd have to find ways of doing this a lot better. With practice, I discovered how to cut straight and thin slices of bread, having buttered each slice before cutting, a skill which has stayed with me ever since.

Extra bread

Even though the food we got for our main meals was (as I remember) quite good and tasty, many of us seemed to have appetites that never tired of wanting extra. For this there was an unlimited supply of fresh bread, huge long loaves of it, in the pantry ("Annie's pantry"). We could take slices of bread from there, during any free time, onto which we would spread whatever we chose. I soon discovered that I could spread apricot jam more thickly than almost any other jam, so that was almost always my choice. We had to buy our own supplies of these spreads and I used to get through a whole pound of jam each week, on these extra slices of bread.

Cakes from home

In those days we had very few occasions when we could visit home during a term. I think we were given permission for this about once a term. For some of my last two years at Winchester my parents were in Germany so I probably didn't go anywhere for a day out.

The one thing that was always special about a home visit was that parents were expected to provide a cake. This would be taken back to the house where it would be eagerly awaited by the other boys, with whom it would always be shared. Mother usually made a fruit cake for this, but once she'd completely forgotten. Not to be put off, she searched through the pantry to see if by any chance she had some other kind of cake. "Oh, good," she called out. "I have a chocolate sponge-roll you could take. I'd quite forgotten I had that."

When I got back to Kenny's that evening we were soon to discover the results of this sponge-roll having been forgotten. It was so old it had become completely solid; almost fossilised. There was absolutely no way we could cut into this, let alone cut a slice off it. In the end, someone found a hack saw which he used while I was tightly gripping the roll against a table top, the other boy cutting it as if sawing logs. We then gnawed our way round the edges of our slices until we had finally been able to eat it.

Using the chemist

I was already interested in matters of the mind, even during my first year at Winchester, in particular the notion of mind over body. It then occurred to me that it might be possible to help people to feel better by simply making them believe that some special medicine had brought this about.

The school had an arrangement at a chemist in the town where boys could buy almost anything on account. I went to ask the pharmacist if he could make up a bottle of "pretend medicine" with a colour, a nasty taste, and a guarantee that it would do absolutely nothing. I explained what I planned to do with this. There were quite a few boys who would complain of feeling depressed, out of sorts, possibly homesick, to whom I planned to offer a teaspoon of this special medicine. I would claim that it had been amazingly helpful to me when I'd felt just the same as they were feeling.

The chemist agreed to make this for me, and he explained that what I was asking for is called a placebo. He said that doctors sometime prescribe a placebo to people who may not be needing medication, but who are expecting to be given something by the doctor.

I tried this placebo out on several boys and most of them reported they felt much better. One boy even came back for more. I got through half of a bottle of this stuff before getting bored with the experiment. It had worked well enough already to demonstrate the point I was interested in.

I still remember with embarrassment that my bill at the chemist got bigger and bigger each term, but no one ever challenged me about this. I don't think that the money was spent on medicines. Instead it was on things like a "posh" razor, when the time came to start shaving, and an expensive badger's hair shaving brush. Also, I frequently bought chemicals there, to make up photographic developer in the chemistry lab, which meant I didn't have to pay for any of the photographic chemicals when I got into doing photography. I have no idea now what else I bought there, but I can remember one bill came to about £25 for a term, which was a truly huge amount in those days. I suspect I was pushing my parents to challenge me, to help me to cut back on this spending, but they never did. I can't think why.

Taking exercise

We all had to take a minimum amount of exercise each week, and a prefect would go round during prep each evening to record the time we'd spent doing this. An hour of football would count as an hour, and so would an hour of gym. However, going on a run, which might take only fifteen minutes, would also count as an hour. A longer run would count as an hour and a half, even though it took about thirty minutes.

My main two forms of exercise were going for solitary runs or going to the gym. There I got on well with the gym instructors, especially an ex-naval sports instructor. He was able to lift boys up to the high bar on one hand, somehow producing the magic that enabled them to get into a swing around it, or whatever. With his help I became quite good at gym and I got top prize at the end of the first year. But in a subsequent year I dislocated my knee, trying to vault, so I never took part in other competitions.

I was not a sports person. Somehow I managed to avoid playing football. The only game of football I can remember playing was one in which, on that day, we had the Earl of Suffolk and Berkshire also playing.

Suffolk, as we called him, was the only person I ever knew who (or so I was told) remained in the bottom class of the school beyond the limit of three terms, after which boys always moved up to the next class; but not Suffolk. He seemed to have failed to satisfy his teachers to such a degree that he was held back for a fourth term, to give him a final chance to prove himself capable of keeping up with other boys. He failed to do that and had to leave. I later heard that he went on to Eton, who doubtless welcomed him with open arms.

When I was doing my pre-National Service time in the RNVR, on *HMS Indefatigable* at Weymouth (see later) I heard tell of Suffolk down there too. We all had to make sure that, when we went ashore, we were at the jetty in time to get the last boat back. We heard that Suffolk had once arrived too late for this, so he'd somehow managed to telephone the duty officer saying: "This is the Earl of Suffolk and Berkshire. The captain is expecting me but there is no boat to be seen." For this, we were told, the duty officer had duly apologised and had quickly arranged for the captain's barge to be sent to collect the earl. Upon arriving at the jetty, the skipper found a sailor wanting to climb in. "Get off. This is not for you. I am here to meet the Earl of Suffolk and Berkshire," to which the man dressed as a sailor had replied: "But *I* am the Earl of Suffolk and Berkshire." I have no way of confirming this story, but I have liked to believe that it may be true.

Mostly I did gym or running, especially running when I wanted to do my quota of exercise as quickly as possible. What I particularly remember was how stiff my legs were after running for the first week of each term.

I was also pretty skilled at avoiding cricket. I played only four games of cricket in my five years at Winchester, being bowled first ball in three of them and bowled by the second ball in the fourth. However, for

76

fielding, I discovered that a good wheeze was to make sure I was put in to play at long stop. This became "long something else" when there was an over, to avoid players having to wait ages while I walked the full length of the pitch. There, at this deep position, I only had to retreat a few yards for me to be able to lie in the long grass where I could read. I would remain there until a shout announced that a ball was coming my way. It was sheer heaven for me, going through the motions of playing cricket like this. And a few times we lost the ball in the long grass, so the game had to be suspended until it was found.

For a while at Winchester I took up fencing, as a left-hander. I offered to do this as I have always been ambidextrous, and I was told that left-handed fencers had an advantage: it confuses the right-handers, who are often not used to fencing against "left-ers". Unfortunately, it confused me too. When we were called to be "on guard at two" or "on guard at four" (these being two positions) I couldn't work out which was which for me, trying to fence left-handedly. I soon gave it up.

Roseveare's suicide

We had a maths master called Dr. Roseveare. He had two sons in College, both scholars. The second of these was someone I knew quite well. We were both in the choir and the orchestra together. He played the cello. We also sat next to each other in at least two different subjects. On the day before he killed himself, we had been talking together about a concert that was happening the next day, at the Guildhall. One of the pieces being played was a cello concerto and Roseveare told me he would definitely be going.

The very next day we learned that Roseveare had been found hanged from one of the chapel bell ropes. I could never understand what had happened to him. How had he changed so suddenly? It worried me at night, for weeks, while not getting to sleep. What then alarmed me was that I realised I admired his courage. I could imagine feeling suicidal like him, especially over the daily problem of how to get from the house to chapel, without being seen and without feeling able to go through the twos and threes ritual. But, fortunately, I didn't have the courage to do what he did.

The choir sang for Roseveare's funeral and I was shocked and moved to see how very small the coffin was in which he was brought into chapel. How utterly devastating it must have been for his parents, I realised.

77

Lord Wavell's funeral

Another funeral, for which the choir also sang, was that of Field Marshal Lord Wavell, one-time viceroy to India and a former Wykehamist. It was he who put together an anthology of poetry, *Other Men's Flowers*, and it was also he who said: "Winston Churchill is always expecting rabbits to come out of an empty hat."

From the funeral service in chapel, we processed to the chantry cloisters, that little church beside chapel, where a grave had been prepared for Wavell. The choir then sang *God Be in My Head and in My Understanding*, which affected me deeply. After that a piper played a bagpipe lament, marching out of the cloister and far away. We never heard the playing stop, it just faded into the distance.

My second radio

Having made my first radio while I was still at Maidwell, I made another at Winchester. This had two valves and was capable of being listened to through a loud speaker. I made a wooden cabinet for this in carpentry, but I kept my smaller radio in what used to be called my "Toys",[1] in the hall of my house. I have no idea why these (with a desk, a seat, and cupboard) were called by that name. They were built around the sides of the hall and each boy had one.

I used sometimes to listen to my radio with a single earpiece from the headphones, including one memorable occasion when there was a heavyweight world title boxing match taking place. I was meant to be doing prep, or whatever it was called at Winchester, but I couldn't resist the temptation of listening to the fight. Unfortunately, at one point I turned up the volume too high, which made it squeal. What I didn't know, but soon learned, was that when it squealed it also transmitted at the wavelength to which it was then tuned. The result was that the prefects, who were allowed to listen to the radio during this prep time, had their listening disturbed by my radio. I don't know how one of them thought to check whether I had my radio on at the time, but I was caught staring at my homework but listening to whatever I had cupped in my left hand. I was made to show what I had there, which revealed the earpiece from my headphones. I was beaten for this.

Having discovered that I could transmit in this way, I tried out an experiment back home during the next holiday. I stretched a long wire across the lawn and connected this, as an aerial, to my radio. I deliberately set the volume too high, so that the familiar high pitched squeal was set off. I then took a portable radio, tuned to the same wavelength, in the basket of my bicycle while I cycled all the way to Nyewood. This was a mile or so from the house. Sure enough, my radio's squeal was the only sound the portable radio could pick up at that wavelength. My transmission from the garden completely obliterated the programme it had been tuned to.

The next day, mother's cleaner said she'd been listening to a wonderful programme of music from Westminster Abbey. She had been really enjoying this until an awful squeal took over. For the whole of the remaining part of the programme that was all she could hear. She wondered if something had gone wrong with her radio, but it was all right the following morning. I felt dreadful when I heard this. I also didn't realise that what I had been doing was completely illegal. If it had gone on much longer there could have been so many complaints that someone might have gone around the area, to detect where the interference was coming from. I never did that again.

My parents being called to see the housemaster

During the holidays a letter came summonsing my parents to see my housemaster (Goddard). I had to go too. When we got there he was holding a plug on a short piece of flex. Goddard told us that a cleaner had found this flex, with its plug, sticking out of the junction box under my desk. Not knowing what it was, the cleaner had pulled it. Instantly, there'd been a big flash and all the lights in the hall had fused. But the cleaner had not immediately reported this. When an electrician had been sent for, he had spent a whole morning testing the circuits to see where the short was, until he found this plug. I'd put this in to feed the mains converter, which had provided my radio with the high voltage and low voltage it needed. My father was told how much the electrician had charged and we would have to pay for it. Fortunately that was the end of the matter.

Coffin stools

I had originally been keen on carpentry. When I heard that Rogate church was needing some coffin stools, I thought it would be a good idea if Michael and I made a pair for the church. He thought this a good idea too, so we both ordered the wood for this and began to make them.

I don't quite know what happened to my stool. By the time Michael had finished his (with carved sides as well) there was practically nothing of mine to be seen. In fact it never materialised at all. Now, instead of there being two coffin stools there was only one, which was not going to be much use with a coffin.

For a long time I could not think why it was I'd given up making this coffin stool, but then I remembered the assistant at "Mill" (which is what the carpentry place was called at Winchester). One day, when I was beginning to work on the coffin stool, he had come and put an arm round me and said he liked me. It felt very odd. I didn't like it and I never went back to Mill again. I didn't tell anyone about this, as I didn't really know what it was about, but I did know that it felt creepy and something to be avoided. So there was never a second coffin stool.

Michael's natural history prize

While Michael was still at Winchester, before he went on to Dartmouth, he took some wonderful photographs of birds, taken from carefully prepared hides. These hides had to be put up in stages, being very gradually moved towards the nest, until it became possible to enter the hide with a camera, and without the birds being too alarmed to return to the nest. Michael had shown me these hides and I had seen some of his photos, which were excellent.

Michael had been taken under the wing of a well-known bird photographer, Eric Hosking. I found the following entry on the internet:

> Hosking's success as bird photographer started when he was attacked in 1937 by a tawny owl in Wales and lost an eye in the process. All the media reported it and overnight he became famous in all of Great Britain. Since then, all bird photographers wear a face mask, like fencers, while photographing owls on these islands. Eric Hosking died on the 22nd of February 1991, in London, at the age of 81.

A time came when Michael was entering for a natural history prize and he'd already written his essay for the prize, needing only to print the photographs he had planned to go with it. I think he'd probably done some of them, or perhaps most, but he then fell ill with flu and was not able to finish printing his photos. I offered to print these for him. He won the prize.

The Master of St. Cross

A few miles down the road from Winchester is the church of St. Cross, attached to which is a set of almshouses for poor pensioners. The priest in charge is known as the Master of St. Cross, who was at that time the Rev Oswald Hunt.

During my first year at Winchester I was invited to tea by Oswald Hunt and his wife. I had learned from mother that he'd officiated at her wedding in Godstone church, and the Hunts remembered this well. I also learned that they quite often invited Winchester boys for tea. A few weeks later, one of the boys in the choir said to me he hadn't realised the Master of St. Cross was my stepfather. How had he arrived at that idea? Oswald Hunt had told him that he had "married" my mother, which (in this boy's mind) seemed to make him my stepfather!

I took a photograph of St. Cross church from the Master's garden, with the tower of the church reflected in the pond in front of it. For this, I'd thrown a brick into the pond to create ripples, taking the photo at the moment when these looked most interesting. The Master was so pleased with this, when I showed it to him, he asked me to make 100 Christmas cards for him, using this photo. He also had this printed in the official guide to St. Cross, which continued to be available in the church for many years later.

There was a sequel to this, during my last year at Winchester, when the (then) mayor of Winchester, having got my name from Oswald Hunt, wrote to me asking if he could use that photo for his official Christmas cards. He had already got permission from the Master of St. Cross to use the printing block he'd had made for the guide. But I didn't let him use it. I explained that the block had been made from a matt photo, rather than a glossy one, which resulted in the reproduction being substandard. I therefore told the mayor I would only give my permission for him to use my photo if he had a new block made, using a glossy photo which I would supply him. I sent him the glossy photo, but he didn't want to go to the expense of having a new block made. So my photo did not end up as the mayor's Christmas card after all.

Eton-Winchester match

Each year there would be a special weekend during which Winchester would play cricket against Eton, playing either at home or away. This was a time when many old boys would come back, walking round the pitch to see who they could recognise from their time at "Win Coll".

One year, when the match was being played at Winchester, my father came for the match and, like many other old boys, he spent most of the time catching up with friends. I felt completely redundant, spending most of the time just standing around while he chatted. One person he met was a friend he'd not seen for ages. I then heard the following interchange between them: "Hello Roddie, what have you been doing?" And later, "Are you married?" … "Yes" … "Children?" … "Yes" … "How many?" … "Masses" … "Well, roughly how many?" … "Four, and here is one of them," introducing me as one of those masses of children.

Winchester v. St. Swithin's

During my last year it had come to the attention of the new headmaster, Desmond Lee, that it might not be a bad idea if boys at Winchester were introduced to the opposite sex during their last year, especially as there was a well-known girls' school not many miles away: St. Swithin's. So, on the school calendar of sporting fixtures for that term, we not only had *Winchester v. Eton* for the cricket match, we also had *Winchester v. St. Swithin's* for what was then to become the annual dance *"against"* St. Swithin's.

We were taken up to St. Swithin's in a bus, and handed over to house mistresses in small groups. The mistress who looked after my group gave us a bit of a pep talk, which ended with her saying: "Well, boys, don't be shy. Just go up to a girl and say the last time I saw you, you were wearing a gymslip. Who are you now?" I did just that, but that is all I remember from that strange dance.

Corps

One of the other "sports" at Winchester was in the Combined Cadet Force, or "Corps", which took up every Wednesday afternoon. We would dress up in khaki, wearing a webbing belt with brasses that we had to keep very shiny, and boots which were meant to have toe-caps shining well enough to see your face reflected in them. For this we learned how to spit and polish, which meant we had to spit on the toecaps and rub in polish, repeatedly, until they really shone. And it was possible to make them very shiny indeed.

One Wednesday, 6th February 1952, when we had been marching around in what was known as "Meads" (a grassy area near to the chapel), we were given the stunning news that King George VI had just died. I can still recall the deep shock of that, and I clearly remember it was a Wednesday.

I also remember that there was a concert in the cathedral that night. One piece planned for this was hardly appropriate for such an occasion, so the slow movement from Beethoven's 7th Symphony was played instead. I still think of the king's death when I hear that movement played.

Field day

Once a year, we would have an all-day military exercise against another school. For this we would dress up in our uniforms and be bussed to an area of open land. There we would be put through exercises of defending a post from attack, or attacking *the enemy over there*, or whatever games were invented for the occasion. But the highlight for us was when we stopped for lunch.

We would fill up our kitbags with goodies from the school "tuck shop", buying more than any of us could comfortably manage. We then gorged ourselves during a lunchtime truce, which we and the enemy school would mutually observe at an allotted time. After pigging ourselves, we were none of us up to much running anywhere. It was just as well we were not expected to engage in real combat after we'd had our picnic lunches.

One year, we had our bit of the field day greatly enhanced by the fact that someone had raided the armoury, stealing literally thousands of blank cartridges for the forthcoming day. So, instead of our usual ration of fifteen blank cartridges each for the whole day, we each had hundreds of these. I can remember our rifle barrels getting so hot we could hardly hold them. We also discovered that, if we balanced an empty cartridge case on top of a vertical barrel, when we next fired the gun this cartridge case would go whizzing through the air making a wonderful noise. It was just as well none of these spinning missiles hit anyone as they could have done a lot of damage.

Monty's visit

"Monty", otherwise known as Field Marshal Bernard Law Montgomery, 1st Viscount Montgomery of Alamein, KG, GCB, DSO, PC, came to give us a lecture about his part in the Alamein offensive, for which he'd become famous. He was a very arrogant man, and he spoke from the back of his throat which made him sound even worse. He had a map beside him on the stage, demonstrating with this (and a long pointer) how he had outmanoeuvred the Germans. "They were *heaar* and I was *theaar*, and I drove in my jeep all around *theaar* so that we could take the Germans by surprise, attacking them from *heaar*." And so it went on.

For the evening service that day, Monty had announced to the head-master that he (Monty) would read the lesson. This was something that no one but a school prefect ever did. It was a school prefect's unquestioned privilege, but on that occasion Monty had his way.

A lecture on colour photography

In about 1952 we had a lecture on colour photography, illustrated with slides. The lecturer explained to us how his colour slides had been produced. This was a very complicated process. First of all, he had to take three different photographs of the same thing, using for each photo a different coloured filter: red, yellow, and blue. He had then to print the photograph three times, each printing to bring out the colour that accorded to the filter being used. Finally, with all three prints made on top of each other, the final photograph would bring back the original colours, combining to produce all shades and tones of colour. The results were truly remarkable. I can well remember the lecturer explaining this process to us and adding: "But it will never be within the pocket of ordinary people as it will remain hugely expensive." How times have changed since then.

Going to the moon

In the same year we had a lecture about space travel. The lecturer took, as his focus, the popular idea that one day we would be able to send men to the moon.

We were shown, with elaborate diagrams and calculations, that the weight of fuel necessary to get a rocket to the moon, a rocket big enough to take a man too, would be so immense there was no material that could possibly withstand the pressures of such a load of fuel on board, let alone the pressures to be experienced throughout a journey to the moon, and that was only for getting to the moon. There would then be the problem of getting back. For this, the amount of fuel needed to lift the return rocket off the surface of the moon would be less, as the moon's gravity is about one sixth of that on earth. Nevertheless, the additional fuel needed for the return journey would make the whole process even more impossible.

This lecturer also ended his talk with a prediction. Having "proved" mathematically that it would be impossible to get a man to the moon and back, it would remain forever impossible. Or, so it seemed then.

Years later, on 26th December 1968, when we were living in Coleridge Walk with our daughter Hanna, we were watching the TV for news of *Apollo 8*. That was the first time men had gone round the moon.

I'd been following this trip very closely, awed by the almost infinite complexity of it. I had realised that, for every second of the journey to the moon, the speed of the rocket would be slowing all the way from the earth until the gravity of the moon would take over, then speeding up again towards the moon. Also, the rocket had initially to be aimed in a direction that was widely different from the position of the moon at the time of launch, leaving the moon to move towards the direction of the rocket's flight path.

I had also understood something of the risks involved. If the rocket was even slightly off course, aiming a bit too close to the moon, it would crash onto the moon. If it was even slightly too wide of the moon, it would fail to be captured by the moon's gravity and would disappear for ever into space. So everything depended upon the calculations working out exactly right.

I can still remember the excitement when we heard the first sounds transmitted from *Apollo 8*, after it came out from behind the radio silence caused by the moon being between the space capsule and the receivers on earth. They made it. So much for the predictions given at Winchester. Later, as we all know, they also landed on the moon and got back.

A school prize in physics

When I went to Winchester I had already been learning about electrics and radios, so it was not surprising I found physics fascinating and quite easy.

After I had dislocated my knee in the gym, and I was not allowed to put any weight on it, I was confined to the house sickroom for about ten days. A physiotherapist came each day to give electric massage to my knee and, gradually, it was getting better.

I had been intending to do well in the annual chemistry exam, mainly in order to placate Dr. Hutton (the chemistry teacher) who seemed to dislike me just as much as I had come to dislike him. I had therefore been revising for his exam. But, being laid up in the sickroom, I was unable to attend his exam.

However, two days later, I was told that I need not miss the physics exam (also annual) as I would be allowed out next day. I thought I ought to do some revision for this too, and asked for my books to be brought up to the sick room. But when I looked at all that stuff, I thought there was really no point in revising. It would only cram my head at a time when it might be better to go into the exam with a clear mind. So I did no revision at all. When the results came out I had come top, and I was awarded that year's prize.

Hutton, however, was furious. He wrote in my report that he thought I should be disallowed the physics prize. He had written: "Casement had clearly missed the Chemistry exam in order to give himself an unfair advantage over other boys, by having lots of time to revise for the Physics exam." I was very angry about this, especially as I hadn't done *any* revision for that exam. Father asked to see the headmaster, Mr. Oakshott, who was also concerned about this.

Chemistry

One of the reasons that Hutton took against me was that I was almost always late for his classes. I was also always full of excuses, as if it was never my fault. He was quite right to object to that and I am now very glad I eventually learned to stop making excuses.

Chemistry could be quite good fun, as when we were testing for gas being given off by a reaction. We would test for oxygen by putting a glowing spill into a test tube, and if it burst into flame it showed it was oxygen. Or, if it produced a "pop", it was hydrogen.

We all enjoyed the time when a boy was doing one of these gas experiments, but he'd got his quantities all wrong. He had ten times what he should have been using. The result was a huge amount of gas pouring out from his experiment, which he proceeded to catch in a gas jar.

86

He then took the jar to a Bunsen burner and there was an enormous explosion. A boy at the back, mimicking Hutton, then said (in Hutton's voice) "And *that* was hydrogen," causing much hilarity in the class.

I also enjoy remembering a story told to me of a time when another experiment had gone wrong, in some other class taken by Hutton. The experiment they were doing was the very basic one of heating iron filings with sulphur, producing a horrid smell of hydrogen sulphide. And, when tested with a magnet, the iron filings no longer responded to the magnet. This showed that the iron had combined with sulphur to make iron sulphide.

Most boys had managed their experiments successfully, with the signs also of a chemical reaction being in process: *it continues to glow red even when taken away from the flame*, but one boy had no reaction showing at all. Hutton had begun to get impatient, as this was holding up the class, so he had got several Bunsen burners together, putting them all under the crucible containing what was meant to be iron filings with sulphur. At first, still nothing happened, but then there had been a really gigantic explosion.

Hutton had suspected that magnesium filings might have been used rather than iron. So, after hours, he had tried to see if a reaction between these might work. He had looked it up and, so I was told, he'd found that magnesium was not known to react with sulphur. But, just to test this, he'd put a mixture of these in a fume cupboard, retreating to a distance to see if anything happened. The result was again a huge explosion, which had blown the thick glass of the fume cupboard out of its frame and across the full width of the classroom. So magnesium is now known to react with sulphur, *if heated enough*.

One relic that I kept from my time with Hutton was, to my shame, a bottle of mercury I'd stolen from the lab. At first I'd used this in the school house to rub on pennies, making them shine. We also played with the silver balls that mercury makes when it is dropped. In those days we knew nothing of the dangers of mercury.

Many years later, in fact 2006, I found that I still had this mercury in a cupboard under the stairs. I asked our dentist if he could use it. No, he couldn't. However, he told me that he could dispose of this, if I took it to his surgery on a day when poisonous materials were collected. I never managed that. Instead I took it to the recycling depot, saying I did not know how this could be safely disposed of. I'd learned, from the chemist near us, that the fumes from mercury are now known to be so dangerous that mercury is usually kept in a sealed jar which is, itself, kept under water. I was glad to be rid of this—after about fifty-four years.

Nick Younger

Nick was the one person from Winchester I continued to keep in touch with and he would invite me to be his guest at his London club (The Athenaeum). When I sent him an earlier draft of this book he replied with his own memories of Dr. Hutton. He wrote:

> Reading the Winchester bit, I wondered how we came to be such friends, being in different houses, but I suppose it was music which brought us together and we were both struggling to fit into an alien world.
>
> I cannot resist capping your stories of Kenneth Hutton. I got on fairly well with him and it is only really to him and to Henry Havergal (the master of music) that I feel any sense of gratitude for my education at Winchester.
>
> I remember two incidents in Kenneth's class which left a lasting impression on me and an inspiration towards chemistry.
>
> In the first, some industrious student told Kenneth that his calculation as to the number of kilocalories generated when Zinc was reacted with Sulphur had produced a surprisingly large number. Was this really the case? Kenneth's experimental instincts were aroused and he strode to the fume cupboard, mixed the appropriate quantities of the Zinc and Sulphur, applied a Bunsen burner and closed the fume cupboard door.
>
> My recollection was that the glass fume cupboard door went straight past Kenneth, leaving his image in the glassware—rather like a Tom and Jerry cartoon.
>
> The second incident was intended to demonstrate the reaction of Hydrogen and Oxygen to create water. A complicated system of glassware sat on the teaching bench with Hydrogen, supported by mercury on one side and Oxygen on the other. The trick is, I gather, to make sure that the elements are not reacted in too exact proportions so that the surplus gas takes the shock. Kenneth, on the other hand had got it just 'right' and, when he added a spark, the whole apparatus

disintegrated with a bang, leaving nothing on the bench and all of us knee-deep in mercury. We were thrilled.

Very sadly, just a few days after writing this lovely letter to me, Nick died in hospital from advanced prostate cancer and secondaries. I wrote immediately to his widow, Mary, copying some of this letter to her as I felt sure she would like to see this evidence of Nick's humour, so close to the end. When I attended his funeral in Ripon Cathedral I was touched to hear his son read from that letter to me, in the homily to his father.

O-level exams

I took my O-levels during the first year of that changed form of examination. Until then it had been known as School Certificate. In the early years of these new exams, no grades were given. They only gave a Pass or a Fail, which offered little incentive to do well, and virtually no challenge at all. I therefore formed my own plans for these exams, which worked extremely well for me.

First of all, I noticed that if I completely ignored the history exam it would leave me with just one subject per night for which to revise. In any case I never wanted to do the history exam, having come to regard myself as a complete dunce in that subject, so it would be no loss if I failed it. I therefore decided to fail history as completely as possible. The other part of my plan was to play with brinkmanship, to see if I could pass some of the other exams by only doing a minimum number of questions, as in maths when it would be possible to tell if I'd got an answer right or not.

When I went in to take the history exam, I wasn't even sure which period I was meant to have been studying so I accepted both of the exam papers being handed out, to choose between them. I don't suppose I would really have been allowed to answer the other paper, for which I would not have been entered. That was for boys in another class who had studied a different period of history.

As I had set my mind on failing history in a spectacular way, I chose to rely entirely upon the only history book I had, until then, ever enjoyed: *1066 and All That*. I therefore put down *1066* for every date that was asked for, including the date of Trafalgar, knowing this to be totally incorrect. I don't suppose that went down at all well. But when the results came out I'd got 16%. I have no idea how it was that I failed to get the zero score I'd aimed for.

When I came to the maths exams, because I only needed to get a Pass, I decided it would make the exams more exciting if I only did half the number of questions asked for, which would get me to the pass mark of 50%. All I then needed to do was to get 100% in each of those questions. So, after about half of the time set for the exam, I handed in my paper and went out to enjoy the sunny day. It seemed a shame to be kept inside on such a hot day. However, on my way out of the exam room, I was looking at one of the questions I hadn't bothered to answer, and I found I'd already answered it in my head before I'd even got to the door.

It did seem rather silly to have thrown away another 10% for just a couple of minutes more in the sun. So, for the next maths exam, I thought it might be fun to have another challenge. I would aim to finish it all and to get 100% in the completed questions. I therefore checked each answer, and it was pretty easy to know in maths whether an answer was correct or not. I was just checking the last question, to see where to put the decimal point, when we were told to stop writing. I dashed a point in as I put my pen down, and I put it in the wrong place. This made my answer ten times what it should've been, but it was too late. I couldn't change it. I got 98% in that exam.

I mention the exam results in my last book.

> I was so little worried by exams that I didn't even notice that I hadn't received the results-letter, which the housemaster had promised to send to each of us during the holiday. Nor did I remember to ask him about this when I returned for the next term. The exams had slipped entirely from my mind until I found other boys comparing their results. (*Learning from Life*, pp. 27–28)

When we were going to bed someone asked me "How many did you get?" I had no idea what he was talking about. "How many *O-levels*!" It was only then that I realised the results had come in and the housemaster had been telling everyone else, because they'd all been asking him. (He'd been ill when he should have sent out the anxiously anticipated results.) It hadn't occurred to me to ask so I ran down to see him and was told that I'd got eight but (and was I surprised?) I had failed in history.

A-levels

When it came to taking my A-levels, the official results still were only recorded as Pass or Fail: there was still no other grading. Once again, I decided to make the exams more exciting by setting myself the task of making sure I got just a bit more than the pass mark (still 50% in the exam) by getting 100% correct answers in half of the required number of questions. I used this method in all of the exams. I took maths, additional maths, and physics. It actually worked very well. We had two and a half hours for each exam, and we were expected to answer no more than nine questions. So I set myself the task of answering five questions in each exam, checking to make sure there were no mistakes. This meant I had half an hour for each question, rather than rushing through in half the time to answer nine. I really enjoyed the challenge I'd set myself, approaching the exams in that way, and I only let myself answer a sixth question, as a kind of insurance against failure, once I was sure of the first five.

Steeplechase

Each year we would have a steeplechase, some twelve miles across rough country, all of the more senior boys being encouraged (or expected) to take part. In my last year, as we neared the finish, I was almost coming last. In the end I slowed down so that I could pair with someone else who *was* coming last. We finished together, coming 113–114 equal.

One perk for taking part in the steeplechase was that anyone who had completed the course was allowed to go to bed after house tea, instead of staying up for prep. But this last year I didn't have that privilege, as I was due to go to Southampton for my National Service medical.

The National Service medical

One thing in particular had been impressed upon us, before we set off by train for our medical: we must not by any means have a pee before we'd been through the tests, as we would have to provide a specimen.

I arrived at Southampton *bursting* for a pee, but I knew I would have to hold on until I'd provided the required specimen. However, when the moment came to give this, I was handed a very small wine glass. There was no way I could make use of such a small receptacle, in the state I was in by then. I needed a bucket. But I could not get this across to the medical orderly who was demanding a specimen. He barked: "You knew you'd have to give this, so you should have held on." He handed me a pint of water, telling me to drink that and wait, which only made my problem worse. When I still couldn't provide a specimen, the same happened again. I was made to drink a second pint of water. Finally, I did manage to get someone to understand my problem. I was eventually provided with a bucket and some privacy, told to run water over my wrists, and the medics finally got the specimen they'd been waiting for: probably all two or three pints of it!

The final part of this medical was to have my eyes tested. By this time I was so exhausted from the steeplechase and the journey to Southampton, not to mention the sample fiasco, I found I could barely focus my eyes. When they asked me to read the test card, with those letters that start very big and go down to being very small, I could hardly get beyond the first line before it all began to go fuzzy. I think they probably recorded my eyesight as blind in one eye and nearly blind in the other. Anyway, I was put down to train as a supply person in the Navy, not an executive. Proper eyes were required for that.

The "plunge"

In our day at Winchester there was no such thing as a swimming bath, such as the boys now have. The only place we had for swimming was called "Gunner's hole" (why, I don't know). This was a section of the river that flowed between concrete sides.

Each year we had some kind of competition, diving and whatever, which included a thing called the "plunge". For this, we had to stand on the low bridge that crossed the river where it flowed into our swimming stretch, seeing how far we could glide before stopping.

In my last year I thought it would be fun to try this, not because I was any good at diving but because I knew I could hold my breath longer than most people. We each had three goes at this. For the first two I took my planned deep breath and waited for the river to glide me past the winning mark left by others. But this didn't really work, and I could hear people shouting, "You've stopped moving," so there was no point continuing to lie there with my head still under the water.

For my final go I chose to swim out of the competition, meaning to indicate that I was withdrawing from it. I thought people would be able to see me swimming. For this, I used my arms to take me down to the bottom and there I swam about fifty yards down river, only coming out when I'd done enough.

While I was still swimming, I could hear people diving in and was glad I hadn't held up the rest of the competition. Then, when I got out, I noticed a lot of alarm around the plunge area. I went to see what was going on and saw a boy diving in, coming up with someone else clutched in his arms, saying "I've got him," only to find that he was holding onto someone else who had dived in along with him.

Only then did it dawn upon me they were looking for *me*! When I hadn't surfaced from my last plunge, disappearing into the murky water, people must have thought I'd got stuck in the muddy bottom. I therefore went up to the master in charge, Mr. Hampton, and said: "Excuse me, sir. I think they are looking for me." He didn't turn round but said, angrily: "Can't you see I'm busy?" "But, sir, I really do think they are looking for me." When he turned round, and saw who was speaking to him, he first looked as if he'd seen a ghost. Then he raged at me, saying he would tell my housemaster of this.

I was by then a house prefect, sitting at the housemaster's table. I therefore told him about this fiasco over lunch, making sure he saw the funny side of it, and he laughed loudly as I told him. After lunch, however, he heard from Mr. Hampton and I was summoned to the study. Goddard (my housemaster) then had to show his disapproval, and I could of course see that I'd been very foolish. It had never occurred to me they wouldn't see me swimming my way out of the competition, but I'd been tempted to do that because I knew I could hold my breath for a very long time.

During my National Service someone started a competition to see who could hold their breath the longest. I won, holding my breath for three minutes and twenty seconds. What was interesting was to find that my stomach began palpating, as if to squeeze out the last dregs of oxygen before passing out. One person did pass out, so I never tried that again.

My first kiss

During my last term, one of the other prefects said to me, in front of all the other prefects, that they'd all decided I was the only prefect not to have kissed the "house tart". This was the name given to a maid who served us at meals and who worked in Annie's pantry (Annie being in charge of the kitchen staff). It was in there that we could always help ourselves to bread. This maid was often to be found in there, doing whatever she had to do, and she was very flirtatious so she'd certainly earned her nickname.

I was not going to be put down by my fellow prefects. Without saying a word in response to their taunt, I walked straight to Annie's pantry where I found the "house tart" doing whatever. I went up to her and, without saying anything to her, I kissed her firmly on the mouth. While doing this I remember thinking that noses do rather get in the way. I then merely said "Thank you" and returned immediately to the prefects' study. "Well," I said, "you can never say *that* again."

Easter holiday alone in England

After the two weeks I'd stayed with the Havergals (see later, under Music) I was left to fend for myself for the rest of that Easter holiday. Mother had decided that, as there were only two weeks left of the holiday, it would not be worth paying for me to go out to Krefeld for such a short time.

For some of the time I stayed with my father's mother (Granny). She gave me an umbrella for Easter, which I decided I would keep for best, having a broken umbrella at Winchester for rainy days. I would therefore keep this new one rolled, especially as I'd just been made a school prefect. One of the privileges for school prefects was that they were allowed to strut around with a rolled umbrella, when it was not raining, as a mark of their status in the school. Everyone else had to leave their brollies unrolled and floppy.

That bank holiday Monday was a wonderfully sunny day, so I decided I'd go for a walk over the Downs, it being a perfect day for that. But Granny didn't want me to go without my brolly: "What if it rains?" I told her there was no way it was going to rain, but she thought she'd seen a bit of a cloud out of her window, so she made me take my new brolly with me. I can remember feeling a total prat walking on the Downs with this rolled umbrella, in front of lots of other people walking there.

94

One night, I had decided to put a new film in my camera, still using the free film I'd been given by the naval photographer. This would normally mean using my changing bag. I would wind "naked" film onto the spool of a film cassette for my camera, but I didn't have the bag with me. So, once it was dark, I got inside a cupboard in the bedroom to load my cassette there. I'd noticed, as I pulled the door closed, that the door had made a slight click but I didn't think any more of it until it was time to get out of the cupboard. Then I found I had shut myself in, with a catch that could only be turned from outside. It looked as if I might be there for the night.

Not to worry anyone else, I decided it might be all right to sleep in the cupboard. Granny and her help, Josephine, would have been asleep by then anyway. But I couldn't sleep. In the end I began to call out, shouting as loud as I could, until Josephine came into my room to see what was going on. She was amazed to find no one there. But then she realised that the voice she could hear was coming from inside the cupboard. She laughed until she cried when she opened the door to find me shut inside.

Going back to Winchester early

Although I was fond of Granny, after some time of staying with her I began to be impatient to get away. I therefore pretended that term was starting the next day and excused myself, having packed to go back to Winchester. I arrived there three days early. I'd hoped to stay with Mrs. Blake, my singing teacher, but she had guests that night. So I went to my house and found the matron, explaining I had come back early. She made up my bed and let me spend the first night there. For the remaining two nights I stayed with Mrs. Blake.

Music

What really saved my sanity at Winchester was music. This became the centre of my life and what I spent most of my spare time doing.

For my first term I had to go to the chantry, this being where the first year boys went rather than to chapel, which wasn't big enough for everyone. My main memory of that was being fascinated by the huge eyebrows of Mr. Hodges, who played the little organ there. His eyebrows were so bushy and long he had to lift them up from behind his glasses before he could play. At the start of my second term I auditioned for the chapel choir and was admitted as an alto.

Singing

I think it was at the beginning of my second year I auditioned again, applying to sing bass. However, the master of music and choir master (Henry Havergal) said he would prefer me to remain as an alto. He wanted to have an alto with experience and I could clearly still sing as an alto. So, for all of my remaining time at Winchester, I continued to sing alto.

In my last year I asked Havergal if I could have singing lessons, as I was having to do some solo parts and I felt nervous without having adequate technique for singing. He was adamant I should not go to just anyone as he thought I had an unusual voice. He didn't want this spoiled by inappropriate tuition. He therefore wanted me to go to Alfred Deller, and he arranged for me to meet him when he was in Winchester for a performance of Haydn's *Creation*. Deller said he would be glad to take me on but his fee would be five guineas an hour. But I could not contemplate asking my parents for that. It would also have meant my missing a whole day from Winchester each week, travelling to London and back. It was just not possible.

I argued with Havergal, saying it would be better for me to have some singing tuition rather than none. He didn't agree but he also did not prevent me going to see Mrs. Blake, a piano and singing teacher on the music staff. She took me on for practically no fee at all.

Under Mrs. Blake's tuition, I discovered I had a much greater range than I'd realised. She would take me up to the treble descant C, as a regular part of warming up. This was most unfortunate, and proved Havergal right in the end. I'm sure this contributed to my eventual voice strain, particularly after I had my tonsils out. That operation had left my throat all twisted and, thereafter, I could not place my voice in the way I had learned to do. I also think that Havergal was proved right in not wanting my voice messed around with, which I think Mrs. Blake had been doing as she was overly excited by my unusual vocal range.

Nevertheless, I had a great deal of fun with my singing. For instance, when the Quiristers (the choir school attached to the College) were in quarantine, after one boy there had got polio, Havergal asked me to sing second treble for the rest of that term. I was about seventeen at the time.

A small group of us (two voices per part) used to sing madrigals, a high spot being when we were invited to sing at a banquet held at the Guildhall in honour of the retiring bishop of Winchester. We sat at the high table and sang our hearts out.

One evening, three of us sang a programme of madrigals and folk-songs in the school library. Havergal decided that, as we were in fine voice that day, he would transpose everything up a tone (I was then singing up to the treble F or G) which made the evening quite special.

One of the works we sang in the cathedral was Handel's *Messiah*. As always, Havergal would get so excited during the rehearsals he would get increasingly hot, taking off his tie, then his jacket and waistcoat, always ending up with his red braces over his shirt.

During the final rehearsal in the cathedral, it had been decided that the drama of the "Amen chorus" could be heightened by using spot-lights that had been set up in front of the reredos, at the far east end of the cathedral. These lights would be turned up, from dim to very bright, as the chorus proceeded. During the rehearsal, when we came to the last "Amen" at the very end, the resonance in the cathedral was utterly amazing. The final chord took all of seven seconds before it faded away. It sent shivers down our spines and we all expected the same to happen at the evening concert.

On the night, when we came to the "Amen chorus" all was going extremely well, with a fantastic slow building of the crescendo towards the end. The lights were being turned up behind us, lighting up the reredos as planned, when suddenly the whole cathedral was plunged into darkness. The extra lights had fused the entire cathedral. The choir continued from memory but the orchestra, most of them professionals who would be playing by sight, soon ground to a halt. Then we heard Havergal's voice calling out to the packed cathedral: "Everyone, please stay in your seats. Lights will be brought to you as soon as possible." It was the biggest anticlimax I'd ever experienced. We never finished that final chorus.

While I was at Winchester we also performed Bach's *Mass in B Minor*, Haydn's *Creation*, Beethoven's *9th Symphony*, Bach's *St. Matthew Passion*, and, I think, the Brahms *Requiem*. All of these took place in the cathedral.

One of the features of music in chapel was the use of the congregation. Once a week Havergal would take some time before a service to have congregation practice, during which he would get them to sing the hymns properly, full voice when appropriate or quietly, as for "... *still small voice of calm*" at the end of one of the hymns. He would also rehearse them for their part in Stanford's *Te Deum*, for which he'd written a congregation part. Practising this, he would stand in front of the congregation, showing with his hand where to find the notes. He held his hand like a large note on a musical stave, and he would move it up and down to indicate where to find the notes; very high, down to very low. It looked comical but it really worked.

During my last summer term we put on Handel's *L'Allegro, Il Penseroso*, and I sang a solo aria. Someone, who had previously been our assistant organist, came up from Exeter for the concert. He told me that he'd heard me singing this aria during the rehearsal, as he was approaching the hall. He had thought he recognised the voice of Alfred Deller, only to find that I was the person singing it.

In the concert, everything went well except for the very first note. Havergal had been trying to give me a big boost, in the introduction to the aria, with the orchestra playing quite loud. My first note, a low A, was at the weakest part of my voice. So, when I tried to match the volume of the introduction, my voice popped. However, I quickly cleared my throat and after that it went fine.

Stop whistling

Another funny thing happened when I was a prefect. I had just had my sinuses washed out, because of recurring infections, with the result that my voice suddenly became much more resonant. I found I could sing almost anything, including both alto and soprano arias from *The Messiah*. As I was a prefect, I had the privilege of being allowed to have a bath whenever I wanted, even during prep time. On this occasion I was having a bath in one of the bathrooms, enjoying the amazing acoustics, singing soprano arias such as "*I Know that My Redeemer Liveth*". I was having a wonderful time until someone came to the bathroom with a message from the housemaster (Mr. Dicker) across the road from us. He'd sent a message: "Tell that prefect to stop whistling." He obviously could not imagine that any prefect could sing as high as that.

The Royal School of Church Music (RSCM)

During my last Easter holidays at Winchester I was invited by Havergal to take part in the RSCM training fortnight, which that year was taking place at Winchester Cathedral. For this, each year, they would make up a choir with the leading voices of cathedral choirs throughout Britain. Havergal put my name down as one of the altos. I was just thrilled to be included.

Each day we would have a practice hour, before matins and again before evensong, or before mass at the weekends. We would also have two hours of sight-reading, going through some of the best music written for cathedral choirs. Then we would have the actual services each day, and in the evenings we would have another two hours of making music for fun. This meant that we sang for about eight hours a day, and it was amazing to find that our voices didn't tire.

Each year the RSCM, as well as having its two weeks of choir training, would broadcast an evensong. That year, the broadcast was on the first Wednesday after we had just met, having only come together on the Friday before. We'd had only those few days for the choir to be trained up for that broadcast, which (I was told) used to be regarded as the cathedral broadcast of the year—setting the standard for cathedral choirs throughout the country. When we got back from the broadcast, we learned that telegrams had been coming from all over the place, saying how well it had gone. It certainly felt a great privilege to have taken part in that.

During that fortnight with the RSCM I was staying as a guest of the Havergals. I really loved his wife Hyacinth. She was the kindest person I'd ever known. She really made me feel a member of the family.

The sons, Malcolm and Giles, were also there for some of the time. Giles, who was then wanting to become a ballet dancer, used to do dance steps and exercises in front of a mirror. But he later became a tubby lad and clearly could not pursue his first ambition. In 1969 Giles became artistic director of the Citizens Theatre in Glasgow where he remained until 2003. In 2002 he received a CBE for his services to theatre.

While I was staying with them, Havergal was preoccupied with composing. At times this completely engrossed him, as became apparent when he went to post some letters on a very rainy day. "Don't forget your umbrella," Hyacinth called out. Henry picked up an umbrella and walked to the post box with this held aloft above his head, completely

99

oblivious of the fact that he'd forgotten to open it! He came back soaking wet and unaware of it.

Also during that time, Joan Dixon (cellist) had been staying with the Havergals. She was rehearsing for a concert to be held at the Guildhall and I was asked to turn pages for her while she played.

Cathedral choir

As a result of my two weeks with the RSCM, the cathedral organist and choir master, then Mr. Surplice (a most suitable name), invited me to become an honorary member of the cathedral choir. So, for my remaining time at Winchester, every weekend I used to run between chapel and the cathedral, for rehearsals or for services. It was an amazing privilege to sing with them.

Bach's Magnificat

Havergal was away for one term on sabbatical leave. While he was away his place was taken by Reginald Moore, a very talented organist, who was a rather cold man and a perfectionist. This was actually quite good for the choir, as he brought us to a level of discipline that Havergal didn't—he being too nice to be a really strong disciplinarian.

When Havergal returned, he found the choir was singing, as he told us, better than he'd ever heard us sing before. As a result he decided to put on a performance of Bach's *Magnificat*. This was a real challenge, as he planned this with only three weeks in which to rehearse for it. The performance, when we came to it, was electric. I think this reflected the excitement we all felt in getting to know this wonderful piece in such a short time. I'd never heard it before.

The organ

There is a very fine organ in the chapel. At the end of each service Havergal would play a voluntary, and after Sunday services he usually played a Bach *Prelude and Fugue*. He would get very excited playing these. We, in the choir, were always allowed (two or three at a time) to go up to the organ loft to watch him play, one of us also to turn the pages. Sometimes, when Havergal wanted to push back some of the stops, but not wanting to take his hands from the keys, he would push them back with his foot. On one occasion he got cramp in his leg while doing that, having to struggle to continue playing as if nothing had happened.

Viola and violin

The reason I started with the viola was that mother used to play that, alongside her sister Joyce (on the violin) and another sister (Barbara) on the cello. Mother had a really *terrible* viola. In fact, it was of such poor quality that, when I took it to a music shop in Winchester to have it valued, they asked me whether I was offering it with the case or on its own. "Would it make much difference?" I asked. "A great deal of difference," was the reply. "If you are offering it *with* the case we could offer you £5. If you are wanting to sell the viola on its own, then I'm afraid we could not give you anything." I only ever heard mother play one thing on it, remembered from her 'teens. It was "*Drink to Me Only with Thine Eyes*".

I was taught by John Sealey, who later became leader of the orchestra at Sadler's Wells. He was fortunately able to find a much better viola for me, which could make a really rather fine sound. I played a viola piece in the school music competitions, part of a viola sonata by Marcello, and I remember being so carried away in playing it that I forgot to breathe. I almost fainted.

Another time when I played solo viola it was for *King Richard II* at the Guildhall. Havergal had composed some Elizabethan sounding music, which I played in the wings. "*Music do I hear? Ha, ha! Keep time ...*" However, it was not long before King Richard tired of my playing: "*This music mads me, let it sound no more,*" at which point I would put my viola back in its case and I'd move to where I could enjoy the rest of the play.

However, in spite of having a much better viola, I became bored with the pieces I was learning to play on it. Nearly all of these had been arranged from violin. Also, in the orchestra, the viola part was probably the most boring of all. So I decided to try playing the violin. First of all, I borrowed other boys' violins to see how easy it was to change from one instrument to the other. I also wanted to get a sense of what different violins sounded like. I soon discovered from these experiments that all one needed to change to the violin was a good ear. The fingers learn to adjust. I therefore went to the music shop to see if

101

they could sell me a violin. There I found one that was being sold for £7. It had a very sweet tone and was at least as good as some of the violins I'd borrowed.

I told mother that I wanted to buy a violin, and I'd found just the thing: it only cost £7. However, mother, who seemed to be worrying about the cost of everything (I don't know why), said she wanted me to wait. She then told me she'd heard of someone in Rogate who was selling a violin for £5. She wanted me to try that first, before making any decision. I did try it, and it was just as awful as her viola had been. I could not believe she wanted to save £2 by getting me to buy a rubbish violin, rather than the one I'd found. In the end I bought the £7 violin and it was a great find.

Orchestra

After I'd played the violin for just a few weeks I said to Sealey that I had become bored with playing viola in the orchestra. I asked him if I could change to violin. He told Havergal of this, and he reported that he had apparently said: "If Casement wants to make a fool of himself, let him. He can play at the back desk of the second violins."

I was so incensed by this idea that I would be making a fool of myself, I did something I'd never done before. I got the music for the next orchestra rehearsal and I actually *practised* for it. Before then I had always been sight-reading for orchestra, or just making do on what I had picked up from each rehearsal. But, on this occasion, I played the music with confidence and great gusto; in fact with so much gusto, Havergal promoted me to become leader of the second violins from that day on. I'd never had a single lesson on the violin as Sealey refused to let me take it to my lessons. With him, my instrument continued to be the viola.

Years later, when I was working for the FWA (Family Welfare Association) in Islington, I used to walk past Sealey's house several times a week. One day, when passing his house, I was shocked to see the doors and windows had been blackened from smoke, so I enquired what had happened. There'd been a fire, and Sealey along with his second wife had been burned to death. I was deeply shocked by this.

Before then, Sealey had done me a very great favour. I'd asked him to find a good violin for me, offering my viola and violin in part exchange, asking him to find the best I might be able to afford. He found me a Richard Duke violin, made in 1767. This had the most wonderful tone and was a treat to play. I could sense that it had played everything before, and all I needed to do was to remind it. Alas, when I got into writing my first book, I had no time to keep up playing this. I don't think Margaret missed it, but I certainly did. Then, after years of not playing this lovely violin, I no longer liked the sound I made, and it was a shame for it to be left unplayed, so I sold it. I was paid something like £3,500, which wasn't bad, considering I'd bought it for £70, plus the value of the viola and violin. We went to India on the proceeds.

Leaving Winchester

I wrote about this in my last book:

> My attachment to the school itself became very evident when the time came for me to leave after my last term. In my final hours there I could see just how attached I had become to the bricks and mortar of the place. When everyone else had packed up and left, with barely a second thought about not seeing them again, I spent a long time walking round, weeping my goodbye to the buildings, the chapel, the music school where I had spent so many hours, and all the places that had been significant to me. I was showing an attachment to places rather than to people. I had too often experienced people as unreliable. They had kept on leaving, and we had kept on leaving people as we moved from one home to another. The school buildings, however, remained the same. (*Learning from Life*, p. 29)

Note

1. *Toys*, in that baffling language of Winchester *Notions*, are the individual "horseboxes" in which a boy has his desk, keeps his books and other possessions and does his "toy time", or prep. This is taken from the Winchester College *Annual Report*, 2008.

CHAPTER FIVE

My parents in Germany

The Duke of Edinburgh slept in my bed

Krefeld (Germany)

In 1952, father was appointed to the Royal Naval Rhine Squadron at Krefeld. The first name in the visitor's book father kept there is that of "Alexander of Tunis", Field Marshal Lord Alexander.

The official house

After the war, various properties were requisitioned for use by the British forces in Germany. There was a castle, where the admiral was placed, and an amazing house in Krefeld which father had as his official residence.

The drawing room had a very wide picture window, which stretched the full width of the room, looking out onto the garden. The window was made with one huge sheet of glass that could be lowered into the basement by means of a winding handle. This meant that, in hot weather, the drawing room could become completely open to the garden.

The inner doors, as between the drawing room and the dining room, were also made of single sheets of glass. When these were opened, the door would slide into a wall cavity. The steward, who looked after father, used to polish the big window and these doors until there was not the slightest mark on them.

One visitor, when he made to go into the dining room, said: "I remember the trick about these doors. They look open but they're actually closed." He then took hold of the upright frame of the door, slid it carefully to one side and walked straight into the glass of the door that he'd, unknowingly, just closed.

There was a lot of room in the house. When I stayed there I had a suite of rooms to myself, with a bedroom, a dressing room, and a bathroom. That was where the Duke of Edinburgh was put when he stayed.

Each evening, except (I think) at weekends, dinner would be a formal affair. The reason for this was said to be that father, and any house guests, should always be properly dressed in case someone official came to visit, or when they had guests for a formal dinner. This meant that we men had to be in dinner jackets almost every evening.

One guest who came to dinner was a retired German officer with a wooden leg. Father, trying to be hospitable, said: "I suppose we did that to your leg." The German replied: "Oh, don't worry about that. I was run over by one of my own tanks."

A very cold bath

As it was extremely cold during the winter I was there, I made a thirty foot icicle. For this I set up a siphon on the ledge of the bathroom window, which slowly poured water from a large jug onto the top of a strong length of string that I had hung over the window sill. The string reached down to the ground, the top end being tied to a towel rail. By constantly filling the jug with water, I was able to get the siphon to feed water down the string, day and night. By the next morning I had an icicle that must have weighed a great many pounds. It was much too heavy to haul up to the bathroom window, so I cut it down and carried up lengths of this to put into the bath, which I filled with water and left my icicle there to melt. The next morning, with ice still floating in the bath, I had the most freezing and refreshing cold bath of my life. But, *Oh my*, I was glad to get out as quickly as I could.

Shopping

It could be very cold out shopping, but mother found a way to deal with this. In those days, many of the shops had open doors to the street, with a curtain of hot air being fanned up from pavement level to ceiling. Mother found it very useful to stand over the hot grille until her skirt had filled up with hot air, which would help to keep her warm until she next needed to fill up at another shop.

When mother went shopping in Krefeld, she would sometimes buy things for the cook, to save her going out specially for some particular item, but she could not speak any German. On one occasion she'd agreed to buy some eggs for the cook, not knowing the word for eggs. Unable to find any she could point to, she went up to a counter and started to make chicken noises. The shop assistant thought she understood, and came back with a chicken. "*Nein, nein,*" said mother, using one of the few words she knew. She then squatted down in the shop (she a captain's wife) and made egg-laying noises, until the assistant finally understood that she was asking for *eggs*!

Speaking German

Father was not much better at speaking German. He knew some words like "*Ein fahrt*" but not much else.

When trying to find his way to Mönchengladbach, he asked the way without using the *umlaut* in Mönchen, so it sounded as if he was asking for Moonchen Gladbach. The German he asked could not make this out at all, nor could the next person who was asked if he knew where Moonchen Gladbach might be. Eventually, someone else joined in and asked whether it could be Mönchengladbach that my father was asking for.

One day, when father was driving, the car radiator began to boil with steam pouring out. He ran into a garage to ask for help, and mother was most impressed when he came back immediately with a man carrying a wateringcan full of water. "How did you manage to explain what you needed?" she asked. "Oh, that was easy. I just told him *mein Fahrter is kaput*," thinking that *Fahrter* would mean the thing he drove in—perhaps related to the road signs he'd got used to—and he knew that *kaput* meant "broken". What he didn't know was that, to a German, it could sound as if he was saying *mein Vater ist kaput*, which would mean *my father is dead*. Clearly this was not likely to be the case, as the car was spewing out clouds of steam, so the man had correctly seen it was water that was needed: regardless of whatever my father might think he was saying about his father.

Miss Inkster

Mother found an extraordinary little woman who went with them to Krefeld, being there to teach my sisters Elisabeth and Susan. When she first came she was already over seventy. She was not much above five feet high, dumpy and round (almost spherical), with a lovely chuckling laugh.

There was a time when Miss Inkster had been teaching Elisabeth the catechism, including the Ten Commandments. A few days after that there was a bit of commotion in the drawing room, Elisabeth slapping something against the sofa. Miss Inkster asked her what she was doing, to which Elisabeth replied: "I think I've just committed *adultery*." Miss Inkster asked her what she meant and Elisabeth replied: "I've just killed a fly." Miss Inkster, realising where Elisabeth's thinking was coming from, said: "In that case you mean *murder*."

The floods in Holland

In 1953, while my parents were still in Krefeld, father heard reports of terrible floods in Holland. He ordered all the landing craft under his command to set off immediately to Holland, steaming down the Rhine at full speed, getting to Holland before any other rescue craft had been able to get there.

What followed was the most strenuous three weeks of his life. Father used his official yacht (the *Prince Charles*)[1] as the place where each day's strategy was planned and where reports were brought back. He said afterwards that he probably got only two hours' sleep a night, as meetings would go on for most of the night, and all of each day was taken up in rescue work, helping to get stranded people to safety.

After this, father was decorated by Queen Juliana of Holland, being made Commander of the Order of Orange Nassau. He was meant to receive this in person from Queen Juliana but, on the day of the investiture, there was so much fog he could not get to the palace.

Father also got a special notice from our queen, an elaborate announcement signed by her, in which it states that although Queen Elizabeth II was pleased to be informed of the decoration father had received from the queen of Holland, and she hereby gave him permission to wear this on formal occasions within her empire, she would not allow him to call himself by any title pertaining to the Orange Nassau within her lands, or words to that effect. What is amusing is that the framed statement from Queen Elizabeth looks even more impressive than the one from Queen Juliana.

My typewriter

I had my eighteenth birthday while in Krefeld and I remember that the most important present I received then was a typewriter, given to me by mother's mother. My cousin Rosemary happened to be staying at the time. Having just done a secretarial course, she immediately told me I must *never* look at the keys. "How will I be able to type if I don't look at the keys?" She then set about showing me how to touch-type. She printed out the keyboard and marked this with the fingers for each letter. "Only ever look at that," she said, giving me the plan she'd made for me. And that was all I ever did look at.

Once I'd learned the fingering for the alphabet, I used to practise words on my knees, or on any surface that was handy, on a bus or whenever I had spare time. I very quickly became fluent so that, by the time I did my National Service training I was already able to type quite fast.

Going to Salzburg

The following summer I was again staying in Krefeld, having just left Winchester. While I was there, I discovered that the Salzburg Festival was on, so I set off for part of it. I went to stay with Baron and Baronin von Salis.

When I got to Salzburg I found my way to 2, Ernst-Grein-Strasse (I remember the address to this day). There I met the charming von Salis family, the baron and baroness with their daughter Hanni.

During my first evening with the family, the baron was very keen to try out his English, which was an incredible mix of Jane Austin and Shakespeare. He had read these extensively but he'd hardly ever had any chance to *speak* English.

109

Trying to speak German

While in Salzburg, someone asked me if I was French. I replied: "Nein. Ich bin *Englander*." This person seriously doubted what I was saying but I insisted, pointing out the evidence: my pronunciation, my grammar, my vocabulary (all being so bad). He asked if I had a dictionary with me, which I did. He was then able to point to the word he was hearing. It seemed that I was insisting in my very poor German that I was *ein Inländer,* which means a native of the country! I should have been pronouncing it as *Engländer* without the English sound of "*ing*" at the beginning.

Mozart's Geburtshaus (birthplace)

While in Salzburg, I went to see round the place where Mozart had been born. I was utterly amazed by the vast amount of music displayed on the shelves, hundreds upon hundreds of scores. It occurred to me, as I looked at them, that it would take a normal person a whole lifetime just to copy out these scores, without even having the task of composing, whereas Mozart had composed and written all of these himself in the space of his very few years. He was just under thirty-six when he died.

Later visits

Sometime later, my parents drove through Salzburg and chose to visit the von Salis family, who were still living at Ernst-Grein-Strasse. Then, when I was at Cambridge, I visited them again during my scooter tour around Europe. When we were there, the baroness told me they had loved meeting my parents: "And your father has very good German," she said. I was amazed at this, and replied: "But he only has *two* sentences in German."… "*Ja,*" she said, "we had them both!"

Meeting Joan Dixon

On one of my trips back to England from Krefeld, I met on a station platform Joan Dixon (for whom I had been turning pages in Havergal's house). Travelling back together, she told me she'd been touring Germany and had ended up having a musical weekend in a castle where musicians had met for the fun of making music together, playing for no audience other than themselves. It had been a wonderful experience. In particular she'd heard a young baritone sing German *Lieder* like no one else had sung them. "I'll tell you his name," she said, "as he will very soon become world-famous. Of that I am sure, even though at the moment he's not known outside of Germany. His name is Dietrich Fischer-Diskau." How right she was.

The Duke of Edinburgh's visit (March 1953)

Soon after the Duke of Edinburgh had been promoted to the most senior positions in the Army, Navy, and Air Force, he went to Germany to inspect the BAOR forces there (British Army of the Rhine), which included all three services. For his visit to inspect the Navy forces, he stayed with father in his official residence in Krefeld, the admiral's official residence being too distant for that to be practicable.

Father had everything prepared for the duke's visit, sailors at the ready to present arms and to salute as he arrived. It had all been timed on the assumption that he would arrive exactly as planned. However, it turned out that the duke had got bored on the *Autobahn*, being driven by his driver, so he'd taken the wheel and driven himself—at great speed. As a result he arrived much earlier than planned.

Father had the sailors salute the royal car and one of them went to open the door, where he'd caught sight of the Duke of Edinburgh. But father was trying to get him to go to the rear door where, properly, the duke should have been sitting. Only then did father realise that he'd been driving himself. The duke got out and laughed, seeing my father's embarrassment. "Oh, don't worry; I drove so fast that I lost all of the accompanying cars. They couldn't keep up." The royal standard was then duly raised on the flagpole by the house.

When the Duke of Edinburgh got into the drawing room, he found a sheet of instructions to the staff on royal etiquette, which he enjoyed reading: "So you've got them all prepared for me, then."

For dinner, mother had chosen the soup and the main course, leaving the cook to choose her favourite dishes for dessert. The cook had chosen to make meringues and éclairs, these being put onto a silver salver with folded napkins to decorate the dish.

Unfortunately, some of the napkins got stuck to the meringues so that the napkins began to float onto the table or floor when people were serving them. The duke thought this very funny. However, when mother wrote to my father's brother John (then at the Imperial Defence College) to tell him about this, John could not read her handwriting. The word for napkins had been written with mother's characteristic high stroke on the "n" which had led John to think that the meringues had been decorated with *hairpins*. He passed this story all around the IDC, where father was well known, and people were later quite disappointed to hear the true story. They said they had much preferred the version that John had been passing around.

When the Duke of Edinburgh was driven down to the naval base, as they approached he lent over mother to turn on the light so that people would be able to see who was sitting in this official car, with the royal standard flying. He laughed when he saw that there was only a handful of German people who'd turned up to see him being driven into the base.

As I have already mentioned, I didn't join my parents in Germany for my last Easter holiday at Winchester. For part of that time I stayed with my father's mother (Granny), and I learned a lot more about her during that time.

Finding Granny's long-lost friend

I give an account of this strange experience in my last book (*Learning from Life*, pp. 168–170). I had been to Terwick church for the Easter Day service and was walking back when a car had stopped to give me a lift. I'd got in beside the chauffeur and thanked the lady in the back, who then asked me if I was at Winchester. When I told her that I was still there, she replied: "I used to know someone called Roddie Casement. He went to Winchester, but that must have been a long time ago now. It was before the war." When I told her that she was speaking of my father, she was delighted and asked: "Is his mother still alive?" I said we would soon be driving past her door, about two miles down the road. The lady then told me she had been trying to trace my grandmother, with whom she had lost touch during the war. "She is my best friend. I would love to see her again."

The week before this, Granny had been telling me an exactly parallel story about trying to find her best friend, who was no longer known at the addresses she'd been writing to. When we arrived at Granny's house I ran in to her, saying: "You remember that friend you'd lost, your best friend. Well, I've just found her for you. She's in the car outside wishing to see you." The two friends spent the rest of the day together and Granny died the following year, very happy to have met her old friend again.

When Granny died, I have a vivid memory of her in her coffin, in the sitting room. She'd been laid out and prepared, with the coffin still open, and what I remember now was how very beautiful she looked. All the lines of pain had been smoothed out of her face. I'm told she had been extremely beautiful when she was young.

Note

1. This had originally been Goering's yacht, previously named (by Goering) *Karin II* after his wife.

CHAPTER SIX

Into uniform—National Service

Several times I am due for a reprimand

Pre-National Service

As a requirement for doing my National Service in the RNVR I had to do three weeks of pre-National Service training in *HMS Indefatigable*, an aircraft carrier anchored in Weymouth.

I had to dress in uniform that made me look just like someone in the St. John Ambulance Service, with a white band around a peaked cap. I was in fact once mistaken for one of them. I was to be known as an "upper yardman", that apparently being my rank, but I never found out where this designation came from. I was simply going to be paid to push a pen, etc., as someone in the supply branch of the service.

For our meals we were all issued with a knife, fork, and spoon, which we had to take with us to the mess, otherwise we would have to eat with our fingers.

We all had hammocks, slung on hooks in rows, in a compartment that was off the hangar deck where aircraft would normally be housed if the ship were ready for action. The first thing we had to learn was how to sling the hammock and, much more important, how to get into it. As the hammock was slung above shoulder height this was quite an enterprise. At first we were hooking an ankle over the side and trying to scramble up that leg to get the rest of the body into line with the hammock. It looked as if we would have to be lifted in by a mate, so impossible did it seem. However, after a day of trial and error, I miraculously discovered that my experience of gym came in handy. I soon managed to spring up and, as it were, levitate level with the side of my hammock. It soon became possible to spring into a hammock in one movement, but how that was achieved I never quite understood.

One of the courses that we had to do on *Indefatigable* was learning how to chart the course of a ship on a navigation map. We were given course and speed, and the distance travelled on each leg. We were meant to be charting an entry into harbour, using these measurements, and a petty officer instructor went round to see how each of us was getting on. One person, when asked if he had managed to reach the anchorage point, replied: "Well, not exactly. At the moment I seem to be cruising along the fairway of the local golf course."

The A-level results came out while I was on *Indefatigable*. One day, I was minding my own business when someone pointed out to me that I was being called for on the loudspeakers: "Would upper yardman Casement please report to the captain's office." I could not imagine what this might be about. Had I unwittingly committed some awful crime? Or had someone in my family died? I rushed to the office only to be congratulated by the captain, some buddy of my father's, who had received a message to say I had passed my A-levels. Once again I had forgotten that there were results to hear about.

We went out in a "whaler" (small sailing boat) a few times, sailing this in the harbour. While we were on this course we also took part in a whaler race, which took place outside the harbour. However, the wind blew up to gale force so the race was abandoned halfway through. We then had a choice, either to wait an hour or more for a boat to tow us back to the ship, or to sail back. We chose to sail.

This was no easy matter. As we approached the entrance to the harbour we had to tack into the wind, which was blowing against us in exactly the opposite direction we needed to go. Every time we tacked, having to be careful not to get too close to the rocks on either side of the entrance, we found we had only made a gain of a few yards beyond the previous tack. So we had to persist for ages until eventually, and only very gradually, we crept our way forward through the entrance.

We then had a clear run back to the ship, sailing close to the wind and going at an incredible speed. At one point it looked as if we would ram straight into the ship, if we didn't stop in time. So, as soon as we got close to the ship we dropped the sails, aiming to catch hold of a rope hanging down to the water from one of the ship's booms, to which we were meant to tie up. But we had lowered our sails a few yards too early. The man at the bow of our boat failed to reach the rope and then, instantly, we found ourselves being blown away from the ship. We hurriedly manned the oars and rowed, most of us having never rowed before, struggling against the wind. It looked as if we were again making no headway at all, but very slowly we managed to get back to the rope and this time we were able to tie up.

Having put the sails and oars away, the next thing was to get out of the boat and up to the boom. To this day I do not know how I managed this. From rowing for what had felt like half an hour against the wind, until we had managed to tie up, I felt utterly exhausted. We then had to climb a rope ladder which took us to the underside of the huge boom. Next, we had to ease ourselves up the side of the boom until we scrambled on top of it. By this time we were at least thirty feet above the water.

What nobody had told me was that, for walking along the boom, there was a steadying rope which had to be used in a special way. The rope was to one side of the boom, slightly loose. What you were meant to do, which I only learned about afterwards, was to lean back towards the boom, away from the rope, bringing the steadying rope with you until it tightened. You were then meant to walk sideways along the boom, to safety in the ship.

What happened to me was that I started out using the steadying rope as if it were a rail, leaning towards it rather than bringing it towards me, and the further I went along the boom the looser the rope became. Eventually, I had to let go of it altogether as the rope was too loose to give me any further support. For the rest of the way along this boom, with a terrifying drop beneath me and the wind gusting this way and that, I did a balancing act until I was able to jump the last bit into the ship. What made this even worse was that I overheard someone talking to his wife, in a group of people being shown over the ship at that time. I heard this man saying, in a broad Yorkshire accent: "*Ee!* I think the lad's in trouble. Do you think he'll make it?" At that moment I was not sure that I would.

That was such a terrifying experience it has virtually blocked out any other memories I might have had from that time on board *Indefatigable*.

117

Call-up for National Service

While visiting Krefeld in the summer of 1953, I received a letter that had been forwarded to me from the Haben address. This was a call-up letter saying I should report to *HMS Victoria*, Portsmouth, on a date in the same week. I replied saying that this was insufficient notice, could they please give me another date?

To this I received a reply apologising for the first letter, which had been sent without them knowing I was abroad. They explained that they could not insist upon my reporting while I was living abroad. So the initiative was left to me, to let them know when it would be convenient to begin my National Service. I forget now exactly how I came to choose a good time, but I did eventually make myself available.

For the first weeks we had to be in a place called Victoria Barracks. I learned later that this had been condemned as unfit for human habitation but it was regarded as good enough for us.

The first day there we all had to be vaccinated and inoculated, against just about everything it seemed. We had to line up, stripped to the waist, with our arms on our hips. Then, gradually walking forward to the next point of action, we received whatever it was into each arm.

Another memory is that of the system for what was called "going ashore". We had to line up for what was referred to as the "liberty boat". This left at predetermined times, about once an hour. If you were in time for one of these you were marched, in line, through the gates of the barracks. This was what was meant by "going ashore". On one occasion, someone came running down to the gate asking to be allowed to join the others. "No, you're too late. The liberty boat has just gone." This was to teach us about only going ashore at the set times as if we were actually on a ship.

We had about four weeks of preliminary training at *HMS Victoria*. Some of us were then sent to another shore establishment which was in Yorkshire. After that, I can remember complaining to someone: "I joined the Navy to see the sea but the nearest I ever got to it in the first six months was the Gosport ferry."

HMS Ceres

This was where they trained people who were to join the Supply and Secretariat branch of the Navy. I was sent there because my eyesight was not good enough for whatever the others were allowed to become. It was a collection of Nissen huts placed in a field, with barbed wire round the perimeter. It too was called a "ship", named after the goddess of plenty—hence the name *HMS Ceres*.

I was given various fill-in jobs while waiting for the next intake course to begin. For some of the time I was washing-up for the canteen. My task in the washing-up department was to be one of a team of three. There was a conveyor belt that took racks through the washing section, then to the rinsing section, and then to the dryer. We stacked at one end and unloaded at the other, re-stacking the plates back into piles, and so on.

One day, a joker had put a huge amount of Teepol into the washing-up machine, this being highly concentrated washing-up liquid. When we turned the machine on, it began to pour out foam in an unstoppable stream. This literally filled the washing-up room to armpit level, and then poured out of the door into the passage. We desperately tried to dilute this, to stop it producing foam, but it took a very long time to get it under control. Meanwhile I was afraid that someone would find us still wading around in foam, perhaps putting us on a charge for whatever crime they might call this. But, finally, we got this in hand.

There were well over 500 people who were fed in this canteen, most of them having their first time away from home. Many of these refused to eat the food provided ("not like mother's cooking"), waiting until they could go "ashore" where they would buy food that was more to their liking. As a result there was a huge waste of food, but the officers had started a pig farm in the grounds of this establishment, where all the waste food was put to good use.

My main memory from those times is from my period with these pigs. I spent several weeks doing odd jobs in the pigsties. On my first day I was using concrete for a job that needed doing in the sty of the prize sow, which was about to have piglets. When I was called away for tea break I'd left a bucket of concrete in the sty, but when I returned I saw to my horror that the sow had eaten the entire contents of my bucket!

I spent a very anxious night, afraid this prize sow would die along with her piglets, and (again) I might be up for some charge, and almost certainly I would not get my commission, which would mean not being promoted to an officer. The next morning I got up very early and rushed to see how the sow was. She was OK, but the sty was not OK. It was

119

covered with *concrete turds*, which I had to chip away in order to hide the evidence of what had happened the previous day. The sow, a few days later, gave birth to fourteen piglets.

I finally got onto the officer training course, but I remember very little of it. However, the one thing that stands out now is the typing course. We all had to learn to type, which was no bother to me as I'd already learned to touch-type, having been tutored in this by my cousin Rosemary.

Once we had got the hang of the typewriter they started playing slow waltz tunes, expecting us to type one letter with each main beat of the waltz. I didn't need to go that slowly, so I typed three times as fast as the others. And when it came to the typing exam I did three copies of everything, handing in the best of each.

We all had to spend a day shooting rifles while we were there but I had an advantage, having had quite a lot of rifle practice at Winchester. It might be that I had rifle shooting in my genes as mother used to get prizes for her rifle shooting. She'd even won a prize when she had been about seven months pregnant with me, lying on top of me at the firing range.

I don't know what happened on that shooting day as I was going down with flu. Anyway, I fired at targets: 100 yards, 200 yards, and 300 yards. I also had to shoot at snap targets, which were raised and quickly lowered again, we having to shoot at them before they disappeared. At the end of the day only two people got scores that entitled them to be given a badge as a "marksman". I was one of them. I still don't know how I managed to do so well when I was shivering with flu. Anyway, it was not an advantage being a marksman. I had to wear the gold badge on my arm so that, if anyone saw me doing something wrong, like walking when I should have been going at the double, I felt it made me into a "marked man": *the tall one with a badge.*

We were all measured for officer's uniforms, in case we got our commissions, and I was relieved to find that I did achieve that in spite of everything. Then, for one crazy evening, we were allowed to dress up in our midshipman's uniforms to eat in the officers' mess, being waited upon by people who'd been our mates until the morning of that same day. Now they had to call us "sir".

When it came to the cheese board, I noticed that there were lots of different cheeses, the names of which I didn't know. I didn't want to show my ignorance, so I asked for a cheese with a name that I remembered hearing. But I had forgotten that the cheese I'd asked for was one of the blue cheeses, which until that day I had always refused to eat, imagining them to be full of living mites or whatever makes them go blue. I couldn't then ask to have this changed to a non-blue cheese, so I ate it and found it to be absolutely delicious. I've specially loved blue cheeses ever since that day.

HMS Glasgow

My first real ship was the flagship of the Mediterranean Fleet, then under the command of Admiral the Earl Mountbatten of Burma, and later Admiral Sir Guy Grantham. This was based in Malta.

When I arrived, wearing my uniform for only the second time since it had been made for me, I walked up the gangway to the quarterdeck, feeling very junior and not a little apprehensive. Then, as I began to reach the top of the gangway, I saw the head of another midshipman saluting me. It was David Starling, someone who'd been with me in the "Pink Dorm" at Maidwell for my first term. I immediately felt in familiar company.

I was shown where I would hang my hammock when the time came for bed, which was under three enormous fans that supplied most of the ship. They were on all the time and made such a terrific noise that you could not hear anything said to you, even when the other person was shouting. I thought I might never sleep again, with that noise going all night, but I soon got used to it. In fact, I became so used to it I woke in alarm one night when all the fans simultaneously fused and shut down. The silence that followed was deafening.

My job, for most of my time in *Glasgow*, was in the pay office. There I had to keep a duplicate ledger for about half the men on board. Another midshipman did the other half. We had to enter every allowance, every deduction, and whatever else impacted upon what each person would get paid at the next pay day. I then had to read out my results to the senior petty officer, who kept the official ledger, to make sure that there were no differences. If there were any, they had to be reconciled to see which of us had made a mistake. There was no such thing as a computer, or even a calculator, to make any of this easier. It was all a matter of mental arithmetic, which was something I was lucky to find easy.

When Mountbatten came to leave *Glasgow*, handing over to Admiral Grantham, he gave a series of cocktail parties at the admiral's house in Valletta. I went to two of these. For the first, I was one of the many junior officers in the fleet who'd been invited, I being on the admiral's flagship. At the end of this party, Mountbatten stood at the top of the double staircase, saying a rather bored "Goodbye" … "Goodbye" to each of us, shaking our hands as we left.

The second cocktail party was for senior officers. This included my father, then commanding a squadron of four frigates, he being captain of *HMS Wrangler*. Father asked to bring me with him as well as mother (she having moved to Malta) when he went to this second party. At the end of this I met a very different Mountbatten. He chatted with my father and he even seemed interested to be introduced to me, whom he'd never had occasion to notice before.

Mother used to tell of a time when she and father had been to a dinner given by Mountbatten, at the admiral's house. She'd been sitting next to Mountbatten. In conversation, she'd asked him if it was true that he still had the vice-regal gold dinner service (from India) that she'd heard about. He then called a steward and said: "Mrs. Casement has asked for the next course to be served on gold plates," which she hadn't at all. But that is what followed, and mother thought it looked very strange having meat and gravy on gold plates.

While I was in *Glasgow* I kept on getting sore throats. The ship's doctor sent me to the naval hospital at Bighi, where an ENT consultant prescribed what someone told me was his one and only operation, which he apparently performed on people whenever he could find an excuse. This was to give me an SMR or sub-mucous resection.

Bighi hospital

I had my SMR operation under a local anaesthetic. My nose was stuffed with gauze that had been soaked in some kind of a liquid; and I could then hear all the noises of cutting into my nose, a carving and grinding sound that reverberated through my head. I found myself becoming more and more tense during this, and it seemed to go on forever.

While I was still in Bighi, I began to hear news of my father's ship, *Wrangler*, that it had gone aground at Villefranche, on the south coast of France. I couldn't believe this at first, but then it was confirmed that this was indeed so. His ship had been caught in a sudden onshore gale, which had caused his ship to drag anchor, ending up with its stern aground on the rocks.

122

We heard a lot about this later. I gathered that my father had given the responsibility for planning the anchorage of the four ships in his squadron to his navigator, who happened to be the son of a Rogate couple, Captain and Mrs. Lane. This navigator had not taken into account the local conditions, which included the fact that Villefranche was noted for sudden changes of wind direction, with severe gales blowing from the sea to land. For that reason, all other navigators anchoring there would put out a double length of cable. My father's navigator hadn't done this.

Father was on board, writing up a report, when the gale blew up and he then became aware the anchor was dragging. Most of his officers were ashore at the time, and he immediately had the engines brought back to full steam and tried every manoeuvre to try to keep the ship free of the rocks, but to no avail. It was already too late, and there was nothing more he could do to prevent the grounding. He also got the ship's crew to run "as one body", from one side of the ship to the other, trying to rock the ship free. But nothing worked. The ship was ultimately towed away from the rocks, but the damage was so severe that, even though they were able to get back to Malta, the ship was eventually scrapped. My father never really recovered from the shock of that experience. Mother said that, years later, he would wake in the night from nightmares, in which he was back there with his ship on the rocks.

The court martial

I got permission to be absent from *Glasgow*, so that I could attend my father's court martial. It was an unbelievable experience. I saw no way that he could be found guilty; and I was mystified by his navigator having been found not guilty at an earlier court martial, when his part in this had to be judged. I felt sure that my father would also be found not guilty.

During the court martial proceedings, my father sat at a desk with his ceremonial sword, unsheathed, in front of him. It lay sideways, neither pointing towards him nor away, which is the naval custom at a court martial. He sat with solemn dignity throughout the proceedings. He never once blamed his navigator, and he has been proudly remembered for that.

At the end of the hearing, father was marched out of the courtroom, as were we all. After the court had completed its deliberations, we came back and we were the first to see the ceremonial sword in its new position. It was now placed with its point facing *towards* where father would sit. He was the last person in court to see this, being brought in after we'd sat down. This meant that the court had found him guilty.

I just could not believe this. It was shattering news. And my father's long-term career was ended by this, at that moment. Father had already been told that his next post would be as captain of *HMS Excellent*, and it had been assumed that he, like most other previous captains there, would then be promoted to admiral. That was no longer going to be the way for him, and I know he was heartbroken by that. I was just so glad that I'd been able to be there for him then, the only member of our family who could be with him on that day.

HMS Aisne

My next appointment was to a frigate, *HMS Aisne*. I was the only midshipman there, so I was a member of the officers' mess. I was appointed assistant to the supply officer, doing whatever he needed me to do, which sometimes included supplying ship. This meant getting a gang of men together who would form a chain, passing stores from one to the other until all the stores were safely on board. They then had to be stored, and I had to be in charge of operations like that.

Another task I had sometimes to do was to go ashore to get money for the ship's pay day. Once, when I was at the bank for this, I realised that very little of this money was going to come to me. It so happened that I had decided, that weekend, to buy myself a camera for which I'd been saving up from my pay as a midshipman, which was twelve shillings a day.

I therefore went from the bank, carrying £3,500 cash in a holdall, to a post office where I withdrew the money I needed for the camera. I then wandered through the dockyard, looking at various ships that were being serviced in the dry docks. It was a lovely sunny day and I was not in a hurry.

At least I wasn't in a hurry until I remembered I'd come out for some other reason than just going to the post office. I had been to the bank before that and where was the holdall now? I had left it in the post office. I ran, almost flew, back to look for it, imagining myself as the next Casement to be before a court martial. I then could hardly believe

124

my luck when I saw the holdall, still unopened, being kicked around by passing feet while it sat under the counter, stuffed with notes which in today's money would be worth something like £150,000.

That was not the only time I could have been for the high jump. Another time was when I had been given the honour of being allowed to take the salute on the quarterdeck, for evening colours. When I heard them being piped, I dropped what I was doing and went as quickly as possible to the quarterdeck.

When the ceremony started, with a bugler playing the last post and the flag being very slowly lowered, I was standing smartly to attention, saluting. As the flag began to lower, I remembered what I had been doing when I'd heard the piping for evening colours. I had been in the supply officer's cabin, counting the money in the safe, checking piles of money in all the different currencies that were held there, and I had left most of the money on his desk. I had also left the safe open, and I'd left the door to his cabin open. The gangway running past his cabin was frequently used by sailors going between different parts of the ship. What to do? I couldn't abandon my post on the quarterdeck at this solemn moment, but what might happen to the money? And what might happen to me?

As soon as the ceremony on the quarterdeck was ended I flew back to the supply officer's cabin. There I found him in a state of shock, counting piles of money to see if any of it was missing. Once again, luck was on my side. Nothing was missing. "But never *never* do that again!" he warned. He did not report me, for which I was most grateful.

Naples to Rome

Another of my tasks on *Aisne* was to go to the naval attaché in Naples, when the ship was anchored there, to get a pass translated into Italian. Some of the men were going to be allowed to hitchhike to Rome, to spend three days there and to rejoin the ship in Civitavecchia, the port of Rome. The pass said that the bearer was from *HMS Aisne*, having been given permission to go to Rome for three days, then to rejoin the ship by the stated date. Also, in the event of any problem or difficulty, the naval attaché in Rome could be contacted, and he would sort things out. Six men from the ship were given permission, under the auspices of what was known as "MedFoba" (the Mediterranean Fleet Outward Bound Association). This was a scheme that had been dreamed up by

Mountbatten, allowing sailors to benefit from being within reach of places they could visit, Rome being one of them.

After I'd changed money for nearly everyone on board, before they went into Naples, I told the supply officer that I would also like to see Rome. Could he give me permission to do that too? He told me to type out a pass for myself, as for the sailors, and to set off and to be back on ship in Civitavecchia, like the others, in three days' time.

I got a lift in a very slow lorry that travelled all through the night, getting to Rome at about 5.30 am. We had no language in common except when, at one stage, we recited some Latin together: *Amo, amas, amat, amamus, amatis, amant.* The driver cheered this achievement in communication. In the course of that journey we stopped at a café for some food, and the driver taught me how to eat spaghetti the Italian way, with a fork in my right hand and a spoon in my left, twisting the spaghetti until a mouth-sized pile of it was on the fork, then to nip off with my lips whatever didn't get into my mouth. I sometimes think of that time even now, when I'm eating spaghetti the way I was shown during that night-long journey.

When I got to Rome I had nothing much to do at first, as everything was closed. I also wondered what the others might do. Where might they go? It soon struck me that they would probably go to the naval attaché, as the only address they had—as given on their passes, to start from there. So I found my way to that address. I then booked a room in a hotel nearby, where I shaved, and went back to the wall outside the house of the attaché. There I waited to see if the others turned up. By 10 am, all of the other six had arrived at this address, as I had thought they might. They'd all hitchhiked in pairs and each pair had the same idea of starting at the only address they had, as on their passes.

As we were not in uniform, I told these six they could call me whatever they liked, while we were in Rome together. Two called me "sir", two called me "Mr.", and the two National Service sailors called me "Pat". We settled down to do Rome together. For that day, they were able to use my room in the hotel for a wash and shave, but they then set off to find rooms somewhere else.

They came back to tell me they'd found a cheap *Pensione*, which could put them all up; and they asked me if I would like to join them there, after my one night in the hotel, which I did. I had the choice of either sharing a double bed with the ship's postman, or sleeping in a cot with my legs hanging over the side. I thought that it might be going one step too far to share a bed with a sailor, I being an officer, so I chose the cot.

We did Rome together throughout the three days we had there. One person was a whizz with a map, so he took on the role of guide. Another one was great at buying cheaply in markets, so we gave him a kitty from which he bought supplies to keep us fed while we were there. It worked like a dream.

When I got back, I was reprimanded by the MedFoba officer on my ship. He said that I should have been marching the men around Rome, exercising my position as an officer, rather than spending the time with them, and certainly not sleeping in a dormitory with them! But I told him how valuable it had been. I had come to recognise that, under the uniforms that we usually wore, we are all just *men*. Nevertheless, I was asked to write up an account of that time in Rome for Mountbatten and he liked my report. In fact he selected my closing remarks to be used in his annual report on the MedFoba activities. So he didn't concur with that initial reprimand!

During my time on *Aisne*, one day we were suddenly told to supply ship, for an unknown length of time at sea, and within twenty-four hours we set sail for a destination that was not disclosed to us. Only later did we discover that we'd been sent to patrol around Cyprus, looking for gunrunners, who could be supplying arms for the revolution beginning to take place there under Archbishop Makarios.

One night I was following the exercise on the bridge. The radar people had spotted something that could be a boat, so we sailed right up to it until we were within about 100 yards of the object on the screen. Searchlights were turned on and the crew tried to spot this object visually. Then, suddenly, whatever it was took off at great speed. It disappeared silently at a speed that was calculated on the radar screen as being in excess of 100 mph. No one could make out what it was. The captain entered UFO into the ship's log. It must have been flying, to go at that speed, and it had certainly remained unidentified. We never found out what it had been, so it remained a mystery which was quite exciting at the time.

After that we went to Port Said for a few days. Several things happened while we were there. The first was going ashore. After their first visit, there were some sailors who were not at all happy. One lot had been cheated in the market, having bought a leather purse for 100 *whatevers*, in local currency, giving a 500 note for this and waiting for change.

The bag seller swore blind that the sailor had only given a 100 note, not 500. Both notes were the same colour. Clearly what had happened was that the bag seller had palmed the 500 and swopped it for a 100, waiving this around and claiming that the sailor had given him this smaller note. He didn't get his change.

On board we were invaded by Egyptians offering to wash and iron our clothes. I was even persuaded to change out of my white uniform, including the white shorts I was wearing at the time, only to find that I hadn't removed the £15 in my pocket, my month's pay packet. That was a lot of money to lose in those days.

We also had a "gully gully" man ask to do a show on board, all of it being very clever magic tricks that were done right up close under the scrutiny of the sailors. I was left to arrange for this man to put on his show and for the crew to be told about it. When the man had left, his show having been very successful and many men having missed it, I was asked to arrange for a repeat performance. After that the gully gully man asked me to write a reference, which I was glad to do. His performances had been really excellent.

Michael reported to me later that he too had been asked to arrange for a gully gully man to put on a show for the men on his ship, which had put in to Port Said a few weeks after I'd been there. The same man had gone up to Michael and said: "Me very good gully gully man, I have references," showing these to him. Michael saw that one of these was from me, and he told me he'd been tempted to say he wasn't sure how seriously to take *that* one. But his ship's company were also impressed by the show.

While we were at Port Said, with nothing to do, the captain decided we could paint ship. For this, planks were lowered on ropes with two sailors on each, and a bucket of grey paint hanging on a rope between them. I asked if I could join in, as it looked quite good fun and I thought it was a chance to get to know some more of the men on a different basis, as I had in Rome.

This worked very well as a way of getting to know them, but I was almost in trouble with the quartermaster, the man in charge of the paint store. He said to me, "I could have you put on a charge for misappropriating paint. You are meant to be painting the ship, not yourself." Only then did I realise that I was covered with huge drips of grey paint, from head to toe.

Each time I'd dipped my huge paint brush into the bucket, passing it over my head to reach out to the side, paint had been pouring off the brush onto me. It was also extremely hot that day, and I'd been wearing shorts and no shirt. After I had showered, and had used gallons of turps to get the paint off, I found I looked like a negative photograph of a leopard. I'd turned bright red in the sun, except for where the paint had been. All those spots showed up white, and it took quite a few days before the red and the white began to even up.

HMS Falcon: Royal Naval air station (Hal Far)

After *HMS Aisne* I was appointed to *HMS Falcon*, the naval air station in Malta, otherwise known as Hal Far. This airfield was shared with the American forces.

For most of my time at Hal Far I was the only midshipman. I was appointed to be under the supply officer, Commander Bennett. One job was to look after the currencies, of which there were at least twenty. In hot weather the safe smelled of cheese, because so much of the foreign currency was dirty. Another job was to handle the Post Office Savings books, entering savings or letting men take money out of their bank books. I also had to help with the pay day "disbursement of monies". In addition, I sometimes had to check stores, ticking off how many of each item we had in store. This involved going through a list of things, all recorded in "supply" language, with items such as "cruet, salt, silver top, officers for the use of", and all manner of similarly bizarre descriptions.

Once a week I had to get up at about 5.30 am to inspect the galleys (the kitchens), visiting without notice to see that the cooks were doing what they should be doing at that ungodly hour of the morning.

The chief cook excelled himself by making about thirty huge Christmas cakes, all of them elaborately decorated with coloured icing. The captain had previously taken part, stirring a cauldron of cake-mix with an oar, following naval tradition.

One of my other tasks, working for Commander Bennett, was to collect money from the local bank for pay days. There was one memorable time when the cheque I had to cash was for £22,500, which would be getting on for £1m in today's money. I was given a guard of four sailors with truncheons, which didn't inspire me with much confidence, as they were making it very obvious that there was a big amount of cash being collected. If anyone had turned up with a pistol they wouldn't have been able to do anything to protect me, or the cash.

While waiting, I found a little old lady in the queue behind me. She was in a state of shock and had to tell me her story. She'd been widowed about ten years and had just returned from her first holiday since her husband had died. She had come back from three weeks in Sicily when a neighbour had spoken to her in the street, on her way to her house, asking if she liked her new home. But she hadn't moved.

The neighbour was alarmed to hear this as there'd been a removal van outside this lady's house for several days in the previous week. When she got into her house, she found burglars had cleared it of absolutely everything except for the wallpaper. She had nothing to sit on, nothing to sleep in, and nothing to cook with. Did I think the bank manager would be able to lend her some money, as she now had only £60 left in her account? I was full of sympathy and said I wished I could do something to help, but I didn't know what I could do. At that moment I was called to the counter and, in front of this little lady, I had a mountain of cash handed to me, all of which I put into the two large holdalls I'd brought with me. "I do hope the manager will be able to help," I said, as I carried all that money past her in the queue. My sympathy must have seemed very shallow.

When Commander Bennett went on holiday he left me in charge of his desk and diary. I had to record all messages for him, letting people know when he would be back, and whatever else. While sitting at his desk I was fascinated to see in his diary that he had written, in the margin, little sums of money like: + 2/10½ (two shillings and ten pence halfpenny) or −1/6 (one shilling and sixpence). When he got back I asked him what these meant. "Oh, that! I keep a note of what I owe my wife or what she owes me." I could hardly believe it.

I was alone in Malta for Christmas (no family around) but good friends of my father's, Captain and Mrs. Ross, asked me to stay with them. He was captain of the dockyard. The following year, when it was soon to be the 150th anniversary of the Battle of Trafalgar, I overheard Captain Ross saying he would probably be the only captain in Malta not to be attending a Trafalgar night dinner. I'd already asked father to the Hal Far dinner so I asked Captain Ross if he would care to come too, as my guest. He said he would be delighted to.

I had felt free to ask my father to that dinner, and then Captain Ross, as I'd heard that my captain had already invited Admiral of the Fleet Sir Guy Grantham, the C-in-C. I had thought, wrongly as it happened, that this dinner would therefore be crowded with other senior officers coming along too. That was not so.

At first (on the seating plan) I was placed at a little table at the bottom end of the wardroom, with my two guests. I was the most junior officer there. However, when I was asked for the names and ranks of my guests, for their place names to be prepared, it caused a great deal of stir. It turned out that my two guests were the next most senior officers to be at that dinner, second only to the C-in-C. In addition, both of my guests were about ten years senior to my own captain. In the end the captain of HMS Falcon (Hal Far) had Admiral Grantham on his right and my father on his left. I sat between my father and Captain Ross. It was a most memorable evening.

The family in Malta

By coincidence, Michael was also in the Mediterranean while father was posted there. I too came to be posted to *Glasgow*; then, after *Aisne*, to spend the rest of my National Service time in Malta. Having all three of us out there, father arranged for mother to come out too, with Elisabeth and Sue as well when they were not at St. Mary's Calne, their school. So, for some of the time, we had the whole family out there.

Swimming

I became increasingly interested in swimming underwater, using hand flippers as well as feet flippers. I could easily swim 100 yards, or more, with the double use of flippers. I also enjoyed being able to hold my breath for long periods of time.

In one bay, where we had been having a picnic, I had found a cave about thirty feet down from the surface of the sea. I'd swum into this, counting my strokes as I went so that I would be able to time my return, to fit in with how long I could hold my breath. There was then a shocking change of light. What I hadn't realised, when I went into this cave, was that the sun was approaching what is known in science as the "critical angle", at which point nearly all of its light would be reflected by the surface of the sea, and almost none of it refracted into the water. At that moment the cave was plunged into complete darkness. I had to feel my way back along the walls, to get back to the opening and my return to the surface. It felt pretty scary until I got back to where I could see the surface again.

That was not my only swimming scare. When I was still in *Aisne*, on our way back from Port Said, the captain had several times ordered the ship to stop for swimming. Scramble nets were lowered for men to get back on board the ship. Some sailors were timid enough to get into the sea by also scrambling down these nets.

I thought I should not reveal how uneasy I felt about diving in, so I just hoped for the best and dived from the ship's side. The sea was something like thirty feet down and I had never in my life dived from a height such as that. In fact I'd never dived from anything much higher than the edge of a pool. On my way down I became suddenly terrified. I had my eyes wide open and, as I descended, they must have become even wider out of fear. When I hit the surface of the sea my eyes were still staring at it, and they were smashed in by the water—not being protected by my eyelids. It felt as if I had done a bellyflop with my open eyeballs. Never again would I dive like that. Nor, for that matter, would I ever again (after that cruise) dive from any height at all.

Another time, while *Aisne* was stopped for swimming, I began to wonder if I could swim under the ship and out the other side. It felt like a kind of dare I could set myself, so I set off to try this. I did however take the precaution of not trying this anywhere near the stern of the ship, as I knew there were huge intake pumps around there that sucked in sea water. I didn't want to be sucked into a pipe. I therefore chose to swim under where the bridge is located, which happened also to be where the ship's keel is lowest in the water.

I set off down, counting my strokes and leaving plenty of spare room so that I didn't scrape my back against the hull. When I thought I must be near the midpoint of my journey I looked up. I was horrified by what I saw. I was under the deepest part of the ship, exactly halfway between one side and the other, and I was sinking. I'd gone so deep I had reached beyond the point where the body still has buoyancy. Beyond that point (because of being compressed by the water pressure) one begins to sink, and I was sinking.

I began to panic, so I swam back the way I'd come, not realising there was a current flowing under the ship, and I was then swimming against that current. On my way down I had been swimming with it. The result was that it took me twice as many strokes to swim back to the surface as it had taken me to swim down. I was also having problems with my ear drums, as I could feel the pressure was making them feel close to bursting. So I had to break off swimming, from time to time, to equalise the pressure by holding my nose and blowing against the pressure of my fingers. I think that was the closest I ever came to drowning.

One other incident happened when I was being pulled along on what we knew as an "aquaplane". This was a kind of surfboard which was tied to a speedboat. The board had a string across the top which one held onto, first lying on the board and then, as the speed built up and the board became more steady, kneeling and possibly even standing on it. That was the aim, to be able to stand on the board. Once a person had managed to stand, the speedboat skipper would begin to swerve, trying to make him or her fall off the board.

During my turn on the aquaplane, after I'd been shaken off I thought I could feel a small crab holding onto my big toe. I tried to shake it off but without success. I therefore lifted my foot out of the water to see what it was. Only then did I realise that, in falling off the board, I'd lifted the nail right off my big toe. The nail was then held on by one corner and was flapping in the water. What was also interesting about this was that I didn't feel a thing, my concentration being totally occupied at the time by my falling off the aquaplane. I still have the evidence of that accident, as that toenail never grew properly again.

This toenail no longer grows forwards, like other nails. It only grows upwards, getting increasingly thick. From time to time I file this down, to make it as nearly like a normal nail as possible, sometimes using a Black & Decker sander to do this. It works very well.

That is not the only DIY treatment I have undertaken. There was a time when I had cut the end off my left thumb. I slipped the severed end from the knife, putting it back onto my thumb, and held it firmly there while I put a tourniquet on my arm. Then, knowing that superglue had initially been made for use in plastic surgery, I very carefully glued around the edges of my joined-up thumb until it was all holding. After removing the tourniquet it still held, so I put on some tubigauze (tubular dressing), and that was that.

After a couple of weeks my thumb had healed well, except that I had no feeling in the dead skin. I therefore sandpapered the end of my thumb until I could feel it again. At least I did not have to go through the procedures of A & E at the local hospital.

I wrote up this DIY treatment and sent an account of it to *The Lancet*. I got a horrified reply, saying that I was lucky not to have got blood poisoning from the superglue. They were definitely not going to print my letter in case it encouraged other people to try DIY on themselves. Nevertheless, my thumb has continued to be fine ever since.

While at Hal Far I was given some rides in various aircraft. The first was in a helicopter, the only time I have been in one. Before taking off, something was put round my neck and I was put into a flying helmet, with what I had thought were ear protectors. It was necessary to have these as the noise was excessive and it could have been damaging to one's ears. What I didn't know was that the ear protectors also contained earphones, nor did I know that the thing round my neck contained a microphone. The pilot was hugely shocked when I shouted, trying to speak to him.

At one stage of the trip we went over to Sliema harbour, where I could see my father's ship, so I asked the pilot if we could fly over that too, which we did. Father told me later that he'd been trying to have a conference in the ship at the time, but a helicopter had kept on flying round the ship so that nobody could hear until it went away. He'd almost reached the point of ordering the helicopter to move away, and he wasn't much pleased when I told him that it was because of me that the helicopter had been there.

I was also taken up in a jet fighter which was an extraordinary experience. The pilot decided to show off to me, doing some twists and loops, all at immense speed. I could feel my stomach flying between my feet and the top of my head. Fortunately I wasn't sick, at least not until after we landed.

The Americans shared this airbase, and one of them asked me to have lunch in his mess, which I did. This was quite an eye-opener. They were proud of the fact that officers and men all had the same food, which was no hardship for anyone. The choice, that day, included a whole small chicken or half of a large duck. I had the duck, along with a huge helping of vegetables, and then pudding too. Afterwards I was so full I had to go back to my bed to sleep it off. I was told that all the food for the American forces in Malta was flown out each week from America, a huge operation in itself.

Films

From time to time, the ships in Malta would show films that were going around the fleet, each ship having a turn. There was one film about a probation officer which clearly made an impression on me, eventually tipping the balance for me away from the idea of going into personnel management and towards probation, which I later trained for.

Another film that left a deep impression was one called *The Green Scarf*. This was about a monk who had specialised in treating blind children and deaf children. He was then asked to take on a child who'd been born deaf and blind, who was therefore also mute. The film went through the process by which the monk had gradually made contact with this frightened and isolated child. I think it was this film, and later the story of Helen Keller, that played a large part in my subsequent interest in finding ways to tune into the experience of other people, especially when their experiences were so different from my own.

CHAPTER SEVEN

Teaching at a prep school

I am dismissed: all the staff then resign and I am reinstated

W hen I had finished my National Service I had a whole summer spare before going to Cambridge. I therefore decided to apply for a job as an assistant teacher at a prep school, for the summer term.

I had an interview for this school (now closed) on the same day as there was going to be a concert given by the Vienna Boys Choir, in London. I was very keen to get to that. So keen, in fact, I had forgotten to ask what I would be paid. I'd been offered a job to teach Latin and maths, and some English, and I would live in. But then it was time for me to get the train to London for the concert, after which I travelled back to Rogate.

When I got home father asked me how things had gone. I said: "Oh, I got the job and I also got to the concert—the concert was fantastic." I remember it included the Mozart *Coronation Mass*. Father wasn't that keen to hear about the concert; he only wanted to know what salary I'd been offered. I hadn't asked.

Before starting at this school I got in touch with Nigel Jacques, who'd been at Maidwell with me and had recently started teaching at Eton: "Do you have any advice you can give me for teaching?" When Nigel heard I would be teaching maths, he said: "Just do what 'Gwig' used to do. Remember apples and pears." (Gwig was the nickname for

Mr. G. W. Greenish, a teacher at Maidwell.) I had no idea, at first, what Nigel was meaning. He then reminded me that, when doing algebra, Gwig used to say: "You can't add apples to pears, so add apples to apples and pears to pears. You do the same thing when adding a's and b's, or x's and y's." He was quite right.

I also had to "mug up" my Latin, using the same books as we'd used at Maidwell. I remember spending a day at the Goodwood races, not following the horses with my family but going through all the Latin exercises, to make sure I could still do them. It turned out to have been a well-spent afternoon.

At this school I was eventually paid £3.50 a week, with board and lodging provided. An aunt then took me in hand, getting me measured for a suit, she choosing the material. It was a grey suit with pale chalk lines, and large lapels. I wore that suit for years afterwards. I remember it cost £30. Mother was going to pay for it but she forgot. I didn't like to remind her so it cost most of my term's salary.

It was an interesting experience teaching at that school, but in some ways also strange. The boys had no idea how old I was. One of them asked me over lunch: "Sir, what did you do in the war?" I was only twenty-one at the time and didn't want to reveal that I was far too young to have been in the war. I replied: "I left Malta just before the war started," which seemed to be enough of an answer for the boy not to enquire further. I was, in fact, not quite four when I left Malta.

For accommodation, I had one of three rooms in a little cottage in the school grounds, shared with two other bachelor teachers. One of them was the second master, known as "Johnny", who'd been there about twenty-five years. He was a very heavy drinker and would turn up in the mornings smelling hugely of whisky, but he was a good sort and a lot of fun. The other master there was a former ADC to one of the viceroys of India, Mr. Twinberrow, MC. He was known by the boys as "Twinkle-toes" or (sometimes) as "Harpic" because they regarded him as "clean round the bend". In those days this meant crazy. It was also a play on the words used to advertise Harpic which, we were told, would clean round the bend. I believe that my nickname was "Casey".

The headmaster suffered from tunnel vision. He also suffered from vanity, which meant that he tried to pretend he didn't need glasses. When his secretary announced that some parents were outside, want-ing to see him, he replied: "I'll see them straight away." He then took off his glasses, hiding them in a drawer, and groped his way towards these parents to shake their hands. Once, he ended up shaking a woman's handbag! On another occasion he shook a walking stick in the umbrella stand, thinking this was also a parent wanting to shake hands.

One evening at staff dinner, the headmaster insisted on carving the chicken we were about to eat. As he couldn't really see this, he took it to the window sill, claiming that he needed more light. There he pursued the chicken with a carving knife and fork, until the whole thing was on the sill outside the window. At this point his wife rescued the chicken before it fell into the flower bed.

At another of these staff dinners, Johnny mentioned to the headmaster's wife that he thought he really should, after twenty-five years on the staff, be allowed a second chair in his room. When he had guests round, which he usually did when the pubs had closed, someone always had to sit on the bed. The head's wife said there was a spare chair in the drawing room, which he could have if he could get it up the narrow stairs to his room.

The headmaster was also deaf, while his vanity prevented him using his hearing aid, which was most of the time. This, plus his near-blindness, resulted in a disaster with regard to this chair. Johnny and I had tried to get this up the stairs but had found, as the head's wife had suspected, that the legs were just too long to get it round the bend in the stairs. "Not to worry," said Johnny, "it will easily go if we take a couple of inches off each leg."

We were in the process of cutting down these legs when the headmaster came by. Not able to see what we were doing, he asked: "How is it going with the chair?" Johnny replied: "It will soon be OK. We are just making the legs a bit shorter." The head, not being able to hear or see, just grunted a kind of approval and walked on.

At dinner that night the head's wife asked whether the chair had been OK. "Not at first," said Johnny, "but we soon fixed that. We cut the legs down a bit and now it's fine." The head's wife nearly fainted. We had, without knowing it, cut down the legs of a *Chippendale* chair, now sitting squat in Johnny's room and entirely worthless. Staff dinner became very silent that evening, no one able to think of anything further to say.

There was a rather lovely chapel attached to the school, which had something like fifty-five boys so they could all get into this. The head rather liked to show off that he had a pet canon, whom he would ask once a term to come to the school to celebrate Holy Communion.

On one of these occasions, the head had been acting as altar boy, handing the bread and wine to the celebrant. When the wine began to come along the line of teachers at the altar rail, Hilda (the school bottom class teacher) whispered along the line: "Don't take the wine." She'd discovered that the headmaster, acting as server, had mistaken a bottle of *methylated spirits* for altar wine, which had been in a bottle next to it. Someone had been cleaning the silver but hadn't put the meths away, so we were being offered *consecrated meths!* The only people who took this were the head and his pet canon.

I taught at this school for the whole of one summer term, before I went to Cambridge. I also went back there for the remaining eight weeks of the following two summer terms, during my long vacations. I would be allocated either the bright half of the larger classes or the dim half, to give bright boys a chance to get on and the not so bright to have a chance to consolidate.

One boy had been a complete dunce at Latin. He'd never scored more than 17% in the end of term exam, set by the second master, which meant he always had to sit it again as a punishment. This was automatic for anyone who did not exceed 33⅓% in the exam. I decided there was no point making this boy do extra work out of school for doing badly in class, which he regularly did. Instead, I would spend some of the lunch break once a week, teaching him on his own. In his exam at the end of that term he got 33%, and he was thrilled. But he was still made to redo the exam because he'd failed to get more than the stipulated 33⅓%. I thought that was really unfair. I also had to teach some English. When it came to setting an exam in English, one of the questions was: "Write brief sentences to show the different meanings of the words 'advice' and 'advise'; also, the words 'practice' and 'practise'."

One boy, whose father was a French diplomat, wrote a very precise answer to this but I could not immediately understand it. He'd written the words without putting any gaps between them. The first of his two short sentences went like this:

a d v i c e w i s a c i s a n o u n a n d a d v i s e w i s a s i s a v e r b

It took me a few minutes to decipher this, not at first realising that he (being French) was writing "th" as he would be saying it, when it sounded like an "s". Once deciphered, I could see that he understood the difference between these words exactly. He had tried to write: "advice with a c is a noun, advise with an s is a verb."

We had school inspectors come round one term. When they went to see how things were going in Twinberrow's maths class, they found the blackboard was covered with a chalk drawing of a sailing boat, which he'd just drawn. "We are all at sea at the moment," said Mr. T, and the examiners seemed to like that.

Mr. T didn't know any of the boys by name, not even after he'd been there some time. He usually taught maths and he would get boys to exchange books, reading out the answers so that they could mark these for him. He would then call out their names and he would get them to read out the marks that had been given by the boy in the next desk. He wrote his end-of-term reports straight from his list of marks, still not knowing which boy these marks related to.

After this school, Mr. T went on to become headmaster of a classy day school near Chelsea. He told me that he still didn't know any of the boys by name. He would take them by Tube to play soccer at some playing field used by the school. The boys would then go home from the Tube, getting off at whichever stop was nearest their home. When he got back to the school, he'd have almost no boys with him and he had no idea where any of the others were. The remaining boys, he said, would usually be collected in chauffeur-driven Rolls or Bentleys, leaving him with no boys at the end of the day, which he regarded as most satisfactory. I have no idea how he became a headmaster.

I used to be on duty each weekend, except one. I would usually be asked to take the bottom game of cricket, where the pitch was about fifteen yards long instead of twenty-two. I introduced my own rules. We didn't change ends; we didn't have six balls to an over; each boy would bowl until he got a wicket, or until I said he'd had enough; and, if no one was able to get a boy out for too long a time, I would take over the bowling. A cry would then go up: "Oh, Sir's going to bowl." It was fun.

Once, when there was a staff cricket match. I was put in to play with the boys, as a handicap. I was bowled by the under matron, with her second ball to me, and I didn't score at all. That seemed to be just about right and in keeping with my usual form.

Making a glider

During my last term there, I'd bought a kit for making a glider, which had a wingspan of six feet. I invited any of the boys who were

141

interested to help make this. It was to be their project, which they could get on with at weekends, with minimal supervision by me. This project worked wonders. The boys loved doing it. It also meant that the boys were much easier in class because they seemed to like being taught by me. At the end of that last term we had the ultimate launching of this magnificent glider, and it stayed at the school to be used again during the following term.

Speaking up

At one staff dinner, during this term, the head's wife asked me (in front of the head who was not wearing his hearing aid) why it was the staff never co-operated with her husband. I said I would like to answer this important question but I could not do this over dinner.

I later began to answer the question but the head came in and we had to stop talking. It so happened that I was just about to have the first and only weekend off I'd been allowed in all the time I had been teaching at this school. So I said I would write to her in reply. This I did, with great care and in some detail.

I spelled out to the head's wife that the staff had been seriously disillusioned about the school since the standards had been slipping. The reputation of the school had fallen to such a low point that younger brothers were not automatically coming to the school, to join a boy already there. Also, to avoid the numbers being seen to be dropping, the head had been taking in boys from diplomatic parents, boys who often came with little knowledge of English. We therefore had boys who were French, Italian, Turkish, and other foreign children, all of them having to be taught English by the bottom form teacher, Hilda, before being taught Latin (through English) in the next form.

Another way in which the numbers had been kept up was through the head's policy of accepting boys from other schools when they'd been thrown out, for whatever reason.

One result of this policy had been that the staff had to decide whether to focus on teaching those boys who might still pass their public school entrance exam, for which a prep school was meant to be preparing them, or whether to let the brighter boys virtually teach themselves while they took on the slow ones.

The head had already been taken to task by the second master who, on behalf of the other staff, had told him that he should clear the school of the "dross" he'd allowed in, so that they could do the teaching of bright children, which is why the staff had first come to this school. Or he should advise parents to take the brighter boys elsewhere while the present school could then get on with what the head's wife was claiming to be their new policy of being *a happy place for unhappy children*. In that case, the head should make the more scholarly staff redundant, getting in another kind of staff to take on the problem boys he was taking in to fill up the vacancies.

I was able to pass on two other complaints from the staff, which had been made frequently to the head, with no response to either. One was that the school hadn't been repainted for so long that it was looking drab and unkempt, with old paint peeling off all over. The last school inspectors had reported on this and had been told by the head that he was about to do all of that. But nothing had been done ever since, and it looked as if it might not be done at all until the next inspection came around.

The other complaint was about the swimming bath. For all of that term, this had been cracked and was leaking, the water often being at least a foot lower than it should have been. This was now dangerous, as had been demonstrated only that week.

The head insisted that he and no one else would be allowed to oversee the swimming, but he could not *see* or *hear* what was happening. He'd therefore not noticed when a boy had dived into the no-longer-deep end, becoming concussed when his head hit the bottom. The games master, Neil, happened to have gone into the pool area just then, looking for one of the boys, when he saw what had happened. Neil had jumped in to rescue the drowning boy and had carried him up to the matron, where he'd been monitored throughout the rest of the day and evening. He did recover, but he could have drowned.

These, I said in my letter, were some of the reasons why the staff would not co-operate with the head. I kept a copy of the letter to show to the other staff, and it was just as well that I did.

While I was teaching my first class on the Monday morning, having returned from my weekend off, I was summonsed by the head. He told me: "You have the rest of this week to pack your bags, to go. You are now 'persona non grata' at this school. You have been dismissed."

We had a very different coffee break that morning. The staff would usually spend that break comparing their *Times* crosswords, which they'd spent the first two hours doing, while they were meant to be

143

teaching. During the crossword time, they would often leave the boys to work from exercise books instead of being taught. That morning, I told them I'd been dismissed and why, and I showed them my letter. They told me there was only one thing wrong with it: "We should have written a letter like that years ago." The staff decided that if I was going then so were all of them. Each and every one of them handed in their notice, in writing, to the head before the end of that coffee break. By the end of the day he'd asked me to stay.

There was an interesting sequel to this, when Margaret (my wife) and I announced in *The Times* that we were getting married. I received two letters from the school.

One letter was from the headmaster, congratulating me, wishing me well, and saying that he'd just sold the school as *a thriving concern* to another headmaster who would be taking it on.

The other letter was from Johnny, also congratulating me but adding: "You'll never guess what the head has done now. He'd heard that another prep school had been burned down during the summer holiday, so he offered his school to the head, who needed his purchase to be on the basis of 'vacant possession'. This has meant sending letters out to all the parents of the current boys, saying they would have to find somewhere else for their boys." So much for it being a thriving concern. I have no idea how those parents would have been able to place their boys, with only the two or three weeks' notice given that they would not be able to return.

So ended my teaching career. But it had been interesting and a lot of it had been fun. I also learned a lot from trying to teach.

CHAPTER EIGHT

What to read? Cambridge

Anthropology is "the study of man embracing women": that sounds promising

Still avoiding the Navy

I describe in my last book (*Learning from Life*, p. 33) how I got into Cambridge and how I chose to read anthropology. I will summarise that here.

I had originally applied to read physics because I had been awarded a physics prize at Winchester. But I learned that my father was planning for me to apply to the Royal Navy, to become an "electrical officer", because then the Navy would pay all my fees and a salary. I therefore changed my degree subject from physics to economics. However, having taken a book about this out of the library I soon discovered that I would not understand a single word of it. I therefore told my tutor I would not be reading economics after all. So he asked me what else I might wish to read. But I couldn't think of any subject at all that I felt *really inclined* to read, so he picked on anthropology on the grounds that I had said I didn't know what it was. "You go and attend some lectures at the 'Arch and Anth' faculty, and come and see me in a few weeks' time," was his advice.

When I got to the faculty library I asked someone to tell me what anthropology is. Someone there told me that anthropology had been defined as *a study of Man—embracing women*. Well, I thought, that sounds promising. And I settled on that.

Mrs. Pratt (landlady)

For my first year I was in digs in Chesterton Road, with Mrs. Pratt. She had sent me a letter introducing herself before I went there, in which she had explained the rules and what I needed to take with me. I should take my own sheets. "Single sheets will be sufficient," she'd said, but I still had my sheets, *"officers for the use of"*, from the Navy, which were more than single but less than double. When I tried to get into bed, my first night there, I found that Mrs. Pratt had tucked in all of the excess size of my top sheet far under the mattress. The bed was then so tight I couldn't get my feet, let alone my legs, under the sheet. I almost needed a shoe horn to ease myself in, so tightly had she made up my bed. Single sheets would clearly have been preferable.

An audition

During my first term at Cambridge I responded to an invitation to audition with the Cambridge University Drama Society so I went along to find out about this and I had to fill in a form giving my previous acting experience. Of course, I could only give my performance as the March Hare in the Rogate production of *The Mad Hatter's Tea Party*, which must have been the most trivial acting CV handed in to them that day!

The organisers then gave me a list of possible speeches from which to choose an audition piece. Mainly because I recognised it, I chose a passage from *The Merchant of Venice*, which goes as follows:

> If you prick us, do we not bleed? If you tickle us, do we not laugh?
> If you poison us, do we not die? And if you wrong us, shall we
> not revenge? If we are like you in the rest, we will resemble you in
> that …. (Act III, scene 1)

I went off and learned this, choosing to play it with dramatic pauses, gradually increasing the pace as the speech proceeds.

When I went for my audition I arrived early in order to see how things were done, and I saw the person before me (a girl) getting into real trouble with the prompter, who was also acting as one of the judges. He seemed to be so busy writing comments on her not very good performance that he repeatedly failed to prompt her when she dried up. In the end the girl was led off in tears, only halfway through her audition, to be revived with coffee and to be allowed to redo her audition later.

It was then my turn, by which time the prompter had been replaced by someone else who was clearly anxious not to let me down, but he hadn't catered for my dramatic pauses. My audition therefore went roughly like this: *If you prick us, do we not bleed?...* [prompt]. *If you tickle us, do we not laugh?...* [prompt]. *If you poison us, do we not die?...* [prompt].

At this point I turned on the prompter and said: "You are wrecking this for me. Those were meant to be dramatic pauses, not requests for prompts!" He apologised but I then found I'd completely lost my way because of that interruption and I totally dried. Fortunately it didn't matter one bit as I had no intention of taking a part, even if I had been offered one. I was only there for the fun of finding out what it felt like to be auditioned.

As I left, one of the judges told me that I had, without knowing it, chosen one of the speeches they usually gave to someone they were auditioning for a lead part! Anyway, I had enjoyed the experience.

Dr. Pryor

Dr. Pryor remained my tutor for that first year. He was an etymologist. He was also a great character. He invited me, along with a number of his other tutees, to dinner in his rooms. Then he taught us how to eat oysters. They were to be swallowed whole and washed down with beer, something I managed to do on that occasion but I've never brought myself to do it since. He also regaled us with stories, one of which was from the last war.

The War Office had got in touch with Dr. Pryor because he was known to be a world expert on mosquitoes. He had been flown out to Borneo, being given red carpet treatment all the way until he arrived. There, at the local airfield, he found himself waiting to be met, but there seemed to be nobody expecting him. He therefore got into conversation with an airman, who was waiting for somebody who seemed not to have arrived. From this conversation, Dr. Pryor discovered that the airman was meant to be meeting him. So off they drove to the RAF base where he was introduced to a senior officer, who said to him: "Thank

God you've got here, Dr. Pryor. We need you desperately as we can't fly a single one of these damn things. Look, there they are, all of them grounded and we can't make out what is wrong with them." He was pointing to *Mosquito planes*, which were much used in the last war. "Oh, dear," said Dr. Pryor, "I only know about the other kind of mosquito."

Dr. Pryor also told us about worms, that when they hear the sound of rain they come to the surface, which is why blackbirds jump up and down to make worms think it is raining. "Look, I'll show you," he said, taking us down to the lawn with a chandelier of lit candles for light. Then we all began to dance on the lawn until Dr. Pryor was able to show us that it was true. Gradually, a number of worms seemed to have been tricked into thinking it was raining; perhaps raining very hard, with us beer-filled men dancing on the lawn and pretending to be rain.

There were many characters among the fellows of the college and many stories to prove it. There were so many fellows in Trinity, this being the biggest college at Cambridge, that there were some who didn't meet each other for months. One passed another saying: "How is your wife?" The other replied: "Still dead, still dead," walking on without a further word.

Another fellow, a history don who was almost at retirement age, saw my next tutor (the Rev H. A. Williams, later to become Dean of Chapel) and asked him if he could recommend a good book on *sects* that would be useful for his students. "Harry" replied to this ancient don: "I'm rather surprised you are *still* interested in sex."

Some years before I went to Cambridge, there'd been a formal luncheon in the college to honour the Princess Royal of that time, sister of King George VI, and all the fellows had been told to come in their best gowns. There had been speeches, and afterwards there'd been coffee and liqueurs in the master's lodge. I was told that, over coffee, one of the fellows had found himself having to speak to the guest of honour, with no idea who she was. She'd been saying how nice it had been to see her brother's college; her brother this and her brother that. Trying to make conversation, this fellow had said to her: "What does your brother *do*?" She'd replied: "*Actually*, he's king."

F. A. Simpson

Another eccentric in the college was the Rev F. A. Simpson. He was already over the retiring age when they'd introduced an age for retirement, so he stayed on as a fellow until his death. His extraordinary life is beautifully described in a book by a former chaplain of Trinity, Canon Eric James: *F. A. Simpson, The Last Eccentric.*

I got to know Simpson a bit while I was at Trinity, while he went round the fellows garden with pruners in his hand, pruning whatever offended him. He would also, always, be wearing a scarf around his neck, twitching as he walked.

Simpson told me that, as a very young graduate, he'd been offered two fellowships on the same day: "One was to this college, Trinity, and the other was to the college next door, Trinity Hall. I accepted the fellowship to this college, dedicated to the holy and undivided Trinity. I don't know what Trinity Hall is dedicated to: *some local divinity, I presume.*"

In his book Eric James reveals that Simpson was a closet homosexual. He also tells that Simpson had become excited to find that a Casement had been admitted to the college, hoping that I would be of a similar persuasion to that of Sir Roger Casement. I didn't know this at the time, but it might explain why Simpson told me he planned to invite me to be his guest at high table when I had obtained my degree.

Indeed, I went as Simpson's guest some time after I'd started working in Sheffield (see later). I was seated at the table between Simpson and another ancient fellow, this other fellow loudly supping his soup, not talking to anyone until eventually he spoke to me. "What are you doing with yourself now you have your degree, young man?" I replied: "I am working as a bricklayer's mate." He could hardly believe his ears. "*A what?*" he said, and he returned to supping his soup, this time more noisily than before.

Jo Menell[1]

Jo and I shared tutorials in anthropology and archaeology, he driving his VW to these and always taking me with him. He is a great character; multilingual, being fluent in French, Spanish, and Italian, as well as English (of course) and Swahili.

Jo was a persistent womaniser. When we went to see our tutor in anthropology (Doris Wheatley) in her Girton rooms, he would often arrive early so that he could call on one or other of his latest flames. I would be left to amuse myself until the time came for the tutorial to start.

149

I once decided that I too would make a call, while waiting for Jo. I forget who it was I visited, but I found the room of someone I'd got to know, to say a brief hello. I then could not find my way back to the main gate, so I eventually climbed out of a window and ran round the outside of Girton until I got to the main entrance, knowing I would be able to find my way from there to Doris Wheatley's rooms.

I was way behind Jo in the way of entertaining girls. However, just once during my first year, I asked someone called Susan to tea. She was also reading "Arch and Anth", as it was called. For this I bought a tea set and a quarter pound of tea. I never drank tea myself, and I so rarely had further occasion to offer tea to other people I handed over (to the person in the room next to mine) what was left of that packet of tea at the end of my time at Cambridge. It might have become just a little stale by then.

Some lecturers

Professor Burkitt

For archaeology, Jo and I went to see Professor Miles Burkitt, son of Bishop Burkitt. During one of our tutorials, Burkitt had to leave us to attend to the door. He came back to explain that he'd just taken delivery of a part of his father's library, which included *five yards of Bibles*, this being the length of shelf-space these Bibles would take up. Amazing.

Burkitt was proud to tell us that the idea of the Girl Guide movement had been conceived in his garden. His father had been entertaining Baden Powell and his wife, and Mrs. Baden Powell had said (in the garden) that she didn't think it was right that boys should have all the fun. She had therefore decided to start a similar movement for girls, which became the Girl Guides.

Burkitt also told us, again with some pride, that he had once been treated as if he were still a young man (he was nearly eighty) when, a few years earlier, one of his tutees had been ill with rheumatic fever. She had been confined to her room for a term, not being allowed to attend lectures or tutorials. Burkitt had therefore to give tutorials in her room. But, according to the rules of that time, the bed had to be removed from this girl's room before he was allowed in. Each time he visited, he would see the student's bed in the corridor, making sure that she would be safe from any possible sexual advance that Burkitt

150

might make during the tutorial. He laughed about this silly rule: "What would be wrong with the floor, if I were so inclined?"

Dr. Reo Fortune

Another lecturer was Reo Fortune, the author of *Sorcerers of Dobu*, which had been acclaimed as a brilliant research study of a primitive society. He'd described, in vivid detail, how the whole society was apparently regulated on the basis of paranoid suspicions, each of the other.

I heard, sometime later, that there'd been a follow-up study of this society, the new researcher describing them as mild mannered and trusting. It seemed that Fortune may have projected onto the society his own paranoid ideas. Who can tell?

Fortune had for a while been married to another anthropologist, Margaret Mead. I heard her give a lecture, which Fortune also attended. He'd stood at the back of the hall putting strange questions to his ex-wife, which added nothing but hilarity to the proceedings.

Fortune was scheduled to give us a series of lectures. I attended these but they were crazy. For the first lecture he read from a text he'd written on a roll of lining-paper, this being draped over the lectern. He scrolled from the beginning of one line to the end, then scrolling back to the beginning of the next. If he'd been a clown it might have been funny, but from a university lecturer it was sheer madness.

The attendance at Fortune's lectures dropped each week by half, until there were only three girls and myself left, the audience having started at around fifty. He then announced that we would no longer be meeting in the lecture room. He would see those still attending in his study. I was determined not to leave these girls exposed to this madman, so I made a point of being present for what was meant to be the first of these remaining lectures. He told us there was no point him giving us more lectures. Indicating a pile of books on his desk, he said: "All you need is to have read these," and that was the end of that.

Another student was Simon Mackay. After I'd spent a full week reading Malinowski's very long book on the sexual life of Trobriand islanders, I saw Simon sitting in the library, languidly turning pages and looking at the many photographs in this book. I asked him: "Aren't you going to take some notes on what you are reading?" He replied: "Oh, No. I prefer just to get the atmosphere."

151

When it came to the exams, I was terrified I might fail. So, during the term leading up to the exams, I set myself a rigid programme of revision. I also decided to cut out my frequent breaks for coffee. Instead, I had a double strength coffee at breakfast, then again after lunch; one coffee break in the afternoon and another coffee after supper, and I made most of these at double strength. However, what I did not know was that the Continental Nescafé I'd been given, to take back for that term, was already double strength.

The result, without my knowing it for some time, was that I began to develop the symptoms of caffeine poisoning. I began to shake uncontrollably, and to such a degree that I became ashamed of eating in company. At one time I found myself sitting alone in a café, trying to drink a cup of coffee but finding that I could not hold the cup still. I was spilling the coffee into the saucer, which I was holding to catch the drips, with cup and saucer rattling against each other. So I felt it was time I did something about this. Perhaps I was having a nervous breakdown. I needed an afternoon off from my revision.

I therefore went to the "Backs" (along the river) behind Trinity, where I lay on the grass beside the river. But I could not lie still. I just lay there writhing from side to side and twitching. Even that was not working. So, at dinner that night, I asked a medical student if he thought I might be suffering from too much coffee. He asked me of my symptoms, and he asked if I was also getting diarrhoea. I was. "Then you are definitely some way along with caffeine poisoning. Stop taking it." The problem went away.

When the time came for the exams I quickly decided that the best thing was to avoid meeting any of the other students before or after exams. I came to this decision after the first of these, in which I'd written a lengthy essay on: "The function of money in primitive societies."

Unfortunately, I had not even read the reading list for this, so I didn't know that the authority on this subject was someone called Maus, who had written a whole book on it. Instead, I had scanned through all I knew of the many and varied accounts of money, and other exchanges used for currency, that I'd encountered in my studies—arriving at some conclusions merely based upon that.

After that first exam, someone asked me which topic I'd written on. When I told him, he replied: "Well you couldn't go wrong on that as it's all in Maus." I was shocked to hear this, as I hadn't even heard of this bit of essential reading. This clever Dick then listed the conclusions reached by Maus. Fortunately I had arrived at all of these except for one which, he told me, had since been challenged by others. So I might have got away with it.

But, from then on I felt it best to avoid any further post mortem after exams. I would usually leave exams a few minutes early in order to avoid being infected by the exam nerves of others.

One set book I did read was by someone who was making sweeping statements (based on Freud) about the assumed sexual symbolism of musical instruments. I wrote of this in my second book, when I was writing about cliché thinking:

> I came across a salutary warning of this, when I was reading anthropology, in a book about the sexual symbolism of musical instruments. The author, captivated by his reading of Freud, argued that every musical instrument is symbolically male or female. Having got carried away by the shape of violins and cellos he noticed that they are played on with long thin things called bows. These, he claimed, are phallic symbols. He then proceeded to go through the entire orchestra: and how could anyone argue with him?
>
> He pointed out all those other long thin instruments that people put into their mouths; the shape of those wooden drumsticks; and those other drumsticks with large woolly balls; and, what's more, these drumsticks are beaten against the stretched skin of the drums, which (he said) represents the hymen. And what about those inviting hollows at the end of all those brass instruments; and the triangle, which is set ringing by a very small phallic symbol? And so on! After reading all of this, some joker had written in the margin: "If Sir Malcolm Sargent knew what is really going on in front of him, and what he is waving around in his own hand, he would never conduct another concert!" (*Further Learning from the Patient*, p. 18).

When the exam results came out I had been awarded a 2:1. I was told that, had it not been for my paper in archaeology, which had never really interested me, I would have been awarded a first. This was almost unbelievable. I'd been afraid I might fail.

Simon MacKay was awarded what, in Cambridge, was known as a "special pass". This was all but a fail, but (by some special dispensation) a degree was nevertheless awarded to him.

153

When I was in Sheffield (see later) I met Simon again. He was a wealthy landowner in Scotland, and he had thought that he'd discovered some primitive artefacts in a quarry on his land. He told me that he'd sent a sample of these to Professor McBurney, saying he thought these were *burins*.[2] He also offered to let the professor be the first person to explore what (he thought) could become an important archaeological site. Simon told me that McBurney had replied: "I would have thought even you might have recognized that these are not burins. They are flakes of slate, not flakes of flint!" So much for Simon's method of getting the atmosphere, in preparation for his exams.

Meeting a murderer

During the long vacations, it was the custom for college chaplains to take a group of students on a mission to a parish. We were offered as a team for use by the vicar, to provide him with willing hands to visit throughout the parish on his behalf. The first time I did this we went round in pairs, and I was allocated to go with someone called Cynthia.

We usually knocked on doors, saying we were there on behalf of the vicar, and we would ask if we could come in to discuss ways in which the church might be of use to the people we were visiting.

At one door we were met by a man who immediately became very hostile when we identified ourselves as being there from the church. In fact, he was so hostile it seemed to both of us that he could be in some trouble. We therefore suggested it might help if he could talk with us, and maybe we could be of some help.

This man then told us his deepest secret, from his time of fighting in the last war. His best mate had been mortally wounded. He and his friend were both Roman Catholics, and his friend had begged him to fetch one of the RC chaplains to give him the last rites. He'd promised he would do this, leaving his friend bleeding to death while he went to fetch a chaplain. He had gone up to each of the two chaplains and they had, apparently, both said they were too busy and they'd both refused to come. By the time he got back to his mate he had died, without receiving the last rites that he'd promised him.

This man had become so angry about this he'd shot both of these chaplains, under the cover of hostile fire. At the time, it had been thought they'd died from enemy fire, but he knew that he had killed them. He was now a double murderer. Perhaps we could understand why he was so unwilling to have anything further to do with any church, of whatever kind.

We didn't know what to do, so we suggested that he might talk this over with the vicar, which he agreed to do. Cynthia walked with him to the church, while I set off on my scooter to get to the vicarage as quickly as I could. When I got there, I arrived white faced (in shock) and unable to speak. I just beckoned the vicar out of a meeting, and he sensed that it was urgent. He then spent a lot of time with this man and told us afterwards that he'd decided not to report this. The man had suffered enough already. Also, the family and friends of these two chaplains had adjusted to their deaths, as victims of war—not as murdered. What good would it do to bring all of that up again, all these years later? So he had heard this man's confession and he'd given him absolution.

For about ten years after that I always received a Christmas card from this man, and so did Cynthia, thanking us for having helped him to find peace of mind after so many years of self-torture.

Visiting in another parish

During another long vacation the chaplains took us to visit in the parish of Stafford. My main memory from there is that of being expected to accept a cup of tea in every home that we visited.

We were each given an address where we would be expected for lunch, in the home of one of the parishioners. Arriving one day for this lunch I was bursting for a pee. My hostess on that day told me that the meal was ready, the moment I arrived, but I said: "Could I just go upstairs first?" To this she replied: "We don't have an upstairs. We only have the bottom of the garden." This was the first time I'd encountered a privy in the garden, a wooden hut with a loo inside.

Dancing at Cambridge

In my second year I was invited to a party at which there'd be dancing. I found myself with a gorgeous Swedish girl who was unbearably seductive. She began to dance so close that I became terrified and left. I just got on my bicycle and sped back to my room in college.

A few weeks later someone showed me a copy of the Trinity in-house magazine, which included a gossip column. In this there was an entry which said:

> In the college bar, a second year theologian was overheard to say: "You have to watch out with Swedish girls because, if you don't, you might end up getting what you want."

In that year I became a member of the Kitchen Committee, which dealt with complaints, etc. This was under the chairmanship of John Tusa, who later worked for the BBC and then, for a long time, he was managing director of the Barbican Arts Centre. I was on this committee for my last two years.

Beginning to speak Italian

In the summer after my second year at Cambridge, I went round Europe on the Lambretta scooter which I'd recently bought. I went with John Kirkham (later a bishop) who also had a Lambretta. We did 3,500 miles in thirty-five days, camping all the way, and it cost us each £35 for the round trip. We were very proud of those statistics.

From France we went over the Alps to get to Italy, but I hadn't catered for the sunburn I got as we travelled through the Swiss mountains. Travelling at that altitude there was much less protection from ultraviolet light, and I became badly sunburned. I then had to cover every bit of me as a protection from the sun, even wrapping my wrists with handkerchiefs as well as wearing gloves, and covering my neck. I was in agony and could hardly sleep at night.

When we got into Italy I saw what I knew must be a pharmacy, with a green cross displayed outside. I sought out the pharmacist, but realised I had not a single word of Italian. So I peeled back a sleeve from one arm, revealing the angry red of my sunburn, and pointed to the sun. The pharmacist nodded and went to get something for this, and as he returned I unexpectedly found myself speaking Italian with him. When he said *Forte*, I immediately knew where I was with the language. *Non. Fortissimo*, I replied. He then went to get something else which turned out to be a miracle cream. I put it on straight away and very soon it began to quieten the pain. By the next morning the red had turned to brown and I hadn't been kept awake during the night.

I was telling this story after that trip when someone said they thought the cream given to me was probably Eight Hour Cream, by Elizabeth Arden. I don't know if it was the same, but I've since found that Eight Hour Cream does do the same thing. I now always take some of this on holiday whenever there might be a risk of sunburn.

Giving up speaking Italian

I am jumping ahead many years here, to a time when we took our daughters Hanna and Bella on holiday in Italy. We'd rented a self-catering villa and had arrived on a Saturday to find that the shops would be closed on the Monday, as well as Sunday, so we set off straight away to cater for several days.

We were in a small shop that provided most things we would be needing, with which we'd filled a shopping trolley. But the car was parked some way off from the shop. I therefore tried to ask the lady in the shop if we could take the trolley to the car, and I would then return it.

Speaking in made-up Italian, I put this proposition to the lady in the shop: "*Esse possibile pour comprare ici e apprendere le trollee a auto la, e returnare trollee ici?*" The lady just stared at me. It was clear that my fluent made-up Italian was not getting through quite as I had wished. Eventually, she thought she'd understood: "*Si. You want spaghetti.*" That finished me. I never tried to speak Italian again.

My drinks bill

In my final year, as part of my duties on the kitchen committee, I accepted the task of collecting cash payments in the bar, which I had to convert to what were known as "buttery tokens". This was because the sole currency in the bar was meant to be these tokens, which were then charged to the students' accounts. But if some cash were to be used, this was only allowed so long as it was later converted into tokens, which I volunteered to do. I therefore used to receive huge amounts of cash, all of it having to be exchanged for tokens that were being charged to my account.

At one point I was summonsed to meet with my tutor, who by that time was Harry Williams. He said he'd become very concerned about my bar bill, which was rapidly reaching towards an astronomical amount. "What is all this drinking about?" he asked. I had to explain I was not drinking all of this myself, but I was exchanging the bar cash for tokens. "What a relief," he said. "I thought you might be turning into an alcoholic!"

A visit from my parents

At some stage during my last year I asked my parents to spend a weekend in Cambridge as my guests. I set up a lunch party for them. To this I'd invited some of my most colourful friends, including Jo Menell. But, what I'd not catered for was how these friends might get on with each other. It was a disaster. These friends, being compulsive entertainers, were each wanting to have centre stage—each vying for the spotlight—which made for quite a difficult atmosphere round the table.

After that weekend I found that I'd got seriously behind with my reading, which was a pity as I had one of the most interesting topics for that week's essay. I was meant to explore the use of the concepts of *flesh* and *spirit* in the New Testament. I can't now remember much about this, but at the time I was really interested. The books recommended for this were great but I'd lost three days of study time.

In the end, I set myself the task of reading all of the books and writing my essay before I would take time for any proper sleep. I therefore worked right through Monday and Tuesday nights, writing my essay on the Wednesday which I handed in to Harry Williams that evening. I'd slept for no more than an hour or two in either night, and yet my essay was awarded an *Alpha*, my best essay so far. Harry was a brilliant teacher. It was largely in order to be taught by him that I had chosen to read theology.

Some more lecturers

Professor Donald McKinnon

McKinnon became Norris Hulse Professor of Divinity at Cambridge. There were several stories circulating about his eccentricities.

One day, McKinnon had set off to give a lecture at the Divinity School, having just bought a new pair of trousers. But his wife believed he had only one pair, which he used to wear all the time. So, when she'd found his usual pair still on the back of his chair, she had imagined that he'd set off in his gown but without trousers. She therefore telephoned the Divinity School to alert them to this possibility. However, all was well. It was found that McKinnon *was* wearing trousers, his new trousers, but being eccentric he might not have been.

It was also said that McKinnon would sometimes lock himself in a cupboard in the bedroom when he was due to give a tutorial. His wife was reported to have told one student to go into the bedroom, and to read the essay loudly: "The professor will probably be able to hear."

At one tea party, being given by the McKinnons, the professor was nowhere to be found. It was later said that, halfway through tea, a hand had emerged from under the table. McKinnon having hidden himself there, shielded by the table cloth, was groping for one of the cakes being offered to the students.

When he lectured he had the habit of sharpening a pencil with a knife, carrying on with this activity until the end of the lecture, by which time there would be hardly any pencil left.

John Robinson

Robinson was a fine New Testament scholar, who later became Bishop of Woolwich. He was a shy man but very brilliant. He came to fame in particular with his book *Honest to God*, published in 1963.

I was introduced to Robinson when he was at Woolwich, as a result of a recorded interview by Geoffrey Parkinson (a probation officer). I met Geoffrey when I was doing a student placement at Old Street probation office (see later), and he'd interviewed me on what he called my "theological position". I had described myself as a "Christian agnostic". This infuriated Geoffrey and it showed in the tape, during which he became increasingly fanatical, he being fiercely atheistic. It seemed to be a matter of great importance to him, he the son of a pastor (or so I believe), to be adamantly against any kind of religious belief.

Someone had heard this tape and told Robinson of it, because of his reputation around *Honest to God*. He asked to hear the tape and then recommended it be sent to the head of religious broadcasting at the BBC, saying he thought it should be broadcast. In the end it wasn't used, the quality of recording not being up to BBC standards, but I was pleased that Robinson had been interested in it.

As a result of meeting Robinson socially he invited me to lunch. There I met his wife and children. I learned during that meal that

Mrs. Robinson was looking for a violin for one of her daughters. So I told her that I had a spare violin, a pretend Stradivarius, which I'd acquired when I was a student social worker in Oldham (see later). This violin had been offered to me as a gift, as no one in the family was musical. It had a label inside, indicating it had been made by Stradivarius. Even though it was clearly a fake label, it gave some curiosity value to the violin. However, I hadn't been prepared to accept this as a gift, so the would-be donor asked me if I would let him sell it to me for a token amount. "Like what?" I'd asked. "How about a shilling?" So I had bought this violin for a shilling, and I then sold it to Mrs. Robinson for the price of the strings I'd bought for it. The violin had quite a sweet tone but it was clearly not a Stradivarius.

Henry Chadwick

I had the good fortune to have been able to attend lectures by Henry Chadwick, whose erudition on early Church history was legendary and whose style of lecturing could hardly be equalled.

I attended Henry's very last lecture in Cambridge, given at the Divinity School, before going to Oxford where he'd been appointed Regis Professor of divinity. This lecture was attended by a crowd of people who'd been queuing to hear it. Finally, there was standing room only and many couldn't get in. When he finished speaking he was given a standing ovation, and the clapping seemed to be almost unstoppable.

Owen Chadwick

Owen was one of Henry's brothers, all of them becoming very distinguished. He was master of Selwyn College and became professor of ecclesiastical history while I was studying theology.

Like his brother, Owen was also a very fine lecturer. For one series of lectures he read extracts from a set of diaries that illustrated how the Church had been challenged and shaken by the publication of Darwin's *The Origin of Species*. I found these diaries so interesting I chose to look into them further during the summer vacation term (sic) for which I stayed on after I'd taken my final exams.

I later heard a nice story about Owen Chadwick. Patrick Gowers (a friend and composer) had met him walking along the Backs, and Owen (then Dr. Chadwick) had told him of an experience he'd had just a few days before. He had been to Ridley Hall, to visit a student there, and had stayed late. When he'd returned to the main entrance he found it locked, Ridley closing their doors early, perhaps because of being a theological college. A student, upon seeing the then young-looking Dr. Chadwick trying to find a porter to let him out, told him he needn't trouble the porters. Chadwick had then been shown where he could climb over the wall. This student was very surprised, the next morning, to find that the person he went to hear lecture (the master of Selwyn) was none other than the man he'd helped over the wall the previous evening.

Sherry at Ridley

During my final term, I was surprised to receive an invitation to a sherry party to be held at Ridley Hall. The person who'd sent this invitation was someone who had earned a reputation in the theological faculty for being such a stuck-up prig that there were several students who had come to dislike him quite intensely, and I was one of them. So how was it I'd been invited to sherry by this man? I continued to wonder about this until I was at Ridley, drinking this man's sherry. I then recognised a number of other students, especially those who had (like me) come to dislike this man. Gradually, these others and I drifted towards each other and the topic of conversation became one of shared incredulity that any of us had been invited, let alone so many of us who didn't like this man.

After my third glass of sherry I went to ask our host how it was he'd invited us. "Oh," he replied: "It was in answer to prayer. I'd being praying to Jesus, concerned about the fact that there were so many people I hated. What should I do about it? Jesus replied to my prayer by showing me the way. I should invite you all to sherry." So most of the people invited to this party were there with this one thing in common. *We were all people whom this religious man had come to realise he hated.* Quite an original basis for a party!

Receiving my degree

The day before I was due to receive my degree, I booked my parents into the hotel opposite Trinity, and I was allowed back in my previous room in college. We were also allowed to leave our clothes in our rooms for the time of the degree ceremony.

161

After having breakfast with the parents at their hotel, I rushed back to my room to change. There on a hanger was my dinner jacket coat, which I would be wearing. But where were the trousers? To my horror, I realised I'd taken the trousers to Whale Island (*HMS Excellent*) for a ball I'd attended there, for which I had been wearing evening tails. But I'd forgotten to bring the trousers back with me for the degree ceremony.

For a few moments I had the dreadful thought that this was going to be an utter disaster, made much worse by the fact that father had taken a day's leave specially to be present, and it could all prove to have been in vain.

I rushed into the court, outside my room, and shouted at the top of my voice: *"Anyone able to lend me a pair of black trousers? My kingdom for some trousers. Please, anyone."* By some good luck, I did get some trousers—from someone who was very short and very tubby. The trousers certainly got round my waist but they were far too short. I looked a real sight.

Harry Williams had to inspect us, to see that we were correctly dressed for the occasion, in dinner jacket, white tie (strangely) and with an undergraduate gown plus a BA hood. I just about passed muster with the baggy trousers lowered to cover my ankles.

In the senate house we were introduced by the *praelector* who had to take four students at a time, one holding onto each finger of his left hand, introducing them to the vice chancellor while he said, in Latin, something like: "I am presenting these persons to be admitted to graduate status of this university, they being deemed to be worthy of this honour, not only on account of their scholarship but also, I know (*scio*), of their good living." Harry told us later that, when he'd been *praelector*, he would only say *scio* when he didn't really know the students in question. When he did know them, he would mutter *spero* (I hope) instead of *scio*, this being more honest: to be saying that he hoped they were worthy of this honour, despite what he may have known of their so-called good living. That was Harry being very Harry!

An extra term at Cambridge

I had loved being at Cambridge, and I had nothing much to look forward to after leaving, so I booked myself in to stay for what is known as the summer vacation term. This was for six weeks.

As mentioned earlier, I'd decided that one of the things I would do would be to read the diaries that had so fascinated me, when Owen Chadwick had been illustrating from them the impact of Darwin on the Church. I forget now whose diaries these were, but I knew they were kept in the university library.

I had to sign a request form for these diaries to be fetched, and I was asked which years was I wanting to see. I had no idea, so I asked to see them all. "They will be ready for you by tomorrow morning." When I arrived, the next day, I was horrified to see a complete table filled with these diaries, all forty years or so. I therefore spent most of the week looking through them, and it was indeed fascinating.

I found entries such as when the diarist had called in to hear a sermon in Trinity, only to find that the preacher was someone he could not stand, so he'd set off hot foot to the University Church where the preacher was more to his liking. There were many other such entries.

While I was busy at the university library I got to know a fellow who would join me over lunch in the café. He boasted one day: "You might like to know that I have been stolen from this library more often than any other author." An original claim for fame, I thought.

Notes

1. Jo Menell later received much acclaim for his film *Mandela: Son of Africa, Father of a Nation* (1995) which he co-directed with Angus Gibson.
2. In archaeology a *burin* is defined as *a stone tool with a chisel-like head.*

Me as a brickie's mate, having not gone into the city.

CHAPTER NINE

What to do with a degree?

Into the City? Or bricklaying?

Joining the Sheffield Industrial Mission

After my summer term at Cambridge I went up to Sheffield to join the Rev Canon Roland Walls and five ordinands, each of them having done their first (of two) years at theological college. The scheme, set up by Roland (as part of what was known as the Industrial Mission), was to give ordinands an opportunity to see life in the raw before they finally committed themselves to ordination.

I was privileged to be included in the second of three years that Roland ran this course, on account of my having read theology and the fact that I hadn't completely made up my mind whether (or not) to be ordained.

We were to spend our first six months working in Sheffield, mostly in steelworks, during which time we would save what we could from our meagre wages, to be put into a common pool. We would then live for the following four months from what we'd saved. During that second period we would be living in community with Roland at 393, Fulwood Road.

We were all allocated digs where we would stay while we were working. I was to be with someone called Mrs. Marsh, near to Darnell and not far from the place where I was to work, Swift Levick & Sons, steelworks and magnet makers.

At Mrs. Marsh's I met David Beevers, who later became my best man. He was a real rough diamond, having first worked down a coal pit (aged fifteen). He later went into the rolling mills, working with hot steel. When I met him he was studying metallurgy at the Sheffield Technical College. He was the first person out of the rolling mills to get some higher qualification, and he subsequently became the youngest person to be admitted as an Associate of the Institute of Metallurgy (AIM), without any secondary education. He subsequently became MIM, Member of the Institute of Metallurgy.

When I met David, he was earning about £12 per week, working in a metallurgical laboratory as well as doing his studies, and he was earning something like £30 for a Friday night shift (8 pm to 6 am) back in the rolling mills, on a high bonus system for those that wanted it. The original idea was that he was saving up to get married to Jean.

David later used his savings towards setting Jean up in a hairdressing salon, she being a medal-winning hairdresser. They found an ideal and central place for this in Worksop, but they didn't have enough capital to pay for this. I therefore offered to stand surety for a bank loan that they needed to get started.

My job, for the first six months in Sheffield, was to be a bricklayer's mate, or brickie's mate. I was paid three shillings ten pence halfpenny per hour.

I worked in a team of men who became fantastic mates. They soon forgave me my different way of speaking, realising I couldn't help talking posh as they called it, and they set about trying to teach me how to speak *"Sheffull"* with sayings like *"A th'alreet?"* for "Are you well?" To this the reply would be a short *"Ah"*; later in the day, when passing each other, the formality was simply to ask *"Ah?"* (with a lift in the voice) to which the reply would be *"Ah!"* with the voice dropping.

For my first week, my job was to be safety-man at the bottom of a sixty foot ladder, at the top of which one of the painters was applying red, anti-rust paint to the inside of the roof where the magnets were made.

I had to stand all day on the bottom rung. That was all I had to do, and it embarrasses me now to recall how I spent my time there. I had my Greek New Testament with me, and I read that while my mate painted. Towards the end of the week, I asked the painter if there was anything

166

more I could be doing, but he was adamant that he couldn't let me shift the ladder. However, he did let me carry his paint pot while he did that.

All went well, at first. But, one time that the ladder was being moved, I carried the pot of red paint too close to one of the giant magnets which were used for making little magnets.

The system was to put shapes of very hot steel into an extremely powerful magnetic field, allowing the hot steel to cool down. This process would retain the magnetism in the steel shapes, later to be sold as magnets for whatever use.

The pot of paint I'd been carrying flew out of my hand, becoming firmly attached to one of these giant magnets, spilling red paint all over it. The painter rushed over, and together we mopped up the paint, doing our best to clean the giant magnet with turps. When we'd made it look almost OK, the painter said: *"I can see thee'll be a raght reel pant'mime, Pat."* I was soon welcomed by all of the team as a mate.

During my second week I was put on the job of digging foundations. This meant digging a very deep hole, into which there would eventually be steel uprights set in concrete, and other girders later fixed to them. I set about this with great gusto, digging as fast as I could, flinging the loose earth over my shoulder, the same way as the others did, to where the loose earth was collecting around the perimeter of the hole.

As the day drew on, the pile of earth round the hole got higher and higher, while I went deeper and deeper, so that I had to fling the earth over my shoulder with ever increasing force and energy. By the end of the day, the pile of earth was so high I could no longer get any of the earth to stay put. I finally had the rest of the team standing around laughing, while I threw the earth up and then ducked while nearly all of it poured back onto my head. I was also told off: "Pat," (as they called me), "you mustn't work so fast. We'll all get into trouble if we don't work as fast as you."

Mrs. Marsh (landlady)

I found my landlady, Mrs. Marsh, to be an impossible woman. We were constantly being watched for things she would disapprove of, and there was plenty of that.

David Beevers made sure I knew about her rule with regard to meals. If we ever left any food she would never serve us any of that same food again. This meant that, when we had uneatable potatoes (not adequately cooked) it would have been fatal if we'd left any of these, or complained. Instead, David taught me to feed these half-cooked potatoes to the dog, which would be sitting around the table waiting for titbits.

One day I told Mrs. Marsh I would be going out that evening, so I would not need any supper. But I'd used the wrong word. I should have said "tea". When I got back from work, I found that my evening meal was all ready for me and I had to eat every bit of it before going out, where I then had to eat a second meal. For Mrs. Marsh, "supper" meant the few sandwiches or biscuits she would provide before we went to bed.

Breakfast would always be on the table for 6.30, usually fried egg and bacon. If we were late, which often we were, the eggs would be cold and the bacon congealed onto the plate; and we could never leave any of it. So, as the dog was never around in the mornings, David would put the cold fried eggs down the loo.

Some days later we found a notice in the bathroom,[1] which I now wish I'd kept. It said: "In future use smaller peices of toilet paper and flush after each peice" (her spelling). Just imagine doing that!

The fried eggs had probably blocked the loo, mainly because Mrs. Marsh (a DIY fanatic) had extended her kitchen so that the down-pipe from the toilet had to slope along the roof of this extension, before proceeding to the drain. After that, David took any cold and congealed eggs to work where he would throw them to the seagulls.

On the landing, Mrs. Marsh had a fifteen watt bulb, which gave so little light it was not surprising I once failed to turn it off when I went to bed. In the morning she fined me a half crown (£2 to £3 in today's money) for the waste of her electricity. That money, I worked out, would have paid for her fifteen watt bulb to be left on for more than a year, not just for one night. She would often say to us: "It is not that I'm mean but I can't stand waste."

An interview with ICI

While I was still at Mrs. Marsh's I had an interview with ICI, having applied to train with them to become a personnel manager. One problem about this was that I had spelled "personnel" incorrectly in my application. Another problem was getting there on the day.

168

It so happened that the M1 motorway had been opened the same week that I was due to travel to London for this interview. I mentioned to David that I'd been sent a significant amount of money to cover travel expenses. He therefore looked into travel costs and found that, if we hired a car, it would not cost much more for the day and we could share the difference. He would report in sick and we could both go to London, he wanting to spend the day taking photos around London. He's a fine photographer.

This seemed a great idea until the morning of my interview. We already had the car, hired from the evening before, but we woke to the thickest fog I've ever witnessed. Not to be deterred, we set off to get to the start of the motorway. It took us two hours to travel the first ten miles to get there. At this point I stopped the car and spelled out our options. We had three hours left before I was due to report for my interview. We could either call the day off and I'd ask for another date, or we could take advantage of this being the first week that the M1 had been open.

Every evening, for some weeks before this, they had been explaining on the TV how the new motorway should be used. We had been told, repeatedly, that there were to be three lanes: a slow lane, a fast lane, and the outside lane was for "overtaking only".

I reckoned that hardly anyone would dare to be driving on the motorway, and anyone who did would almost certainly be crawling along. No one at all, I thought, would be mad enough to be in the outside lane: "So let's drive very fast, using that outside lane all the way." We agreed to give it a go.

Throughout this journey, I was ready to pull the car onto the central reservation (grass) which, in those days, had no barrier. I would simply steer the car, as gently as possible in order not to skid, onto the reservation. I would then not attempt to brake on the grass, I'd just concentrate on steering. But I didn't actually think we'd meet any cars at all in that lane.

As it turned out, I drove at 85 mph all the way, not able to see more that two cats-eyes at a time, just enough to steer by. And David kept his eyes skinned, as did I, for the slightest sign of another car in front of us. We actually didn't see a single car in our lane, but David counted each of the few cars we passed in the lane to our left, about a dozen during the whole journey.

When we arrived, in record time, I found that the elbows of my coat were soaked through with sweat from nervous tension. It was a once in a lifetime chance to do something as mad as that on a motorway. It could easily have been fatal. And, after all that, I didn't get a training place with ICI.

Another interview

I was subsequently offered an interview for a place at Barnett House, Oxford (see later), but I had broken my glasses about a week before I was due to go for this. My best chance for getting these repaired in time, I thought, would be to send them to the opticians in Cambridge where I'd recently got them. They were most likely able to get a side piece to replace the one I'd sat on, but I didn't know the name of the opticians or their address.

Having packed up my glasses I made a map which I put on the outside of the package. I had written *CAMBRIDGE* across the label, with a map of Trinity Street going past Trinity and St. John's colleges. I then put a large arrow pointing to *Opticians here*.

I did get my repaired spectacles back in time for my interview, and when I next went to Cambridge I called in at the opticians to thank them for their speedy help in this. I then learned that they had been so impressed with the postal service, delivering this package to them without any proper address, they'd put the envelope on their notice board.

Back to Mrs. Marsh

Mrs. Marsh didn't like me sitting on the floor (we were only to sit on chairs) and there were all sorts of other things she took objection to. As a result, on several different occasions, she asked me to leave, and David also. Finally, when I'd been told to leave for a third and final time, David was gloating over me at the supper table, saying it shifted the score between us, now "three to you and two to me". But, at the end of the meal, Mrs. Marsh asked David to go into the kitchen. She wanted to have a word with him.

I was waiting for David outside, sitting on my scooter, as we were about to drive down to see Jean and her family for the evening. David then joined me, laughing his head off, saying: "It is now three all."

Mrs. Marsh had decided that, as David was firmly standing up for me, it would be best if we both left. We had a week to find somewhere else to live.

Mrs. Leary (landlady)

I was able to find a room quite quickly, not far away, with someone called Mrs. Leary; an Irish lady with a shaky arm. I told David I'd found somewhere, but he was very upset I hadn't included him in my search for a room. He remonstrated: "I thought we were mates, and there you go and fix yourself up without me." I felt so bad about this, I asked Mrs. Leary if she could put David up as well. I was in a room with a double bed. If she didn't mind, I could share this with David. So she put David and me together in a double bed.

The teddy bear

As the double bed was a large one, there was space enough for David and me—if he kept to his side. However, not to leave that to chance, I bought David a teddy bear which I placed firmly between us, where it served its purpose well.

When David got married I gave him a little clock, set into a silver teddy bear, as a reminder of those days. And when I was asked to make a speech at their wedding, I said it had been *absolute Hell* having to share a bed with David. I just hoped that Jean would fare a lot better than I had.

Mrs. Leary would quite often talk to us while we had our evening meal. She would hold her shaky hand in the other hand, while she stood by the table. But sometimes the shaky hand would slip free, and David would duck as if she was about to hit him. We laughed a lot while we were there.

The first thing I was asked to do, when I moved in at Mrs. Leary's, was to cut her father's toenails. He lived a few doors down from her. She, of course, could not do this because of her shakes. It felt rather like a Maundy Thursday ritual, I being "girded with a towel" and washing this old man's feet before cutting his nails.

For our own washing, we had the kitchen basin in the evenings. But on Saturdays we would be treated to a hipbath in the kitchen, while Mrs. Leary made herself scarce. David took some photos of me (naked) sitting in this bath, as a joke. I took these up to "393"to show the others, but on my way back I fell asleep on the bus and forgot the photos. I've often wondered what became of them.

Back at Swift Levick & Sons

While at Swift Levick's, one of the jobs I had to do was to go with a lorry driver to a coal depot at the Sheffield railway station. There we had to bag up a ton of coal, which we had to deliver to a house recently bought by one of the directors. We'd heard that he was getting married to an Italian contessa, and we were to fill the coal cellar before they moved in.

After we had carried these heavy sacks on our shoulders down to the cellar, we were invited to stay for some tea, both of us black with coal. The tea was served by someone I took to be the contessa's maid, she being dressed in black with a pretty little lace apron. She was very attractive, and I was probably quite flirtatious with her while we chatted.

During our chatter I heard this "maid" say something about having visited Cambridge. I, of course, said I'd just graduated there, which seemed to surprise her. She then peered at my coal covered face, beginning to see me in a different light. How come I was now delivering coal?

I too began to see this maid in a different light, as it slowly dawned on me that she too was not quite what she seemed. It turned out that it was she who was about to marry the director, to whose house we had been delivering this coal. *She* was the contessa!

Swinging bricks

One of the many skills I learned while working with this building gang was that of swinging bricks, which meant swinging them back through the legs and then up. Instead of climbing up a ladder with a hod of bricks over one shoulder (which we also did when we had to) we would swing bricks up to a second storey, some thirty feet up, to be caught by one of the bricklayers.

The skill was in being able to swing the bricks just hard enough for them to reach the catching point, and to swing them with one's fingers keeping the brick level at the moment of letting go. This would keep the brick from spinning. When I first started doing this I had many failed attempts, the gang standing back laughing while I practised. But after not so very long I got the hang of it, and it was most satisfying to find that I could get bricks to stop exactly at the point where a bricklayer would catch them, at the moment when they were "weightless", then stacking them on the scaffolding.

Roland Walls

When our time of labouring was over the six of us students went to join Roland.

One of the things that was remarkable about the community house was the little chapel at the top of the building. It was extraordinarily simple, peaceful, and beautiful, lending itself well to the quiet of prayer and meditation. This was the centre of our lives while we were there.

I found Roland inspirational in lots of ways. But, as well as studying together and much else, Roland made sure that we always took time out to watch *Hancock's Half Hour*.[2] We watched this together as if it were a weekly vigil, laughing a great deal.

While we were in community we all had our jobs. Mine was to do the laundry for the eight of us living together: Roland, Miss Black (his housekeeper), and the six of us "students".

For the laundry, I had what was probably the very first Hotpoint combination washing machine, picked up at some second-hand place. This was made in the same material as water troughs; galvanised steel. The tub had an electric motor that would churn the washing with some kind of paddle at the bottom. Attached to the side of this was an electric mangle, with a draining board beneath it to take the water back into the tub. I had to rinse everything several times until the water coming from the mangle was clear.

In the garden there was an array of washing lines, about eight in all, and I became expert in hanging up all the shirts, underwear, sheets and pillow cases, and whatever else on these lines.

After the washing was dry, or dry enough, there was an electric roller-iron that was also attached to this antiquated Hotpoint. I had to learn how to roll shirts, and whatever else, through this iron, eventually handing back to the household all of the washing once it had been completed.

Another thing that I remember especially about our time with Roland was how much fun we had with him. He used to regale us with his stories, many of which I still remember and some of which I was delighted to find retold in the book about Roland, *The Mole under the Fence*.[3]

Purple ink

One story was of the time when Roland was quite recently ordained, or so I believe, and he'd been invited to preach at the church of some rather smart village. For the night before, he had been put up in the squire's big house. Sitting up in bed on the Saturday evening, Roland had been checking through his sermon for the next day, using the only writing implement he could find in his room, a pen with purple ink.

The pen had leaked and Roland told us how alarmed he'd become when he found purple ink all over the pristine white sheets on the bed. Then, trying to make good the damage, he'd tried washing the sheet, only to find that this made matters much worse. The ink just spread further and further. I don't know that we ever heard how this was received the next day by the lady of the house.

Miss Black

One weekend, while Roland had been lecturing abroad, Miss Black (the housekeeper) had taken it upon herself to tidy up Roland's study. When he got back she proudly announced that she'd done a big sort out, saying: "I've thrown out those magazines you were hoarding, but I kept the most recent one of each kind." When Roland asked where she had put the ones she'd thrown out, she said she'd made a big bonfire and burned them.

As these magazines were from complete sets of theological journals, Roland had said to her it might be as well if she got out of his presence before he did something terrible; he might even kill her! These journals were not generally available. They'd been carefully collected during his time in the world of theological scholarship, and he would never be able to replace them.

Another time, Roland was in a meeting, with the archdeacon and other clergy from the cathedral, when Miss Black had taken it upon herself to barge into the room pretending to be a ghost. She had just ironed his surplice which she'd put over her head, coming into the room saying "Boo!" not realising that Roland wasn't alone. He had to explain to those present that this was just his housekeeper being a bit strange, which she was. But she always cooked excellent meals for us.

174

Roland's "cell"

Roland had made a bedroom for himself in the garage, putting a mattress onto a ping-pong table. Beside this he had put the remains of the paschal candle, which he used as a bedside light while he read his way through D. H. Lawrence novels. They were part of his reading at that time.

Going down a coal mine

One really crazy memory I have, from my time at "393", was when Roland had arranged for us to visit a coal mine.

We had been warned that we should wear warm clothes, as it could be quite cold. I happened not to have any warm trousers but one of the students (Peter Hipkin) came to my rescue, offering me a pair of his that would certainly be warmer than anything I had.

As I didn't know we would actually be going *down* the coal mine, it didn't occur to me that these trousers, which were pristine white, would not be the most ideal trousers for the occasion. So we set off, I oblivious of the problems I was about to encounter.

When, as it turned out, we were then taken down the coal mine, we were also taken along the galleries being currently worked by the miners. The space got lower and lower as we made progress along them until, in the end, it was almost impossible to carry on unless we were on all fours. But I, with Peter's white corduroys to consider, had to proceed in a squatting position, shuffling along crabwise, in order not to have them spoiled. I certainly felt extremely foolish, and wondered what on earth these miners must have thought of this college prat turning up in white trousers when going down a coal mine.

Going to the island of Iona

Roland had often told us stories about Iona, some of them quite strange.

One story was of George Macleod, who had founded the Iona Community. He had apparently gone to view the work of a silversmith, who'd recently died, somewhere on the east side of Scotland. There he'd seen a Celtic cross that was just right for Iona Abbey. The silversmith's widow was pleased he liked this, but she explained it was not for sale. Her husband had intended to offer this to Iona Abbey. George had then explained it was from Iona that he'd come, and he was looking for just such a cross for the high alter. So that was the story behind how the abbey came to get its altar cross.

Roland also told us of the glass chalices that had been made for George by an engraver who happened to be an atheist. There was a set of these chalices, each with gospel words engraved round them, such as *I am the true vine; This is my blood; Drink ye all of this*. We were told that this engraver had also been invited to choose whatever he liked for the last of these chalices, as long as they were some words of Jesus, and George didn't want to know what words he'd chosen until the engraving had been completed. It was therefore only when George unpacked the chalices that he saw that this engraver had chosen the words *Friend, wherefore art thou come?* I have always thought how profound that choice was, and that question has remained with me ever since.

Another story was of a time that Roland had been travelling up to Iona, stopping off somewhere on the way. He had been having some kind of meal in a café, at a table with another man who got talking. This man had become very interested when he heard that Roland was going to Iona, wanting to tell him of an experience he'd had when visiting there a year or so before.

This unknown man told Roland he had been in the abbey on a Good Friday when he'd heard repeated chanting coming from a side aisle, but there was no one there. Then, according to this man, it felt as if a hand had gripped him behind the neck—making him walk up towards the altar. On the way, the pressure on his neck had made him kneel down three times, and eventually he had been pushed down to become prostrate before the altar. During all of this he'd heard these words being chanted, over and over.

This man asked if Roland might understand the meaning of the words, as he could still remember what he'd heard. He wrote the words down *phonetically* and Roland managed to decipher from this the Latin words that used to be chanted many centuries ago, on Good Friday, *in the Abbey*. During this chanting, monks would be going in procession towards the altar until they each prostrated themselves before it. I forget how long ago this was, but I believe that it was in the thirteenth century or soon after. Very strange.

Well, these are just some memories I've recalled from our shared life with Roland, an experience I have always regarded as a profoundly altering time in my life, during which I began to find a mind of my own.

This eventually led me away from the priesthood, and I chose to work with people in a different way.

Roland later left Sheffield, going to Rosslyn, near Edinburgh, where he started a little community: the Monastery of the Transfiguration. He remained there, until he died in 2011, along with his faithful friend and follower, Brother John Halsey—one of those who had been in Sheffield with me.

Around 1987, I went to stay with Roland and John for a couple of nights. I much enjoyed being with them again and I recall that we laughed so much, and for so long into the night, that it was nearly ten o'clock when Roland noticed the time. We'd somehow laughed our way into the "Time of Silence", which they usually observed after 9 pm.

I went to see Roland again in 2007, and spent an hour with him, both of us reminiscing. I loved seeing him light up with that same impish grin, with Roland (then over ninety) laughing again, as he so often did, as we went through some of our shared memories. What I was particularly pleased to see was how he had these same memories fully preserved in the recesses of his mind, connecting back to them when I reminded him, as if they had happened only yesterday. He would take up a story, adding his own bits to it, as in: "Oh yes, that pen. And the ink was *purple*. All that purple ink on those white sheets. It was terrible." John told me that Roland often came alive again in company, even if he might forget within minutes who it was who had just visited him.

"Where did you meet her?"

Visiting Iona was the final thing we did together as a group after our time together in Sheffield. I had no idea of the problems this could lead to, for me. On the way to Iona, travelling from Glasgow to Oban, I ran into a lovely girl called Helen who sat next to me in the bus. She'd been very flattering to me, liking my chatter and I don't know what else, and I agreed to meet up with her after leaving Iona.

However, I soon realised that Helen was becoming far too attached to me. I therefore went to see her to end the relationship. But she pushed aside my protestations that we were not suited, and persuaded me instead that I hadn't come to end the relationship: "You really want to get married to me but you don't have the courage to ask me." I'd never been proposed to before. Alas, this ended up with the two of us being formally engaged.

I felt terrible about this and went to see my brother Michael and Christina (my sister-in-law), half hoping they might recognise my ambivalence about this engagement when I told them of it. However, far from that, they seemed delighted that I (at last) seemed to be on my way to getting married. They wanted to know all about this girl, starting with *where had I met her?* When I remained stuck without words, Christina said: "Don't be bashful. If you met her on a bus, just tell us." This was *terrible*. I *had* met her on a bus.

It was some time before I was able to disentangle myself from this unfortunate engagement. I was very distressed that this had happened as Helen was a lovely person, and I know she was very hurt by this.

However, Helen felt able to remain in touch and she later came to stay with Margaret and me, bringing her husband and small baby boy, while we were living at Pindock Mews (see later). Funnily enough, there was a census taken the night they stayed, which meant we had to fill in the three of them (put up in the sitting room), two of us and a lodger, all six of us in a two bedroomed house on the night of the census.

Notes

1. The bath also had a notice saying: "Use only two inches of water, starting with cold."
2. This was when the programme was being broadcast for the first time.
3. *The Mole under the Fence: Conversations with Roland Walls.* Mark Chater and Ron Ferguson. St. Andrew's Press.

CHAPTER TEN

Back to college—Oxford

Several brushes with the police

Oxford—Barnett House

By the time I had decided to train as a probation officer, most of the courses like LSE were fully subscribed. The first course I found still having places was at Barnett House, Oxford. In my opinion this was then not a very good course.

Mrs. Layard (landlady)

I found rooms with someone called Mrs. Layard (Doris). It turned out that she was a Jungian analyst, married to (but subsequently divorced from) the anthropologist John Layard, who had also become a Jungian analyst.

I met John Layard on one occasion. He was reminiscing with Doris, talking throughout with a length of ash dangling from the cigarette he kept permanently between his lips.

Among other things, Layard told me of the time when their son Richard was being born, he sitting beside Doris (probably with a cigarette between his lips then too) saying: "Push, Doris, *push.*" He then claimed that, as soon as the cord had been cut, he'd taken the infant

Richard and *hung him on the clothes line* to see if it was true that we are born with the inherited grasp of monkeys still intact. Richard really was able to hold his own weight on the clothes line, while his mother was calling out: "Bring the baby back *immediately*."

Richard subsequently became Lord Layard and wrote a book called *Happiness*, and it is he who has been pushing for the government to endorse CBT (cognitive behaviour therapy) to be the government's recommended treatment for most (if not all) psychological problems, much to the despair of psychoanalysts and psychotherapists.

Matriculating at Oxford

At Barnett House, I was encouraged to become a member of Christ Church, this being the sister college to Trinity, as the Barnett House staff liked to foster connections with the colleges. I therefore went to see the moral tutor (a pastoral role) at Christ Church, who explained to me the procedure. I would first have to matriculate, as an undergraduate, and three weeks later I would go through another ceremony at which I would be incorporated as an honorary graduate of Oxford.

This matriculation required me to be sworn in, placing my hand on a book while I solemnly stated that I would observe all of the statutes contained *"in hoc librum"*. I was then declared to have become an undergraduate of Oxford, which it turns out *I still am!*

Soon after this I received a letter of apology from the moral tutor, explaining that, since I had last met him, there'd been a meeting of the Hebdominal Council who, he said, had *in their wisdom* decreed that Cambridge graduates at Barnett House would no longer qualify for automatic incorporation.

When I subsequently met the moral tutor again, he explained that I would now remain an undergraduate of Oxford, *in perpetuity*, unless I saw fit to take a further degree at Oxford. Nevertheless, I was allowed to be a member of the graduate common room at Christ Church, and I was entitled to wear the Cambridge graduate gown as a visiting graduate. Even now, I am still listed as an undergraduate of Oxford University.

Anna Simmonds

I soon learned, at Barnett House, that I was being paired with someone called Anna Simmonds, an Oxford graduate. She too was training to become a probation officer. I later found that she had a room about two houses down from Mrs. Layard, which was very convenient.

Anna was one of the best friends I've ever had. She was engaged to Derek Hyland, so the friendship remained firmly platonic and it was a great deal of fun. We did almost everything together during the week and then, at the weekends, Anna would be with Derek (also from Oxford) who would come down from Birmingham, where he was working.

Quite often, Anna and I would have a pub lunch. She remained fiercely independent, never allowing me to buy her any lunch or even a drink. The only thing she ever allowed me to buy for her was just one pickled onion. The landlord, where we often had our lunch, came to think we were "an item", even though we never gave any cause or grounds for that assumption. One weekend, when Anna was with Derek, this landlord took pity on me—seeing me there without her. He must have thought we'd broken up as he gave me the usual pickled onion free: "To cheer you up," he said.

The graduate ladies dinner

While I was there, Christ Church took what was then felt to be a momentous step. It allowed the graduate common room to have *a ladies night dinner*, which was the first of its kind since the college was founded.

I was without a girlfriend at the time, so I asked Anna if she would partner me for this dinner, which she agreed to do. It was nearly a disaster, but it all ended well.

It had been expected that there would be about 100 people at the dinner, but on the day there were only twelve couples. The men each took a bottle of wine and we had sherry in the common room beforehand. Anna didn't feel like much wine, so I had all of the bottle after she'd taken just one glass from it.

After dinner someone announced that the senior common room had donated, from their wine cellars, a case of 1927 port to launch these ladies nights, it being assumed that there would be a series of these after this first one had set the trend.

The ladies were given one glass of port and then they were asked to retire to the graduate common room for coffee, while the men had more port: that old tradition, of course. The port was very good. In fact it was *exceedingly* good, and there were twelve bottles of it and twelve men.

181

The port continued being passed round the table until we discovered there was none left! At this point we made our rather wobbly way across the court to the graduate common room.

Not surprisingly, the atmosphere that greeted us was frosty to an extreme. The men had kept the ladies waiting for well over an hour, and the coffee was stone cold—as were the ladies. None of them wanted to speak to any of the men, so we stood in a drunken huddle with our backs to the ladies until it was time to go.

I told Anna I'd drive her home. But, before doing that, I walked round the perimeter of the huge college court, to check that my legs were working OK, and I was relieved to find that they still seemed to be connected to the rest of my body. Anna thought it would be best if we got a taxi. But I was going to be the proper gentleman and I would drive her.

It is shocking to think back on this, but I drove back all the way, being over the limit by many times, fortunately without incident. I was saying aloud to myself: "Change up; don't drive too fast; change down; don't drive too slowly: look in the mirror; signal; turn very carefully," until we got to Mrs. Layard's. Anna came in with me, to see that I was OK, which I wasn't. She was terrific and stayed until she could see that I was going to be all right.

I felt pretty bad about the end of that evening, with Anna having been so kind as to be my partner for it. I therefore gave a copy of *Summoned by Bells* by Betjeman, with the dedication: "To Derek and Anna, for lending and for being lent". I was delighted then to receive a copy of *Selected Poems* by William Blake, in which Derek had written: "To Patrick, for borrowing and returning". They were such good friends.

Parking without lights

While staying in my room at Doris Layard's, I would always park my car in the road outside. It was a quiet side road, one block away from an artery road which ran from the centre of Oxford. In those days there were regulations about having side lights on at night, for which I had a clip-on light that could be fixed to a window. But I never used this outside Mrs. Layard's.

One day I received a parking ticket, charging me with the offence of not displaying side lights on my car at night, outside Mrs. Layard's house. I looked up the regulations, finding that it was only on bus routes that side lights were required. I therefore wrote to the police stating that, as far as I knew, no buses ever went down this side road. So I would not be paying the penalty charge, believing that I had not committed any offence. I heard no more.

Dangerous parking

Later on, I was looking for somewhere to park near Carfax (at the centre of Oxford) and I found a row of cars parked, backs to the wall, along Cornmarket Street, which was close to the junction with Queen Street. There was just room for one more car, very close to that junction, so I parked there while I used a public telephone in the Randolph Hotel opposite.

When I came back to my car an hour later, I found that all the other cars had disappeared, leaving my car sticking out like a sore thumb on that corner. I also saw a policeman, standing with his back to me, most probably wanting to speak to the driver of this car. With less confidence in my innocence than I later claimed in court, *I crept on all fours* behind him to the door of my car, which I opened as silently as I could. I managed to get in without the policeman seeing me, but when I started the engine he turned round. He then said he was charging me with "dangerous parking".

When I received the summons for this I chose to appeal. I then attended court, carrying the book I happened to be reading at the time: *Crime and Punishment* (Dostoevsky). It amused me to have this with me.

I had rejected the offer of a solicitor, choosing to defend myself. While standing in the dock, I was told I had placed my car in a dangerous position, particularly as approaching cars might not be able to see it until it would be too late to avoid an accident. I retorted that it was clearly visible to any car coming up the adjoining street (Queen Street).

"But," the prosecution continued, "that view of your car would be obstructed by pedestrians on the crossing, just before where you had parked your car." I questioned this, saying there was no way that a view of my car could be obstructed by pedestrians, unless there was a very large group of them waiting to cross just there.

The prosecution seemed to be prepared for this. They gleefully pointed out that, at the time there would have been a large crowd of pedestrians waiting to cross, as they would be coming back from theatres and cinemas at exactly that time.

183

I thought quickly about this and I replied, just as gleefully: "I think it is relevant to note that every single theatre and cinema in the neighbourhood of that crossing is on the *other side* of the crossing. Any group of pedestrians waiting to cross would therefore have been on the other side." The magistrate reflected upon this and the case was dismissed.

Taking and driving away

One evening, over dinner in Christ Church, I was asked by someone what the present trends of adolescent crime were, the questioner knowing that I was training to become a probation officer. I happened to know that TDA (taking and driving away a car without the owner's permission) was a prevalent crime at the time, so we discussed this at some length over the meal.

When I went to drive home, I got into my car and began to drive back to Mrs. Layard's. My car at that time was a Morris Minor, with a maroon collapsible roof. I had used one of my keys to open the door and the other for the ignition. But (without knowing) I had got into the *wrong* car; one exactly like mine.

As I was driving away, I noticed that the clutch pedal was not quite how it had been when I'd driven it before. But it so happened that my sister Elisabeth had borrowed my car for a few days before this, and had returned it to me that same evening, having had it serviced in return for the loan of it. No problem, I thought. I could take it back to a garage and have the clutch readjusted.

I then noticed that there was a racecourse ticket left on the windscreen. I was a bit surprised that Elisabeth hadn't removed this, but I it didn't seem impossible that she'd been to the races.

However, when I looked at the mileage showing on the dashboard, the car had been driven much further than Elisabeth could have driven in the few days she'd been using it. I therefore got out of the car and checked the number plate. *It wasn't my car!* So, unwittingly, I'd taken and driven away someone else's car, without their permission. I could be charged with TDA. How could I explain this to the police?

I turned round, to return this alien car to where I'd found it. But when I arrived back at Christ Church, the space from which I'd taken this car had another car parked in it. The only remaining space was now right next to my own car.

I parked the car I'd taken, locking it with the key I had for my own car. I then unlocked my car (one key) and started the engine (the second key) and drove off. But as I left, I saw a row of people at the bus stop opposite—all agog at this rapid change over from one car to another, both of the cars being almost identical. I have often wondered what they made of that. I had also been somewhat alarmed that my two keys could fit another car as well as my own.

Dinner at Trinity College

While I was at Oxford I got to know the chaplain of Trinity, the Rev Leslie Houlden. He was a good friend to me, and several times I dined with him at the high table.

On the first of these occasions, Leslie warned me beforehand that I was the only guest that night. This meant, according to college custom, that I would sit next to the college president who was also then the vice chancellor of Oxford, Professor Norrington.

I had met Norrington briefly in Christ Church, and I'd noticed that he smoked a particular brand of cigarettes. So, to be prepared, I had bought a packet of his brand specially for after dinner. But, on my way to the college, to settle my nerves for this occasion, I'd had a few puffs from one of these cigarettes, putting the half-smoked cigarette back into the packet.

Before dinner, Leslie treated me to some very fine sherry. Two glasses seemed to be in order, the ordeal being still ahead of me. I forget now, but I vaguely recall that we had more sherry somewhere before going into dinner at the high table. Following that, over dinner, we had excellent wines throughout; two glasses of white wine with the fish, and two glasses of red wine with the meat. Then, when we'd finished dinner we went elsewhere for port. This was where Leslie introduced me to yet another custom, that the senior guest was taken by the president, away from his host, to be introduced to other members of the college. So I was taken from the only person whom I knew, and the port proceeded to go round the table for what seemed to be for ever. But, as I gained in my courage, I joined in with the rest of them—keeping my end up as best I could—beside the president and whoever else was sitting next to me.

Finally, we repaired to an annexe room where we had coffee and liqueurs. At this point I began to notice that I seemed to have slipped into something like *Alice in Wonderland*. I can vividly recall looking down at the little tables beneath me, on which there was coffee (the one thing that might save me from passing out). But how to get down to the level of the coffee? I seemed to have grown twice as tall as usual, and I felt almost certain that if I tried to bend down for a cup of coffee I would fall over. What to do?

The answer seemed to be in having a cigarette. I'd read somewhere that nicotine and alcohol somehow cancel each other out. So now seemed to be the right moment to offer the vice-chancellor the cigarettes I'd bought in preparation. In the usual manner, I pulled out two cigarettes from the full packet and offered these to him. He took one and I took the other. But when I made to light his cigarette I saw, to my absolute horror, that he was holding the half-smoked stub I'd pushed back into the packet on my way into the college!

Fortunately, this shocked some part of my mind into quick action and I found myself saying to him: "Bad luck, sir, have another go," as if we'd been drawing lots and he'd drawn the short straw! I was pleased to find that the vice-chancellor was taking this in good grace and we were both able to laugh about it. But it has remained as one of the most embarrassing moments in my life.

A misdirected parcel

I used to subscribe to a record club, *Concert Hall*, which would send a record each month on approval. The system was that the monthly record would be posted and could be returned within seven days without having to pay. I had given my Haben address, as I kept moving around, and mother would usually forward this to wherever I was.

On one occasion, however, my monthly record had been forwarded by mistake to my sister Elisabeth's address in Gloucester Road. She was not yet dressed when the postman rang the doorbell for her to take delivery. So, when she'd got herself into a dressing gown, she checked to see if the postman was still waiting at the door. There she saw him *bending the record over his knee* before pushing it through the letter box!

I sent the two pieces of record back to *Concert Hall*, pointing out that it might have helped if they'd added the usual notice: "Fragile—Do not bend". They sent me a replacement.

Christ Church Ball

I was not going to go to the May Ball at Christ Church as I had no partner to invite. However, I was driving through Oxford in my new car, which by then was an open MG Midget, when I saw a girl I knew looking very fed up about something. She was banging her handbag against a wall as she walked, so I stopped to ask what was up with her.

This was someone called Helena, who'd been one of the people taking the jive classes I'd been going to, so I knew her a bit. She had also, a few weeks before, been written up in *Cherwell* (the Oxford magazine) and had been voted "the most beautiful girl at Oxford".

Helena explained to me what was upsetting her: "All the wrong people are trying to invite me to a Ball, and the right person isn't asking me, so I won't be going to any Ball at all." I replied: "We can't have that. Why don't you come to the Christ Church Ball with me?" She immediately said she'd love to do that.

So there I was, at the Ball with the most beautiful girl at Oxford as my partner, but I was just not used to that kind of thing. I jived away with great gusto, having this jive teacher all to myself, until the excitement got too much for me. I developed a nose bleed. How humiliating! But it was soon better and I got through the evening without further ado.

CHAPTER ELEVEN

Back to engaging with the real world—probation training

I follow Sir Roger Casement into Pentonville prison

Oldham

While doing my course at Barnett House, Oxford, I was required to do a casework placement, which meant being assigned to a supervisor in a social work agency where I would be given a chance to work with some clients under supervision. I was sent to the Family Service Units (FSU) in Oldham, where my supervisor was a Stephen Wyatt, a gentle person who was just a few years older than me.

Visiting the mother of a sixth child

For a while I went round with Stephen when he was visiting his clients. My first solo assignment was to babysit an Irish family called Murphy, to allow the husband to visit his wife in hospital where she had just given birth to her sixth child.

When I got to the home in question, the husband was quite clear *he didn't want to visit his wife*. He would stay at home with the other children and I could go to the hospital. Not knowing how to go about that kind of visit I went and bought a small bunch of flowers, to give to this mother whom I'd previously never met, and set off to the hospital.

When I arrived, I was directed towards the maternity ward, where I would be able to visit Mrs. Murphy, but I had arrived too early for the allocated visiting hour. Until the due time, I had to sit in the waiting room with a number of other visiting fathers. "Is it your first?" asked one of the fathers. I had to explain that I was actually not the father. "Oh!" he replied, as if there might be something peculiar going on. I tried to avoid further questions.

When I got to the ward I was introduced to Mrs. Murphy and the baby. It all felt very strange, visiting someone I didn't even know, to congratulate her on her new baby—born earlier that day. What was also strange was that Mrs. Murphy seemed to be almost totally uninterested in her latest baby, a girl. I peered into the cot and saw the baby was really rather beautiful, so I said to her, trying to make conversation: "Oh, isn't she beautiful?" Mrs. Murphy just replied: "Oh, you think so? Well, I suppose she is. They are all the same to me. All a bloody nuisance."

I was really glad when the visiting hour was ended, as it had been almost impossible to make any conversation with this Mrs. Murphy.

Visiting a prospective foster mother

Another task set me was to visit a woman (Mrs. O'Reilly) who'd recently answered a newspaper advertisement in which the local Children's Department had been inviting people with spare accommodation to contact them if interested in the possibility of taking some foster-children into their home.

Mrs. O'Reilly had seen this advertisement and had indicated on the phone that she was really very interested. She had room for four foster-children, if the children's department could let her take them in. As there had been so many people writing or telephoning about this advert, the FSU had been asked if they could do some of the preliminary interviewing. This was how I'd been asked to visit this woman.

When I went into her home, Mrs. O'Reilly proudly showed me round, including the spare rooms she had. The house had four bedrooms; a double one which was hers, another double one and two single rooms. She was living alone and thought it would be easy to have four children, if two were prepared to share.

As part of my preliminary enquiry, I asked Mrs. O'Reilly if she'd had children of her own. She was about fifty, so it was possible her children had grown up and left home, leaving her now with this big, but mostly empty, house. "Oh, yes. I have four children," she replied. "Where are the children now?" I naturally enquired. "Oh. The Children's Department took them away. *They are all now in care.* That is why I'd really like to have some more children in the house."

I had to tell Mrs. O'Reilly, as gently as I could, that I did not think the Children's Department would be willing to let her look after other children. "Oh. What a pity," she replied. "I'd got quite excited at the idea of having kids here again."

Mrs. Starkey (landlady)

While I was in Oldham I was placed in the home of Mrs. Starkey and her daughter, whose name I don't now recall. This landlady was a homely soul who prided herself in providing a good evening meal.

For one weekend I had to stay somewhere else, as Mrs. Starkey was having relatives in my room for a wedding in the Oldham church. I was placed with friends from the church, whose names I don't remember now. What I do remember is that they had their very first telly delivered to their home the day I was there.

We all watched this TV until broadcasting came to an end, which in those days was about midnight. Then, when the last programme closed down, and the light on the screen had reduced to a spot before disappearing altogether, the husband was trying to turn the TV off. But he didn't know where the right knob was. He was leaning over the telly, trying to find a switch or something at the back, when a woman's voice came over the TV saying: "Don't forget to turn off your set," which was the usual announcement at the end of broadcasting in those days. The husband thought the voice was his wife's, and I remember him shouting over his shoulder: "What on earth do think I'm trying to do, stupid?" Only then did he realise that the voice had come from the telly.

Climbing in

Before my last night in Oldham, I spent several hours finishing off all that I still had to do in the office. I then returned the office keys to my supervisor's flat, putting them through the letter box.

Unfortunately, when I got back to the house of Mrs. Starkey, I found that I'd left her door key in the office. I just could not bear to wake her at 2 am, nor to go round to Stephen at that late hour. So the best thing seemed to be to go round the back of the house where I might be able to climb up a drainpipe, to get into the back bathroom. They were back-to-back houses, with a long alleyway running between them.

Having negotiated the drainpipe without much difficulty, I climbed through the bathroom window and stepped warily into the bath, not wanting to frighten Mrs. Starkey. I didn't want her to wake up thinking a burglar was getting into her house.

Unfortunately, when I looked around the bathroom, by such light as there was from the moon, I noticed something rather alarming. The bath was the wrong way round. *I'd climbed into the wrong house!* So, before all hell broke loose, I now being a "burglar" in someone else's house, I climbed back down that drainpipe and up the next one, this time into the correct house.

Over breakfast next morning I confessed to Mrs. Starkey what had happened. She was so shocked that she felt she couldn't possibly tell her neighbours how the footmarks in their bath had come about. She just left them to wonder.

Home office interview

I forget now at which stage I was interviewed to be accepted for probation. That interview process took place at Horseferry House.

There were ten of us and we all had to endure a morning of group interviews, where we were left to discuss given topics amongst ourselves, while also being watched to see who was showing the qualities that were being looked for in probation officers.

For the afternoon interviews, which were to be individual, we were put on a list indicating the order in which we were to be called. I was last on the list, so I reckoned it might be about three hours before I would be called.

I stayed long enough to see the first person come back from being interviewed. I was then determined not to hang around. The waiting room was filling up with cigarette smoke, and as soon as the first person returned he was leaped upon by the others with questions about the interview, and what kind of things were being asked. I immediately made for the door.

Along the road was the Tate Museum. I knew there was a major exhibition of Picasso on at the time, so I walked smartly down to see this.

I spent the first hour looking at the paintings and the next hour looking at people looking at the paintings. Then I returned to the waiting room.

When my turn came, the interviewer apologised that I'd been kept waiting so long. "It was not a problem. In fact it was a pleasure," I said. "I didn't stay around but went to have a couple of hours at the Picasso exhibition." I think this probably contributed to my being the only one of that group who was accepted for the probation service. For some reason I don't recall, the other nine people insisted we all exchange addresses. We were to write to all of the others to say if we got in. I felt rather embarrassed when I heard that all the others had been rejected.

Rayner House

After Oxford I had to do the probation training course at Rayner House, London. This was residential and, as I thought, not very inspiring. I know that I was pretty bolshy for a lot of the time there, which was acknowledged by the one tutor whom I most respected, Herschel Prins. He later became a professor at Loughborough University, and he referred to his experience of me on that course, at the beginning of his review of *Learning from Life*, a statement that I much enjoy:

> In his latest book he [Casement] acknowledges, in very frank fashion, that he was a somewhat "rebellious" and "difficult" student (I can vouch for that). [However, he goes on] ... His current book indicates how such difficulties cannot only be overcome, but can engender an ability for helping others at the deepest levels. (*Probation Journal*, Sept 2008)

Prins was the one good thing about the Rayner House course. I don't remember much else that I valued.

When it came to the exams, we all had to put a code on our papers so that they would be marked without our names being known to the examiners. I could see the sense of this but for my last exam I didn't have the code on me when the exam started. I just put my room number. This was a law exam.

I was anxious to get away from that exam early, as I hadn't yet bought a present for Flora (my god-daughter) and it was the last shopping day before Christmas. I made sure that my answers were as brief as possible and then handed in my paper about three quarters of an hour early.

I didn't think it mattered as I reckoned I'd put down just about all the law I knew, which wasn't much, and off I went to shop at Harrods.

That particular afternoon was notable for the exceptional smog, for which London used to be truly infamous. It was difficult to see and difficult to breathe. Nevertheless, I got to Harrods in time to choose a toy carpet sweeper, which cost about as much as a proper one. I just hoped that it had been worth skimping the exam for that.

Coventry probation office

My second placement was at the probation office in Coventry. There I was supervised by someone called Mr. Robbins, a very serious man but a good supervisor.

I don't remember much of my time on this placement, but I do vividly recall a time when one of the probation officers came back from a home visit that had gone disastrously wrong. This colleague had been visiting a probationer's home, to meet the parents, when they had got into a tremendous row. This probation officer, a man who was not much more than five foot tall, said he hadn't quite managed to assert his authority as he had wished, in trying to get the couple to stop screaming at each other. So, when they had taken no notice of him at all, he'd jumped onto the settee—to give himself added stature. But the settee had collapsed and he'd found himself standing back on the ground, his legs having gone through the seat, he waving his arms and trying to bring things to order. He had the whole office in fits when he was describing this. I'm not sure how this had ended, but it was clear that he'd not managed to be the assertive and containing presence he'd hoped to be on that occasion.

Music

My main memories of Coventry are of music in the new cathedral. It was there that I heard Beethoven's *Missa Solemnis* for the first time. I was so moved by this that I left immediately after it, in order not to experience the anticlimax of other music still to be played in the programme. I really think the Beethoven should have been at the end of the programme, not in the middle.

I also heard (in the cathedral) the first performance of Britten's *War Requiem*, which was an extraordinary experience. It was inspirational to

194

have soloists from Russia and Germany, as well as from Britain, taking part in this historic performance. I now think that was the most important music of the last century and I am so glad to have been present for its first performance.

Old Street Probation Office

I was required by the Home Office to do two placements in probation offices, which I believe were for about three months each. The second of these was in the Old Street Probation Office. I was to be supervised by someone called John Ferguson, whom I'd not yet met.

John later became my most valued male friend, alas dying of a heart attack while my wife and I were in Pakistan, in 1986. We first learned of this from our answerphone when we got back. It was devastating news. We still see his widow, Andreé, who has also been a good friend, going to stay with her in Digoin, Burgundy.

Before my first week at Old Street, I rang John to ask how I should be dressed. He said that it would be fine if I came in a tidy jacket and trousers. So that I could look smart for this placement I went to Marks and Spencer and chose clothes to John's description. However, when I arrived at the probation office I found that (by chance) I was wearing *exactly identical* jacket and trousers to those worn by John. Geoffrey Parkinson, another probation officer and office joker, immediately said: "Patrick, you really don't have to identify with your supervisor instantly, or so completely!"

Some years later, after I'd left the probation service, I called in for a sandwich lunch at Old Street probation office. I had been riding my scooter in the rain, for which I was wearing black leathers, looking as if I had dropped from a plane. Geoffrey jumped up from his chair, putting a reassuring hand on my arm, saying: "Relax, Patrick. The war is *over*." That was typical Geoffrey Parkinson humour.

For the first few weeks I would either accompany John on some of his visits or I would sit with him in the magistrates court, which was on the other side of Old Street, just opposite the probation office. I describe more fully in my last book (*Learning from Life*, pp. 46–49) the occasion when I was asked to do my first social inquiry for court.

I had been asked to do an inquiry on a man called (in my book) John Macmillan. He had forty-seven previous convictions, all of them trivial, and he'd never been out of prison for longer than two weeks. So it seemed to be worth trying him on probation, even if he didn't last for much longer than he had previously.

John Macmillan was remanded in custody—in Pentonville prison—which inevitably reminded me of my relative, Sir Roger Casement, who had also been there. The familiarity of name also didn't escape the attention of the prison officer who let me in at the main gate. He greeted me with: "Casement, *Eh*? We hanged one of you. Come on in. There is always room for another!" And so it was that I found myself inside the prison where Sir Roger had been before he was hanged.

I went to see the magistrate, Mr. McGelligot, to discuss my recommendation. To remind him about the case, I said that I'd come to discuss the man he had remanded in custody for social inquiries. "You may remember him. I think you might call him *an incorrigible rogue*." He replied: "Quite probably, but what is his name?" I then got mixed up between the similar names and said: "His name is McGelligot. *Oh, No!* I'm so sorry, sir. I mean Macmillan." Fortunately he also saw this as funny.

CHAPTER TWELVE

My first real job: probation officer

"Never, ever do that again": Sir Ewan Montagu, QC

Willesden probation office

In 1963 I was appointed probation officer at Willesden on a salary of £1,000 p.a. This was my first real job.

Elgin Avenue

My first task, before starting, was to find somewhere to live. I was only able to find a temporary flat, where I could remain until I found somewhere more permanent. Meanwhile, my senior (Sheila Himmel) said she would put feelers out for anyone who might have a room that I could rent. She didn't find anyone.

I eventually found somewhere in Elgin Avenue, an attic flat for £3 10s. p.w. I told Sheila that she needn't go on looking for me as I'd now found a room. "Where?" she asked. When I told her it was in Elgin Avenue, Sheila asked which number. It turned out that I was exactly next door to her.

I soon set about making some curtains for this flat. I bought some appropriate material and some lining, and I borrowed a sewing machine from a neighbour. It was so simple. I just whizzed round the edges, having pinned the main material and the lining with the edges turned over. Some weeks later, after the material had hung for a while, I found that the main material had started to sag at the knees. When I mentioned this at the probation office, I was told I should not have sewn the bottoms together as the two materials had different degrees of stretch. No problem. I just took a razor blade and cut along the bottom of the lining. The knees no longer sagged. Problem solved.

When I later called on Sheila, next door, I saw that she shared a door-bell with someone named as "D. Dawes". I wondered if this could by any chance be Daphne Dawes, of whom I'd heard so much in Oldham. Yes, it was Daphne, but she was taking a sabbatical year off, in Greece.

When I subsequently met Daphne, after her sabbatical, I heard that she had begun to run out of money in Greece, so she'd started offering herself to teach English. However, her notice saying *Lady offers English lessons* had resulted in crowds of men turning up at her door, expecting something quite different. She had then made things much worse by saying: *Nay, Nay*, thinking this was the Greek for *No*, but it didn't have the effect she'd intended. Instead, it seemed to have excited these men even more. She later learned that *Nay* was the Greek for *Yes*!

As a result of having Sheila living next door, I soon came to recog-nise the sound of her trying to start her old Hillman car. This would usually take several minutes, with the engine spluttering but not firing properly, requiring of her these repeated attempts at getting it started. This sound would often be the noise that awakened me from sleep. I would then finish dressing as I ran down the four flights of stairs. And I'd shave (with my battery razor) in the car, while I drove through back streets as fast as I could, to arrive at the office before Sheila. I felt it nec-essary to do this as she expected everyone to be at the office before her, and she would always see my car parked outside my flat when she left. By these means I usually did manage to get there before her.

Just before I joined this office, which was situated in Harlesden, there'd been an upgrading of several local roads, to accommodate a new bus route. The surface outside the office was pristine new, but it only stayed that way for a very short while.

In the following weeks, the road was dug up on at least *five* separate occasions. It was dug up for the water; for the electricity supply; for the telephones; for the gas, and for the drains and sewers. After each of these times the road had to be made good where the latest digging had been. No "joined-up thinking" there! Quite why there had been no co-ordination, I don't know. The inefficiency of this just beggared belief. The end result was a total mess, with the road pitted along its length where there had been these five different lines of digging.

One fortuitous result of the new bus route was that, in an adjacent road, the flow had been changed to make it one-way. This meant there was a pedestrian crossing that now had the new zigzag lines on both sides of it, on the approach side (which was correct) and on the far side which was then wrong.

We had recently been educated to know that zigzags were there to preserve a clear view for motorists as they approached a crossing. So I knew there was no need for a zigzag on the *far* side of this one. Therefore, finding that this bit of zigzag had not been removed after the road had been made one-way, I chose to use that as my easiest place to park. This was made even easier by the fact that most other people felt obliged to respect this bit of zigzag, even though it had become redundant.

Inevitably, after some weeks, I found a policeman about to put a notice on my car. Fortunately, I was able to explain the logic of my parking, which he eventually came to accept. After that, my bit of zigzag became my own personal parking space, having enjoyed (once again) pitting my wits against the police, as in Oxford.

Who is this?

Not long after I'd started at the probation office, I had to do court reports on two boys who'd been involved in the same crime. These boys were then required to report to me the following Monday evening.

When the first boy arrived, I just could not remember which boy it was that I was seeing, and I didn't like to let him know that I had already forgotten his name. So I interviewed him, as I was expected to do, explaining the conditions of his probation and asking him more about himself and his family. I would then be expected to dictate this interview to my secretary, but I still didn't know which boy this was. I therefore asked him to remind me of his address, so that I could give him some idea of when I would be calling on his parents. When he'd left I rushed to my secretary to find out which boy lived at this address. My record of the interview could then be recorded in the right file. But it had felt very odd, interviewing him without knowing who he was.

199

Having no pen

I once had to do a court report on someone (a teenager) who had been remanded in custody at the Feltham Remand Centre. Having driven quite a distance to get there, I was shown to an interview room while a prison officer went to collect him. I then discovered that I'd come without any pen or pencil. Having failed to find any prison officer from whom I could borrow a pen, I was soon faced with this lad in the interview room.

I didn't want to lose face by saying I hadn't got a pen, so I put a writing pad on my knee, out of sight behind the desk, I then used my car key to engrave on the pad the names and ages of the brothers and sisters, and all other relevant details that I would need for the court report. All went well until I began sneezing. (In those days I had something like hay fever). Grabbing my handkerchief, I put my pad and car key on the table. The lad could then see that there seemed to be *nothing* written on my pad, and I wondered what he'd made of this interview.

When I got back to the office, I held my engraved pad up to the light and dictated my report from the shadows cast on it, where my key had left its marks. My report then had all the details, even though my pad had seemed to be blank when the lad in Feltham had been looking at it.

Being mistaken for a would-be murderer

One day, while I was interviewing, another probation officer (Tom Quinn from the next office) knocked on my door asking to have a word with me. He said he was about to see a couple who were probably going to separate, permanently, after this last time of meeting. He was afraid that the husband might become violent. So, if I heard any sign of violence happening in his office, would I please come in *immediately*? I agreed to this, and continued interviewing with an anxious ear listening out for signs that I might be needed next door.

After some time, Tom came back to my office to say that all was well. He didn't need me to be on the alert any more. I was then just about to resume my interviewing when I heard a dreadful commotion on the stairs. I rushed out to find that the husband had a fierce grip around his wife's neck, trying to strangle her with both hands. Another probation officer, Charles Hocking, also rushed out to help. I had one of the man's hands and Charles had the other. Between us we struggled to prise these murderous hands off the wife's neck, while Tom was trying to drag him off from behind.

Eventually, and with great difficulty, the three of us managed to overpower the man. His wife was taken to the secretaries' office and I was asked to sit with the man in another, while the police were called for, Tom having hurt his back when he fell down part of the stairs.

The man, after this outburst of rage, seemed to become calm and relaxed—remaining silent. I, on the other hand, was brimful of adrenalin, white-faced, and shaking from the shock of it.

When the police arrived, they were shown into the office where I was sitting with this man. They looked at the two of us (I still shocked and white in the face) and one officer turned to me saying: "Now, just come quietly. You are coming with us." I had to explain that it was the other man, not me, that they had come to take away.

Peter Ely, probation officer

For some time I shared an office with a Peter Ely. He was about my age, a nice chap but often he was quite scruffy.

Peter once had to take a probationer to the Henderson Hospital, where they might take his client in for a period. They ran what was known as a therapeutic community.

The usual practice, before someone was accepted into the community, was for the prospective new member to be interviewed by the community as a whole. Peter and his client were waiting for his client to be called when somebody came and asked Peter to go into the interview room. They then began asking why he wanted to come to the Henderson and in what ways did he think they could help him? Peter soon realised they'd asked the wrong person in. The client, in his best suit, had to be fetched from the waiting room while Peter, in his scruffy clothes, returned to it.

A new probation office at Acton

Sheila, as senior probation officer, found herself having to be responsible for setting up a second office that was being opened in Acton. She therefore had to choose one male officer and one woman officer to join the new team.

Sheila asked to see me and then told me that she had thought long and hard over this, having had quite a sleepless night before deciding that I had to be the male officer who would be transferred to Acton. I was very upset about this, saying it had been very important for me that I'd settled into this office at Harlesden. It had come to feel like home for me. I then went into a sob story about how many times my childhood home had been moved, and told her I just could not accept that I was the best person to be transferred.

Sheila had to think this through all over again, with another sleepless night. She then asked to see Peter. He told me later that she'd gone through the same process with him, but he had given her a much more direct response than I had. He'd just said to her: "You make me sick!" and walked out of her office, not giving her a chance to say anything further.

Finally, Sheila fixed on someone else to be transferred, and he accepted this without a murmur.

Standing up to a magistrate

As a probation officer I was a servant of the court, there to be told what to do and, when asked but only when asked, to give reports to the court; sometimes also to answer questions put by the court.

A condition of a probation order, spelled out carefully at the outset of anyone being placed on probation, was that if an offender failed to keep the conditions of the probation order, or if he offended again, he would be brought back to court and could still be sentenced for the original offence. The conditions included a requirement to report, when told to do so, to the probation officer and also to keep the probation officer informed of any change of address.

I had one client who'd been put on probation for a serious offence, for which he could have gone to prison, but he was allowed a chance on probation. The court placing him on probation was the Middlesex Quarter Sessions, then at Parliament Square.

This client had got into a minor bit of trouble the night that his wife had given birth to their first baby. He'd gone out to celebrate becoming a father, ending up drunk—along with his friends. He was then being driven home in someone's car when the police stopped the driver to check if he was over the limit.

202

My client didn't want his friend to get into trouble, so he'd started shouting at the police to leave him alone. They had then arrested him for *disorderly behaviour*, and he was brought (next day) to the local magistrates court, where he was fined. But this incident put him in breach of his probation order.

As this client would then have to be brought before the court that had placed him on probation, because of this breach, he knew that he could be remanded in custody, on the grounds that his earlier offence had been much more serious. He had therefore asked his solicitor to be present at the magistrates court.

This solicitor sought me out, and I made it clear that I thought this man should definitely be at home, helping his wife with her newborn baby, rather than languishing in prison until he appeared at the next Quarter Sessions.

When the time came for the magistrate to be making a decision about my client, the solicitor said he wanted to call the probation officer. "You can't call anyone," said this magistrate. "That is my prerogative, and I do not want to call the probation officer in this case." He was a stipendiary magistrate, who was well known for being a bit of a bully.

I was not prepared to let this magistrate get away with this. I therefore spoke to the clerk of the court, saying I wished to exercise my rights as a citizen. I said I was prepared to *stand surety*, thereby indicating I would see to it that this man would attend the Quarter Sessions, whenever he was called to appear, and I believed that this entitled me to speak to the court in support of my offer.

The clerk of the court agreed to grant me my right to speak, but the magistrate, to prove that he was not going to be "beaten" by me, still made an order for my client to be remanded in prison. It could have been nearly three months before his case would be heard at Quarter Sessions. My client had therefore appealed to a judge in chambers, the following week, and was granted bail. He then appeared, without any problems, when the case was heard those many weeks later.

When I presented my report at the Quarter Sessions, before Judge Montagu, QC, I was grilled by the prosecution. They pointed out that I had stood bail for this man, I being his probation officer, which the prosecution said proved I was prejudiced in his favour. Therefore, my recommendation that he be allowed to remain on probation should be disregarded as a biased opinion.

I replied that I had offered to stand surety because I was convinced that more benefit would come from this man being at home, supporting his wife and becoming a more responsible husband, rather than being in prison. I was also entirely confident that he would not break his bail, his presence in the court now proving my point.

Judge Montagu accepted my recommendation and agreed to let this man remain on probation. However, immediately after the court hearing, when I was walking back to the probation office in the court building, Judge Montagu ran down the corridor to speak to me. He took me by the elbow and said: "You were absolutely right, doing what you did. But *never, ever*, do that again."

Another breach of probation

I had someone on my list whom I will call James. He had been on probation for some time before I met him, having been found guilty of attempted rape. At the Oxford Assizes, the judge hearing his case had given him a chance by placing him on probation for three years. He would otherwise, undoubtedly, have been sent to prison.

Before he came to me, James had moved from one town to another until he came to London. There he started to live in the area covered by my office and he was allocated to me.

I saw from his record that James had been transferred every few months, from one probation office to another, because of his frequent moves. He had been living a restless and unsettled life. I therefore told him I thought it would be better for him if he stayed on probation to me, even if he did move again in London. That would give me a chance to get to know him and for him to know me. I was recommending this because I sensed he had difficulties in forming relationships, and his offence seemed to have been an expression of that, as it could have been a clumsy attempt at forming a relationship with a girl.

This arrangement worked well, and James remained on probation to me, cycling to see me for his reporting nights from wherever he was living. This sometimes meant a long journey but he never failed to report.

Unfortunately, over the Easter period, James had got drunk and he'd thrown a brick through a shop window. The police were able to identify him and I learned that they had a warrant out for his arrest, as they had not been able to find him at his last known address.

James telephoned me, the evening he was next due to report, to say he might be a bit late as he had a long way to come. I told him it was very important he did come, as he seemed to have changed his address without informing me and the police now had a warrant out for his arrest. I told him to come to the office and I'd arrange for this matter to be dealt with, while he was with me.

James did report, and the police came while he was there, arresting him for his latest offence and now for his failure to report the change in his address. As he was on probation, after the serious offence for which he had not yet been sentenced, they were obliged to arrest him and to keep him in custody until he appeared again before the Oxford Assizes.

I assured James that I would be present at the hearing, and I would make it clear how important I believed it to be for him to be allowed to continue being on probation. I would also make it clear to the court that he had remained in work throughout the year that I'd known him, and he had always reported; even this last time when he knew that this would mean being arrested.

In court, I presented my report to Mr. Justice Stable.[1] He had seen from the police record that James had been fined for the charge of malicious damage (the broken window), and I heard him say to the prosecution: "What a stupid decision, to *fine* a man like this. How is he going to pay a fine unless he steals money for it?" He also had my report, but he seemed totally uninterested in it. In fact it sounded as if he hadn't even looked at it, as his only question to me was: "Has this man done *any* work during the time you have known him?"

I replied that I had made this clear in my report, that James had actually been in work throughout the year I'd known him. I then reiterated my recommendation for him to be allowed to continue his probation, stressing that his relationship to me was the longest relationship he'd had with anyone since he left home, adding my opinion that his earlier offence seemed to have been largely because of his difficulties in making relationships.

Mr. Justice Stable took no notice of anything I'd said. He sentenced James to eighteen months in prison, for the original offence and the breach of probation.

I went to see James in the cells. At the Oxford Assizes, going to visit the cells was in itself quite a traumatic experience. I had to be shown down gloomy stone steps to the dungeons beneath the court. There I saw my client.

Understandably, James was extremely angry, shouting at me that he had thought I was someone he could trust, but I had deceived him. I had promised that I would speak up for him, and I'd said I would recommend that he be allowed to continue on probation, but now he was being sent down for eighteen months. He would never trust anyone again.

This was clearly a moment of crisis. I let James continue shouting until eventually I had to bring this to a close. I put my hands on his shoulders and said as firmly as I could: "James, I can understand why you are so angry. I am angry too. I really don't think it is necessary for you to be going to prison. But what is also very important is that you do continue to trust me. I will continue to be there for you, throughout this sentence and afterwards. I want you to remember that."

James stopped shouting. He said: "I can now see that you do care. Yes, I can still trust you." James then remained in contact with me throughout his prison sentence. And when he was discharged, the prison services arranged (at his request) for him to have a rail warrant that allowed him to break his journey in London, on his way back to his parents in Ireland.

James came to see me and proudly showed me his driving licence. He'd paid to have this renewed while he was in prison. "Look inside," he said. When he told me what he wanted me to be looking at, I saw that he'd given his permanent address as *c/o Mr. Casement*, at the address of the probation office. He was grateful that I had cared enough to have remained there for him. Alas, I never heard from him again, but he had kept in touch with me until then. After that he would be back at his home in Ireland, and back to whatever that might have in store for him.

Don't buy that boat

While I was still working as a probation officer I looked for somewhere I could buy, rather than go on paying rent.

For a time I'd been interested in the idea of buying a Thames barge, having met someone called Jack who lived on a barge in Little Venice.

I could not find a barge for sale but I did come across a houseboat, moored near Hammersmith. It seemed to be quite a romantic idea to live on the river, so I asked Jack what I should be looking for, to make sure that I was investing in something worth buying. He told me he'd come with me to investigate. "For this we need a penknife," he claimed.

I didn't know what the purpose of this might be, until we arrived at the boat.

Jack had chosen low tide as a good time to visit the boat, and we sloshed our way round it in the boots he'd insisted we both wear. He then showed me what the penknife was for. "If the wood is sound the penknife won't go in. Let's see." He proceeded to walk around the whole of the hull, there being nobody onboard, sticking the penknife in at regular intervals. It sank into the wood right up to the neck of the blade. "It's rotten the whole way round. Don't buy it."

A few weeks later, when driving over Hammersmith bridge, I noticed that the boat I'd thought of buying was no longer there. I have since had the dreadful sense that Jack might have left it holed, like a colander, to the point where it may have sunk at the next high tide. I'll never know.

Pindock Mews (Maida Vale)

I eventually found a flat in Pindock Mews, a little way off Elgin Avenue. This had two bedrooms, a living room, a kitchen, and bathroom. It seemed ideal but it was completely unfurnished. I therefore took some holiday time to sort things out.

A three piece suite

I needed some furniture for my new sitting room and I found a suitable suite, as I thought, at a second-hand shop. I bought this for £15. It was delivered later that day to Pindock Mews. There, on my own, I managed to manhandle the really huge settee up the narrow stairs, to the sitting room, and then one of the chairs. But there was no way the room could accommodate any more furniture of that kind. I therefore took the remaining chair back to the second-hand shop, saying I didn't want any money for it. I was just bringing it back as I could not use it, and he could have it for free.

The man wasn't interested in taking the chair back and I didn't want it either, so I left it on the pavement outside his shop. That, I thought, would be the end of it. He could still make a few pounds selling that one chair.

I returned to Pindock Mews where I was greeted by a cheery voice from a woman sitting in the sun, on her little balcony overlooking my front door. Would I like some tea?

I was pleased to have this chance to meet one of the neighbours, not knowing until later that this woman was said to be a *retired prostitute*. So there I was, having tea with a retired prostitute, when a police car stopped outside. "They seem to be wanting someone at your door," she said. I thought I should find out what they were after.

"You are going to be charged with leaving litter unless you remove the chair you left outside the second-hand shop." I could not see how this chair, which had just been sold to me, was now deemed to be litter. They said it was now regarded as litter because I'd left it on the pavement without permission, and I had no right to do that. So I had to remove it immediately. But I had nowhere to put it, so what should I do? They said the procedure now was for me to bring this back to my flat and to arrange for the council to collect it. They would then take it to the refuse tip.

I wasn't going to go through all of that procedure, especially as I had absolutely nowhere I could put it. I therefore collected it from the pavement, putting it on the back of my MG, and drove straight to the local refuse tip to take it there myself. There I was greeted with a large notice saying: *NO ADMISSION EXCEPT TO AUTHORISED COUNCIL WORKERS*. Well, I thought, I could think of myself as a council worker. So I just drove into the tip, a huge place full of stinking rubbish.

Very soon someone shouted at me: "You're not allowed in here." I replied to this: "But I'm a probation officer." The man who'd challenged me, to my amazement, said: "Oh. That's OK then." How could my being a probation officer allow me to be in the council tip, I wondered, but I wasn't going to challenge him. I just dumped the chair and went away.

Buying at an auction

I had never been to an auction before, so I didn't know how things were done there.

All I wanted was to buy some bedroom chairs and two bedside cabinets. The chairs were easy. We still have these rather charming chairs, in our bedroom, which my wife Margaret has since reupholstered.

The cabinets caused me more trouble. I got one very cheaply, but the other seemed to be going for an extraordinarily high price. In the end I settled for just the one I'd successfully bid for. Only later did I discover that I had already bid for a pair, and it was another pair that

I had continued bidding for without realising. I was very glad not to have ended up with both sets, the second going for a ridiculous price.

When I was leaving the auction I met a very angry man in the car park. He'd been bidding against me for the second pair of cabinets, ending up having to pay a huge and unnecessary price for them. He told me that he didn't even want them. He had just wanted to make me bid higher. I explained that I'd been bidding by mistake, not realising I'd already bought a pair, not just a single cabinet. He then flew into a rage, smashing both of his cabinets, stamping on them before my eyes, saying it was all my fault and he'd absolutely no use for them. Serve him right, I thought, for trying to trick me into paying too much.

That was not my only near escape at that auction. After I had bought what I'd come for, I began to watch how the experts were going about their bidding. It was fascinating to watch. They would raise one finger, or a pencil; they would nod, or they might just give a slight tilt to the head; and the auctioneer would take this as a bid.

While watching the proceedings I was also fascinated by the auction-eer. It looked to me as if he had a false eye, but I wasn't sure. One way of telling might be to see if both eyes moved together, or did one stay largely unmoving? So, each time he looked in my direction, I peered at his face to see if both eyes moved together.

Meanwhile, there was much lively bidding for a huge wooden settle, such as you might see in the hall of a stately home. Finally, the auc-tioneer said: "The bid is with the gentleman sitting on the object itself. Any further bids?" I was utterly shocked. I looked around me to find that I was the *only* person sitting on the settle, and it seemed that my researches into this man's possible glass eye had each time been mis-taken for a bid. What would I do with this huge item? And how would I pay for it? The bid was already astronomical. Or could I tell the auction-eer that I was only trying to see if he had a glass eye? At last someone else rounded off the bidding, paying a price he need never have paid if I hadn't been curious about the auctioneer's eye. If I ever go to another auction I will not be so curious about the auctioneer.

During the time when I was furnishing the flat at Pindock Mews I went to Hungerford to see my sister Sue and her husband Bill, to get some carpet under felt. On my way back on the M4, it being a fine sunny day, I regretted not having taken down the roof of my MG car. Instead I turned my attention to the aerodynamics of the roof, whereby the can-vas was being lifted away from the frame it usually rested on, as a result of the wind sweeping over the curve of the roof while I was driving very fast. At that speed the canvas was being lifted more than an inch above the frame, demonstrating something of the lift that occurs over the wings of an aeroplane. I found this most interesting.

Suddenly there was a momentary bang and the entire roof disappeared, having been stretched beyond its limit of tolerance. So I needn't have worried about the roof spoiling my drive on that sunny day. However, I quickly brought the car to a stop so that I could recover what was left of the roof, which soon turned out to have been important as the front and back fixtures were essential for making a replacement. But where would I find someone who could do that for me?

As I was approaching Pindock Mews it started to rain, which could have added to my troubles, my car now having no protection without its roof. But fortune was smiling on me that day. As I was parking my car outside my front door, a man approached me from the garage next door. It turned out that one of the things they specialised in was making replacement roofs for cars. He invited me to drive my open car straight into the garage, out of the rain, and two days later the new roof had been made and my car was again as good as new.

Returning to work

After spending all of my holiday on the flat, carpeting it and furnishing it, etc., I had to get ready for going back to work.

I hadn't completely left my flat in Elgin Avenue, still having a lot of my stuff not packed up and not yet transferred. Among those things was my alarm clock. I would need this as I still didn't have a telephone connected at Pindock Mews, so I would not be able to get an alarm call. It would be a bad thing with Sheila (my boss) if I arrived late on my first day back.

Having to go back to Elgin Avenue for my alarm clock, even though it was about 1 am, it seemed a good idea to do more packing up. I eventually emerged, with a large suitcase of stuff, at about 2 am. But when I had tied this case onto the back of my car, I discovered that I'd mislaid my keys; my car keys and the keys to both flats. I just hoped that they had slipped into my suitcase.

I had no choice but to open my case, now on the back of my car, and I was rummaging around the edges inside this case when a police car stopped. What was I doing?

210

The police were very suspicious of me at this late hour, going through a suitcase on the back of a car. They eventually asked me where I lived. "Now, that is a really interesting point. I used to live here, but I am now living at Pindock Mews." So what was I doing back here, and did I have any proof of my identity? "Well, if you really want to find out who I am, there is a probation officer who lives up there," I said pointing to Sheila's attic window, "but I don't think she'd be well pleased if you woke her up now. She's my boss." The police gradually shifted from thinking of me as a criminal, and just maybe I too was a probation officer, even though I seemed to be behaving rather strangely. I finally found my keys and all was well.

Note

1. Within the probation service, Mr. Justice Stable was called by a much less positive version of his name and title.

CHAPTER THIRTEEN

Catching up on life back at Rogate

Carrying a child in a carrycot who turns out to be Hugh Grant

While I was still at Cambridge, my parents had moved back to Rogate, and they'd bought the Old Rectory at Terwick.

Terwick Old Rectory

"Terwick" had previously been lived in by the Barker family, at which time it seemed rather gloomy, but mother transformed it.

The house had been built over several centuries, being added to in a topsy-turvy kind of way. As a result there were seven different levels which included a cellar. The cellar used to flood quite regularly. To deal with this a pump was installed, which would automatically turn on whenever the water table rose above the level of the cellar floor.

The very top room in the house was an attic that was converted into a snug little bedroom, the ceiling being extended out to the eaves, with the shape of the room then being just like a ridge tent. That used to be my room when I was there, when not at Cambridge or when visiting from London.

My sister's boyfriend had to be told how things stood

When Elisabeth had decided that her then boyfriend was really not her kind of person, she told me she was taking two cups of coffee to her bedroom and she would be telling him that it was *not on* with her, and would *never be "on"*. I don't know why she told me this, except I think she just needed some time to get this over to him, hoping not to be disturbed.

Mother got into a terrible state over this. She came to me in the kitchen and said I must do something. "About what?" I asked. "About Elisabeth and *that man*." When I asked what the problem was, mother said: "They are *in the bedroom together*." I was not going to get drawn into this, so I asked what was the problem about that? Mother said: "The problem is that there's *a bed* in the room. Elisabeth should never be alone with a man in a room where there is a bed." I thought this was really quite funny, as the bed in that room was the least of Elisabeth's problems at the time.

My father and "that word"

There was an incident over supper one evening, sometime after Elisabeth married Anthony. It was while she was expecting her first child. Father got into a big upset over the word *pregnant* being used in a TV programme which had been in one of his favourites: some weekly comedy—I forget which one it was.

Over supper, father said it had really spoiled his enjoyment of that programme, now that one of the actors had used "that word". When I asked which word he was speaking of, he said: "The word *pregnant*. That word should never be used." I asked why not, and he went on: "You wouldn't want anyone to be saying that Elisabeth is *pregnant*!" "Why not?" I asked, still not making it any easier for him. He answered: "It is so much nicer when they use the way they speak of it in the Bible. They use the phrase 'with child', which is so much better than pregnant." Still choosing to be difficult with him, I replied: "Well, you certainly can't say that Elisabeth is *with child by the Holy Ghost*." That seemed to end the conversation.

Christmas dinners at Terwick

Every year, mother would put on a family dinner for Boxing Day. These dinners got bigger every year, and mother would get increasingly

214

worked up in preparing them. She would set her alarm clock for some very early time in the morning, so that she could get up to do more of the preparation.

As the family grew, with each marriage adding to it, the dinner would also be added to. This included some of my brother's family and at least for one year we had his sister-in-law's family, including their two boys. On that occasion I was given the task of carrying the younger boy upstairs, in a carrycot, to be put in our parents' bedroom. That younger boy happened to be Hugh Grant whose fame blossomed later, in particular with the film *Four Weddings and a Funeral*.

Years later, when that film came out, mother had already been widowed and was by then living in her last home in Rogate, Wistaria Cottage (for some reason it was spelled that way and not Wisteria).

One of the carers then looking after mother thought she might like to see *Four Weddings*, especially as Hugh Grant (being "extended family") figures largely in it. "Do you think I will like this film?" mother asked, just before they were leaving. The carer replied: "I'm sure you will, as long as you don't mind the *'f' word* ..." "What is the *'f' word*?" asked mother. "Well, it begins with *'f'* and it rhymes with *duck*." Mother then said: "You've completely lost me now." Anyway, she did enjoy the film.

Mother and father after parties

When I was living at Terwick, supper was usually our main time for being together. I remember one particular occasion when mother and father had been to a cocktail party in the village, staying rather longer than usual as they'd met so many people they knew and wanted to speak to.

During supper that evening mother announced: "I smoked a cigarette at that party," knowing this would enormously shock father as neither of them ever smoked. With shock in the tone of his voice, he replied: "You *didn't!*" Mother grinned back at him and said: "Yes I did. And what is more to the point, *you* lit it."

Once, after another party (mother never being much of a drinker) I found her having some difficulty going up the stairs to her bathroom. She eventually resorted to going upstairs on all fours. That really was the first and only time I'd seen her even a bit tipsy. I felt quite proud of her.

The national anthem

Father was a stickler (whatever that is) about doing things properly, especially when it came to the national anthem.

Of course, on Christmas Day we all had to stand in front of the TV before the queen's speech, while the national anthem was played. But it used also to be played at the end of BBC broadcasting, every night. The ritual then was that, if father could get to the radio—in time to turn it off before the drum roll ended—he would feel excused from standing to attention, as he had turned the radio off just in time. But if the first note of the national anthem sounded before he'd got to the radio, he would stand to attention, usually in his pyjamas, for the duration. Only then would he finish changing before getting into bed.

A good time to talk

Mother regarded bedtime as the best time to talk, as she'd often spent the entire day rushing from one thing to another. Or we might have been watching TV, when it would not have been appropriate to be talking. Therefore, I was quite often lured into her bedroom while she prepared for bed.

So that she didn't have to stop her changing while I was there, mother developed her own style of undressing, which was to put her nightie over her clothes, undoing everything beneath this until it all fell around her ankles. She would then step out of her day clothes. Behind her, while this was going on, she often had her bedside light on in readiness for reading herself to sleep. I once felt I ought to point out to her that there was really very little point in her doing all this under her nightie, as this became almost completely translucent with the light behind. She might just as well be standing before me naked. I think things changed a bit after that.

"Where did you meet her?"—a second time

During my first weeks at the probation office in Harlesden, Sheila (my boss) had suggested that I should take sandwiches along to a monthly lunch group at which some of the local social workers met. It was an opportunity for getting to know other colleagues in the area.

It was at one of those lunch groups that I first met Margaret. She was then working with the FSU (Family Services Units) visiting some families in my area. Neither of us was unattached at the time so nothing came of this. Even though I sort of fell in love with her at first sight, I did nothing about that. It was more than two years later that we began to meet. Even then Margaret was not seeing me regularly and I became increasingly concerned about why she was sometimes not available.

Not being faint-hearted

One time, when Margaret was not at her flat, I heard that she'd gone to see her family in Tottenham. As I really wanted to see her (and Margaret's family name was Lloyd) I telephoned every Lloyd in that area of London, of which there were many, saying to each one: "I may have the wrong number but I am trying to get in touch with Margaret." I eventually found myself talking to someone who said that Margaret had just left, walking round to her parents who lived quite close. That was how I first came to speak to other members of her family.

Another time when Margaret was not available, I went round to her flat, which she was then sharing with friends, Barbara and Peter Dale. I could hear Margaret's voice through the basement window and there was another man there too. Who could this be? I was so keen not to be displaced by a rival I waited outside, sitting under a bush near the gate to this flat.

I waited for about two hours, sheltered by a bush. Then, to my horror, I saw someone coming out from the flat I might then have described (being less PC in those days) as a hunchback. I was asking myself: "What does that man have that I don't?" and I didn't like what first came to my mind. How could Margaret prefer a little man like that? I wrote a note to her, which I pushed through the sash window of their basement flat. I then heard Barbara's voice saying, rather loudly: "We seem to have a *'missive'*. It's for you, Margaret."

That letter

Things had not been going very well between Margaret and me, which left me feeling deeply downhearted, so I went home to see my parents at Terwick for a week's holiday.

217

After breakfast, mother (in her usual way) said: "What do you want to *achieve* today?" (She always thought and spoke in terms of achievements). I replied, in a desultory way: "I have no idea. Nothing really. I'll probably hang around and may play the piano for a bit."

Then the post arrived, and in it was a letter from Margaret. She wanted to come back to me! I just could not believe it. This was amazing. I ran upstairs, packed immediately, and tore back down again. There I saw mother looking rather surprised. "Where are you going?" I didn't explain. I just told her I was off back to London. And that was that.

Getting married

This was the greatest moment of my life. I had almost despaired of ever finding someone I could marry, so at last this was happening.

We were married at the Paddington registry office, where we were met by key members of our families. My father and my brother Michael were in bowler hats, standing outside as if they were attending a funeral, which rather amused us.

We then had our marriage blessed by the Rev Perceval Hayman, our much loved vicar from Rogate, with the assistance of the Rev Tony Bridge whose church we were allowed to use at Lancaster Gate.

The only music that we had was the singing of the *Nunc dimittis*, sung by a tenor from the choir. This seemed most appropriate, as the journey Margaret and I had both travelled, before getting to this point in our lives, had not been easy. Someone remarked afterwards that the tenor's voice was so good it showed that he was not a professional. His voice was completely straight, unaffected, and without any vibrato. It was very simple and truly memorable.

Honeymoon

Margaret had found a hotel near Bath then called Combe Grove Hotel, and the advertising photos made it look rather splendid. It was a bit off the main road, approached by a rather rough track, so we were beginning to wonder when we might be getting to it, arriving when it was starting to get dark.

We then came upon a door with a very dim light over it. This, we thought, might be the gatehouse to the hotel. So I rang at the door and enquired where we might find the hotel itself. "This is it," I was told, and indeed it was. But the hall and the staircase inside were really very small compared with the photos we'd seen. They had clearly been taken with a wide angle lens.

There were several strange things about this hotel. The bath was an antiquated thing with sides so high that it was almost a struggle to step into it. The brass taps were fed by gigantic pipes, allowing water to gush from the taps at an amazing rate, filling the bath in almost no time at all.

The person running the hotel explained to us that, just two nights before we arrived, the chef had been found dead in the kitchen having drunk himself to death. She was now filling in as chef, on top of running the hotel. Actually, she managed that quite well.

There was just one resident in the hotel who was clearly very wealthy. She seemed to dominate her relatives, who came to visit her daily, and we had a fantasy of her shaking her diamond necklace at them if ever it looked as if she might not be getting her way with them, perhaps threatening to change her will if she didn't. But of course that was just our view of her.

We then moved on to Wells where we had booked the final night of our honeymoon in a four-poster bed, overlooking the cathedral.

That night was almost disastrous because I'd heard, on *The Sky at Night* with Patrick Moore, that this particular night was when there was expected to be the greatest display of shooting stars since the 1920s. I was therefore peering out of the window until after midnight, waiting for this display. Some shooting stars were around but the display that had been forecast was definitely not happening. It was only then that Margaret was able to call me away from the window.

Many years later I happened to find myself getting off a train at Paddington alongside Patrick Moore. I therefore told him that he'd almost brought about a divorce during my honeymoon, as a result of his prediction. "Yes, I got that wrong. It happened over America, some hours later." He said he was glad to hear that my marriage had survived nevertheless.

CHAPTER FOURTEEN

Meanwhile becoming a family

Don't judge a book by its cover

Coleridge Walk (in Hampstead Garden Suburb)

We moved from Pindock Mews soon after I started working for the FWA (see later).

As we were taking our first steps to become a family we looked for somewhere more suitable to live, where we could have space for a baby and a bit of a garden.

We found what seemed to be ideal; a little cottage in Hampstead Garden Suburb, in a cul-de-sac. In the back garden the hedges were so high that there was total privacy. In the front garden there were hedges that, by the local suburb regulation, had to be no higher than three feet. And we were not to use clothes lines on Wednesdays (as I recall) or at weekends.

The house had two rooms and a bathroom, upstairs, and downstairs were two tiny rooms (which we knocked into one) and a kitchen. We did all of the indoor decoration ourselves, except for the very high walls in the stair well. At weekends we would either do some decorating together, or Margaret would lie in a tipped-up lounger, with her feet up because of being pregnant, reading to me while I decorated.

Getting to know the neighbours

In decorating our house, we chose a very pale green for the ceiling in our bedroom. And, as I was into gadgets, I bought a paint sprayer to make this easier to do.

This sprayer did not have an air pump. Instead, it had some kind of vibrator that would shake up the paint before expelling it through a nozzle. The directions stated that it was best to point the sprayer out of a window, if working indoors, while adjusting the nozzle until it produced a fine spray. This I did, taking quite a long time to get to the fine spray that was advertised, but then it worked quite well. However, it hadn't worked so well outside the window.

That evening, having done all the decorating we planned for that day, I saw to my horror that the hedge between us and next door, and the neighbour's roses, were all covered with what looked like some kind of blight. The pale green paint, before becoming a spray, had been ejected as little pellets that had reached down half the length of our garden path. What to do?

I clipped the hedge as close as I dare, removing what I could of the appearance of blight. But I could see no solution for the roses, which looked awful. I therefore left a note of apology for Mrs. Farrell, our neighbour, trying to explain. Imagining that she might be familiar with *Alice in Wonderland* (which she wasn't) I said: "I have done what I can about the hedge. But, as for the roses, I see no solution there except the sentence of the Red Queen." I failed to explain that this was when the Red Queen had commanded *Off with their heads* because the gardeners had been painting the roses to make up for having planted roses of the wrong colour. All of that was completely lost on Mrs. Farrell. She wasn't pleased.

The other next door neighbours

When we moved in we hadn't met the people on the other side, David and Margaret de Berry. They had just married and were away for their honeymoon. So, when Margaret took in a huge dog basket that had been delivered *for next door*, we had assumed this must be for David and Margaret. Perhaps they had a dog. We knew that Mrs. Farrell didn't. She only had a cat.

I therefore went round to the de Berry house, put the dog basket on the doorstep and sat in it while I rang the bell. When I heard someone approaching the door I began barking like a dog until the door was opened by David. What on earth was this? Until that moment we'd never met, so this must have seemed extremely odd. Perhaps their next door neighbour was really crazy, and maybe this is what is meant by being "barking mad", especially when he discovered that I was beginning to train as a psychotherapist. When I explained about the delivery of this basket, they were even more perplexed as they didn't have a dog either. It turned out that Mrs. Farrell had ordered this basket from an advert in a paper, thinking it was just the thing for her cat. She had no idea of its size.

Killing the lawn

As the garden at Coleridge Walk had been left to go wild for two years before we bought the house, we had a lot of clearing to do. We had regular bonfires on the lawn, but this eventually left us with a huge dead patch in the middle of it. I had therefore prepared this, and all the other bad patches, and seeded the lawn to bring it back into shape.

While I was doing this, our new neighbour (David) had been watching over the hedge between our gardens. "I hope you put paraffin in with your seed," he said after I'd finished. He hadn't thought to give me this useful tip before I started! "Will it matter much that I didn't do that?" I asked. He then told me that birds would probably eat most of the seed. "Might it help if I put some paraffin on now?" He said it probably would, so I filled a watering can with paraffin and sprinkled all of the lawn with it.

When I looked out of our bedroom window the next morning I saw that the entire lawn was completely brown and dead. I'd killed every bit of grass and I had to dig it all up before re-turfing it. A few months later it looked fine, but I was not greatly pleased with David just after I had first seeded it.

Other neighbours in Coleridge Walk

As for the other neighbours in this cul-de-sac, hardly anyone spoke to anyone. It may have been because the little gardens were so close together, and the front hedges so low, that people would mow their lawns without looking over the hedge to the neighbours who were in their garden alongside, and they would rarely speak.

It was not a very friendly place and we got to know altogether about five families in three years, in the whole of that cul-de-sac. We came to refer to all other neighbours by the numbers of their houses. For instance, we noticed that "number six" was friendly with "number nine" and they seemed to go on holidays together, but we still did not get to know their names. We were told that it usually took two generations of living in the suburb before neighbours really accepted you as belonging. A shame really, and it was largely because of this that we moved to Mansfield Road, at the edge of Hampstead.

Hanna being born

This was a most amazing experience. Hanna was due to be born in UCH, but this was not without some problems. She was not in a hurry to be born, even though the scheduled date was meant to be Christmas Day. Hanna probably had a sense that it might be better to have her birthday separated from Christmas by as long as she could delay it.

When Margaret was due to be examined again at UCH, already ten days after the due date, we got up in the morning to find that there'd been a huge fall of snow during the night. I tried to get the car moving but I could not get it to go more than about a foot from the curb. I then pushed it back into place and we decided to set off for the bus.

In case Margaret was kept in hospital, we picked up the bag of things she'd been told to take with her, and we set off walking to get to a bus. There was not a single bus running between the North Circular Road, which ran just behind where we were living, and Golders Green. So Margaret and I (she heavily pregnant) had to trudge through deep snow all the way to Golders Green where we finally found a bus that would take us to UCH. But even then Margaret was sent home.

A few days later it looked as if labour had started. We were collected by ambulance and taken to the hospital, where labour went on for ages.

When Margaret was told she had reached the final stage, I rang my mother to let her know, saying I would not ring again until the baby had arrived. Hanna was then born, weighing 9lb 1½ oz, absolutely perfect and looking just amazing. She was filled out, no wrinkled face, with lots of dark hair. She was the most beautiful baby I'd ever set eyes on, and that's not just because I was bound to think that.

I was then asked to leave Margaret with the nurses, while they sorted things out. I therefore rang mother as promised, but I was so overcome with relief that all had gone so well I could not speak straight away. Mother, imagining the worst and trying to comfort me, said: "Don't worry, they can do wonderful things nowadays." At this I burst out laughing, saying that all had gone very well and Hanna was *just perfect*.

I was asked to wait by the nurses' office, until I was called back when all had been done that needed to be done. I then heard some nurses cooing over a baby that one of them had just brought into their office. I felt very shut out from this, thinking that I should be allowed to see my daughter too. Peering over the back of the nurse who was holding the baby, I said: "I think that's my daughter you have there." The nurse looked over her shoulder and replied: "I don't think so, dear." She then turned round to show me the baby she was carrying, and it was absolutely coal black. No, it wasn't Hanna after all!

Margaret stayed in hospital for over a week before coming home, and I could hardly bear to be alone in Coleridge Walk, as the place was so empty and it didn't reflect any of the joyous life that was waiting to come home.

I put an announcement of Hanna's birth in *The Times* and, when this had been published, I took this with me on all my travels. I just had to read the announcement almost every time I was stopped by traffic lights. As it was now in the paper it must be true.

The book and its cover

When we were planning our next baby we learned that it would be wise for Margaret to have a while off the pill before we made our next move on this. So I went to the local chemist and asked for three packets of Durex. To my horror, the chemist came back with three enormous packets, each one marked as a gross. That would mean *three times 144 Durex*! I was so embarrassed I very nearly bought them, just to avoid further discussion, but I found I didn't have enough money on me for all of that. I therefore explained that I'd really been asking for three packets of three. "Oh," said the chemist, "I thought perhaps you were planning a party. But, of course, you should never judge a book by its cover!"

Bella being born

This was the other most extraordinary experience of my life. I had not wanted to have to cope with sons, with all the problems of having to go

225

through football, cricket, and whatever else might go with having sons. I'd even played with the idea of taking out an insurance against the possibility of having a son. So, when Bella (Isabella) was born, it was the final bit of heaven for me—having two daughters. (Having grandsons has been very different. I really love that.)

While Margaret and Bella were in UCH I was looking after Hanna at home, except when I was visiting Margaret, at which times her mother came over to take care of Hanna while I was out.

When I was shopping, in preparation for Margaret to return with Bella, I went into the local Waitrose with Hanna. She was sitting in the trolley, her legs swinging through the leg-holes, and she was engaging anyone she could to announce: "I have a baby sister and she is called *Is-it-bella*!"

While I collected Margaret and Bella from UCH, Margaret's mum took Hanna up the road to one of the people we had come to know. Then, as soon as Margaret got into bed, with Bella settled in her cot, I went to collect Hanna. She ran down the pavement and into the house, straight upstairs and into the bedroom. Then, as soon as Margaret saw Hanna (having not seen her since Bella's birth) Margaret burst into tears. Hanna, without a moment's pause, thrust her hands into a box of tissues and, grabbing a pile of these, she held the tissues to Margaret's eyes, saying: "It's all right Mum, Hanna's here." I've treasured that memory ever since.

Hanna's friend the moon

I am not going to bore the reader with loads of children's sayings, but I do want to record the little ritual that Hanna established, when coming home from visiting Margaret's parents in Tottenham. Sometimes we would see the moon in the sky as we left. This would always be on the left side of the car as we drove home and Hanna came to speak of this as "my friend the moon". She would say: "My friend the moon will follow us all the way home and will be waiting for me outside my window."

Father and things that might come in useful

While writing this I came across the following passage in Jeremy Paxman's book *The English*.

Every traditional English family home has a room, a cupboard, an attic, cellar or garage piled with everything from ancient prams to odd rolls of wallpaper in the patterns of twenty years ago, old light fittings to the boxes in which long-broken electrical appliances were sold. They are kept because "they might come in useful some day". (p. 154)

Father, likewise, believed in this idea of saving for another day. For instance, when they moved from Terwick Old Rectory to Mills Farm House (just across the road), everything that could be taken with them went too. Before this move, father even unscrewed hooks and hinges from almost everything he had erected in the garden, the garage, and the sheds, and he even spent time lifting old tintacks—*to be used again.*

Mills Farm House

When mother had first walked around Mills Farm House, imagining how suitable this could be as a new family home, she had been completely unaware of the low doorways. Being quite short, she'd been able to walk through these doorways with no trouble. But taller people, like my father and me, had to grasp onto their knee caps while walking through these doorways, in order to be safe from hitting their heads on the low beams. Father had decided to pin lengths of rubber to these beams, to lessen the impact of heads banging against them, and I found him having a terrible time trying to get his recycled tacks to pierce this ancient and very hard wood; so I offered to help.

I soon found that barely any of father's old tacks were up to the task, so I immediately set off driving to Petersfield, five miles away, where I bought (for about 50p) a box of new tacks which served the purpose well. But when father found that I had completed the job much more quickly than he had expected, having earlier taken ages to get even a few of his tacks to work for him, he could barely believe that I'd gone to such an extravagance of buying new tacks, especially after he had spent so much time in lifting those old tacks to be used "sometime" again. That was so like my father.

CHAPTER FIFTEEN

My next (and last) real job: Family Welfare Association

Meeting the queen: "I suppose it is always useful to have a man in the house, to mend the fuses and things"

Becoming a family caseworker—in the East End of London

I was given a salary increase by the probation service and, on the same day, I was offered a chance to work at the FWA for the same salary as I'd been receiving until then, £1,000 p.a. I took the FWA opportunity, having decided that I was working far too long hours in probation and I wanted to have time to be with Margaret, and later our children. FWA seemed to offer that opportunity, so I took it.

I was appointed to work in the Islington office, known as the Area 4 office of FWA. The principal at the time was Elspeth Welldon, later to become Elspeth Morley. We got on very well and we have remained friends ever since.

My appraisal letter

When the time came for Elspeth to write my first appraisal, after which (if positive) my appointment would become permanent, I wasn't happy with it. There seemed to be quite a few bits of "analytic" interpretation of me, or of my personality, which I felt she had no right to be making.

She was not my therapist or analyst. So I took exception to those bits that I felt were out of place, or seemed to be unfounded opinion.

Eventually, Elspeth rewrote the whole thing, ending with the comment: "If you want to know the kind of person Patrick *really* is, you should see how he came to rewrite most of this appraisal himself!" I felt that was a fair comment.

My first visit upon joining FWA

During my initial week I was given plenty of time to acquaint myself with the office and the kind of work I would be doing. I was then allocated my first task.

I was to visit an Irish woman who already had six children, but on top of that she then had twins. She'd been to see the local priest who, I learned, was almost certainly Neville Symington (later to become a psychoanalyst). He had then been a Roman Catholic priest in that same area of London. He'd given this woman dispensation to use contraception and she'd been prescribed the "pill" by her GP. I was to visit her, to make sure she really understood how to use this.

After meeting this woman for the first time, hearing generally about her life, about her children and meeting the twins, I gradually steered the conversation round to the purpose of my visit.

"I understand that your local priest has given you permission to be using the contraceptive pill," I said. "I've been asked to visit you to make sure you really understand how you are meant to be taking this." She replied: "Oh, that. Don't worry yourself about it. Every night, my hubby and I, *we both take the pills, religious*: indeed we do." I then had to explain to her that this wasn't quite what was intended. I didn't actually go into the strange effects it might eventually have on her husband, but I certainly wondered about that.

Smoked salmon fish cakes

Another visit I used to make was to a single mother with her brood of children. She told me one day that she had a really useful tip for other poor families. Perhaps I would like to pass this on to them. She'd found a fish shop in Petticoat Lane that offered smoked salmon pieces for one shilling a pound. These were the bits left over after they had sliced the rest of a salmon, which was always sold for a high price. She told me that you could get at least a pound of smoked salmon from two pounds of pieces, using a very sharp knife and cutting along the skin. She showed me how to do it.

I got home and told Margaret about this useful tip. "Don't worry about other poor families," she said: "What about us? Get down there yourself and bring some of those pieces back here." So I did just that, and I would quite often come home with my two pounds of pieces bought for *two shillings*.

Years later, Margaret and I were again walking down Petticoat Lane and the fish shop was still there. I could also see that they were still selling smoked salmon pieces. So, for old time's sake, I asked (as before) for two pounds of pieces. "That will be two pounds," I was told. I was staggered, and said to the man: "The last time I bought two pounds of pieces it only cost me two shillings." With typical Cockney quickness, he immediately replied: "Well, next time, don't leave it so long!" I thought that was marvellous.

Referral meetings

Each week we would have a formal referral meeting at which Doris, the office secretary, would present us with applications and requests for help, along with new referrals that we would need to make decisions about and to allocate.

One week, Doris brought in a letter she'd just received. As this is from at least forty years ago, I feel I can now copy this letter exactly as it was, *the spelling mistakes included*.

The Social Officer,
Advisory Bureau,
59, Myddelton Square.

Dear Sir,
Please advise me what I can do about this matter.

My senior tenant has been living in my house for the past five years. His wife joined him on the first two years he moved to my house.

It appears his wife is not reliable. She develops unusual interest in me though I do not respons. She tempted me on many occasions so that I may have an affairs with her. I warned her seriously on each occasion as it is against my principle.

231

One day she said she wanted to show something to me in her room. Before I got there she had removed her cloth. I ran out immediately.

I sought advise from my friend who was living in my house at the time. The man advised me to tell her the likely consequences if I should be having sex with her and the husband suspected us. He said I could give her ten shillings for her child who is with the nanny so that she may be listening to me. I did as advised but it did not work.

She always invites me to her room when her husband is away. About two years ago when her neighbour—that is a young man living next room to her—suspected her she complained to her husband that that neighbour wanted to have an affair with her. I told that man to be very careful in dealing with her though I knew what kind of lady she is. The man left my house at once.

The new tenant who occupied the room afterwards had not spent more than six months before that lady alleged him again. The man moved out of my house immediately I warned him.

A few days ago or to be more precise on 12.2.1968 a young man who came to this lady was promptly hiden in the toilet. I knocked at the door of the toilet to urinate before I left for Chelmsford and I found the man there. I asked him whom he wanted and he mentioned that lady.

At about 9 pm on that day, 12.2.1968, the husband of this lady told me that I must be careful of his wife. I pressed him to let me know what had happened but he did not say anything.

I realized that it would be very difficult to establish a case of slander on that statement so I invited six men including the husband of that lady and his wife for a further discussion yesterday. The man did not respons. He later said that we could let that matter end like that.

I am sorry to have taken much of your time in reading this long story. What do you think I can do. They do not owe me any arrears of rent.

Yours faithfully,
NB. The two men alleged by that lady are in London.

I do not remember how we chose to respond to this.

232

Poetry by Doris (the office secretary)

Doris had a considerable flair for writing poetry, especially when any member of the staff left, or for other special occasions—as when Elspeth had her first baby. Doris then wrote to her:

To Elspeth

> Welcome to the ranks of "mum"
> Though you've been one for years to some.
> But here's one who you'll not transfer
> whatever cost it may incur.
>
> His "acting out" will make you sad,
> His temper tantrums make you mad.
> The text books then will seem a farce
> so turn him up and smack his arse.

A group dynamics course

While I was at the FWA I was invited to take part, as a member of staff, in a fortnight's group dynamics course put on by the BAP (British Association of Psychotherapists). We met for four evenings each week, starting in what were known as "primary groups" and then moving into "inter-group" exercises. It was run by Paul de Berker, Ilse Seglow, and Robert Andry.

One thing from that course that I've always remembered was in the first group I was in. There was one participant called Dr. Wonchonsky. When we introduced ourselves, this man (assuming that we would not be able to pronounce his name) told us we should call him "Wong".

Throughout the two weeks, this man, who came to be known as *"Call me Wong"*, became a natural scapegoat. This scapegoat problem eventually took over each group he was in. And, on the last evening but one, this came to paralyse the plenary session too.

During this plenary, "Call me Wong" got into some extraordinary interaction with the "plenary group", eventually complaining that everyone was misunderstanding him. He ended by standing up, shaking his finger at the group, and said: "I have been saying *this, this, and this*. But you have been telling me I have been saying *that, that, and that*. So who is right? *Am I right or am I wrong?*"

233

At the staff meeting, after that evening, people were demanding to know who had allowed "Wong" on the course? It turned out to have been Ilse Seglow; thereafter everyone was turning on her, saying she had spoiled the whole course. Eventually, Paul de Berker pointed out that the scapegoat dynamic had now begun to take over the staff group as well.

That night I had a dream about the course. The next evening, when we came to the final plenary the same thing began to happen, with "Wong" again becoming the focus of the entire group, and nobody seemed to be able to shift the focus away from him.

Eventually, in an attempt to do something about this relentless dynamic that was holding the whole group in its grip, I said I'd had a dream the previous night, which could be about this, and I told it to them:

> In my dream I was in a room full of people, just like this one, and I found myself getting into an argument with the group. I had been accusing this large group of having failed to understand me. I then found myself saying exactly what had been said here last night and my words to the group were: "I've been saying this, this, and this. But you have been telling me I've been saying that, that, and that. So who is right? Am I right *or am I "Wong"*?

I had woken up laughing. When the group heard the reported slip of my tongue from my dream, there was a burst of laughter that was quickly followed by an embarrassed silence. Then someone said the room had become rather hot, could he open the window?

It soon became clear that "Wong" had been behaving in a way that we all regarded as a bit mad. But it seemed we had not been able to let go of him as our scapegoat, perhaps because he seemed to represent some madness that we, the participants, wished not to see in ourselves. So, having found a scapegoat to hand, who so readily represented all the madness we did not want to find in ourselves, the group seemed to have held "Wong" caught in that role. It was only when they were confronted with this dynamic, and their disowning of madness into "Wong", that the group could move onto other matters.

A lecture on "non accidental injury"

During the time I was principal at the Area 4 office of FWA, I arranged for the staff to attend a lecture at the London Hospital on the subject of non accidental injury (NAI). We were told of the signs we should look for, when a child was found to have been injured and the explanations given to account for this seeming to be a bit suspect. We would then be better able to recognise the possibility that a child could be at risk when suspicious injuries were noticed.

After the lecture we all came back to the office in Myddelton Square, for the weekly lunch that had become a tradition in our office. This had been started by Elspeth (principal) who is a fine cook. She then managed to sell the idea to the staff that they would take it in turns to cook a lunch for all of us. We put money in a kitty so that we could be all together for this office meal. However, when I became principal I'd made it clear I was not going to be one of the cooks, there being seven female members of staff who took turns between them.

On the day of this NAI lecture, it had been arranged that Margaret would come to join us for that week's lunch, bringing Hanna with her. But, when she arrived, I was shocked to see that Hanna had the biggest black eye I'd ever seen on a child. How about that for NAI?

Margaret explained that they had been spending the morning with friends and Hanna had fallen down the entire flight of stairs. She had stepped on a loose end of her tights. Then, stepping off with the other foot now trapped, she'd fallen headlong. It was quite embarrassing having to hear Margaret giving us this explanation on that day of all days.

Mrs. Elliott

One of my jobs was to visit some people who had been allocated a small pension administered by the FWA. One of the recipients was Mrs. Elliott, in her early nineties. She was a tiny little lady, very frail, and her only companion was her granddaughter Stevie, who once came to babysit Hanna and Bella.

Mrs. Elliott had recently tried to get a job but she hadn't been offered it. They'd said she was too old. She had tried to get away with saying she was *only seventy*, but they said they would not appoint anyone who was over retiring age. "Perhaps I should have said I was sixty," she said. "Maybe they would've given me a chance then."

Mrs. Elliott was extremely deaf, so much so that it was almost impossible to speak to her except by shouting. Her hearing aid was nearly always squealing, whenever she tried to turn it up, because the microphone part of it would be too close to her ear—picking up the noise from the earpiece. It was that feedback which made it squeal.

After several abortive efforts at making myself heard, I had the bright idea of getting Mrs. Elliott to hand me the microphone part of her hearing aid, taking it out from where she usually kept it. This made it possible for me to hold this as far away from her earpiece as the wire would allow, and I could then turn up the volume without any feedback problem at all. By these means she could hear me quite well even when I was talking at a normal level.

One Christmas Eve, Stevie telephoned the office to say Mrs. Elliott had been hit by a car on a pedestrian crossing just by her block of flats. She'd dashed out to the shops to get some last thing for Christmas, and a car had knocked her down. She was in the Whittington Hospital.

I went to visit Mrs. Elliott. She was in a huge ward with about twenty other people. There she was, seeming to be even more small and frail than ever, with her main hearing pack stuffed down her nightie. I had to shout until we got things organised in the way that I'd shown her.

"Hello, Mrs. Elliott," I shouted. Everyone turned to see who was speaking so loud. "Get it out then, Mrs. Elliott," I shouted again, but I hadn't catered for having an audience. All eyes turned to see what I was up to now, while Mrs. Elliott began digging into her nightie as if she was looking for one of her breasts. I was most relieved when she was able to hand me her hearing pack and I was then able to say, in a much quieter voice: "Are you hearing me now? Loud and clear?" After that we could proceed as usual without any further shouting.

Meeting the queen

While I was still with the FWA we celebrated our centenary. The queen, being our patron, came to meet the staff.

We were all drilled on the matter of how to behave when meeting the queen. Amongst other things, we were not to speak to her unless spoken to. I was tempted to say that this would mean I could not ask the queen if she realised her husband had slept in my bed (thinking of the time when the Duke of Edinburgh had stayed with my parents at Krefeld). On the other hand, if she happened to ask me if it was true that her husband had slept in my bed, I could say to her: "Yes, ma'am."

When the day came, the queen was going round the room in which we had about thirty members of FWA staff ready to meet her. I could hear the questions she was asking the others, stopping to speak to every third person, so I knew what would be her question to me: "What kind of problems do you come across, working here?"

I'd already decided that I wasn't going to go into things like rent arrears, or relationship difficulties. Instead I replied: "Not enough men in this organisation." The queen looked round the room and said: "Yes. I can see that, now you point it out to me. *I suppose it is always useful to have a man in the house, to mend the fuses and things.*" I just loved her response and this indication of her view of a man in the house.

Our centenary appeal

The FWA was granted a five minute slot on the radio in which we could appeal for funds to further the work of the agency, this being allowed us on account of that being our centenary year.

All had been going well, and it is possible we might have received a big boost for the work of the FWA had it not been for the last few moments of the appeal. The person reading out the prepared text for this had ended by saying: "The FWA caters for all kinds of people in need, *from the cradle until the grave: until the final solution.*" We never found out who had approved that text, but it was fatal for our appeal as it repeated the dreaded words of Hitler in his plan for the Holocaust. We imagined many wealthy Jewish people putting away their cheque-books in disgust, no longer wanting to donate to the FWA.

Travel expenses

One of my chores as principal was to check the expense claims for travel. We were paid something like sixpence a mile and we were meant to note down how far we'd driven on days when we were home visiting.

One person, however, was always behind with this; sometimes as much as three months behind. This was Julia Laurence. Trying to help her to see that her travel expenses did not have to be calculated with an obsessional attention to accuracy, I said to her: "Don't think that you have to note every journey, how far it was. After a while, you will get a sense of how far your most usual journeys are. Just put down *how far it feels.*"

Julia took me at my word. Very promptly after that I received three months of her expenses, which I duly checked. However, there was one visit each week that didn't make sense. Most journeys were about eight or ten miles, sometimes twelve or fifteen. But each week there was one journey that Julia had noted as being thirty miles. We didn't see any families that could take us that far, even on a journey there and back. When I asked Julia about this she replied: "You did tell me to say *how far it feels*. Well, *that journey feels like thirty miles*. I hate visiting that family!"

"Power person" or "people person"?

At this time I was working a few hours as a psychotherapist, having completed my training with the BAP. I had also begun a further training, with the London Institute of Psychoanalysis, to become a psychoanalyst.

Even though I had become principal of Area 4 in the FWA, I began to be restless for a better paid job. But I didn't want to lose working face to face with clients, which I was so enjoying. It therefore began to look as if I might have to remain a fieldworker if I was not going to lose that contact, and I knew that I didn't want to get involved in management.

However, Margaret noticed a post being advertised in Ealing, where the Rev Nick Stacey was director of social services. This looked ideal as it was for an assistant director of social services (fieldwork), much better paid, and I already knew something about Nick Stacey. He was ordained and I had read theology. Also, he was said to have fancied Christina (my sister-in-law) at some time, as well as each of her three sisters, so I would have some points of contact with him if I met him.

I wrote to Stacey asking if I could meet him to discuss the possibility of applying for this job that he was advertising. We did meet, and at the end of an hour he summed up the issues: "Well, Patrick, I am going to be perfectly frank with you. There are two kinds of people: 'power people' and 'people people'. I, Patrick, am a power person and I'm looking for another power person to work alongside me. You, Patrick, are a people person so I will not be short listing you for this job." That was very clear and a most useful comment. I didn't apply.

I soon had the opportunity to train again, to become a psychoanalyst.[1]

Julia's death

When Julia joined the office it was known that she had a serious heart condition. Indeed, she often had blue lips which kept us mindful of this.

Not long after I'd left, Julia had the heart attack we had all dreaded and she died at home in the arms of her partner, who was banging on the party wall trying to get help.

Doris, of course, came up trumps as always. As soon as I heard of Julia's death I wrote to the office and I received the following letter from Doris. I quote it here as it gives a real sense of the family feeling that had grown up in that office.

> Dear Patrick,
>
> I was very glad to hear from you as I know how this news must have affected you, knowing Julia for as long as you did.
>
> It has been something of a relief to work here because everyone wants to talk about her. Laraine (Doris's daughter) was very upset and wanted to come to the office to be with people who knew Julia, and she was reduced to tears on reading your letter.
>
> I've put what I feel down as usual on paper. Perhaps you would like to see it. I'll enclose it. [The poem is below.]
>
> I was telling the group here (we had a sort of sit down discussion yesterday to bring it all out) that when Julia first came here you told us straight away about her health hazard and we were almost following her about to catch her when it happened, but somehow that passed and the shock of the actual thing happening is very great indeed. On Friday she just went, and all we said was: "Cheerio. See you."
>
> Must close now Patrick. Love, Doris.

Doris, of course, also wrote one of her poems for Julia:

> To Julia
>
> The gnarled black hand of death has teased,
> played with, prodded, paused ... and seized
> OUR JULIA

239

No time to say how much we care
No chance for us to ask "Please spare"
OUR JULIA

Life to us all is just on loan
But richer now for having known
OUR JULIA.

Doris had a terrible relationship with her husband Ron. As she said of him: "He played away something awful," but he still expected her to look after him, which she did.

When Ron died, Doris told me the next day (while typing my letters) that he'd been "playing ill" in the kitchen, as he often had, saying that he was about to die. He then collapsed with a heart attack, and that was that.

Doris was naturally sad, but also relieved, and she subsequently wrote the following poem which alludes to her relationship with Ron. She told me that it had been inspired by a challenge set her at the writing course she'd been going to. The teacher had given them three words which they each had to incorporate in a poem or short story. This is the poem Doris wrote on the three words given: *Inspiration—Dandelion—Horse*:

She was your **inspiration** for better times ahead.
At least that's what you told her, to get her into bed.
Accusing brought denials with no signs of remorse.
You'd found a shallow new love and I had found a **horse**.
She had become your orchid and I your **dandelion**,
But all through your illness the hassle was all mine!
How could my love survive it—the anguish and the pain?
The answer is it didn't—but I miss you all the same.

Doris later told me about the funeral. She had spoken to the priest beforehand, asking him not to treat this as a very sad occasion. "It really isn't that sad," she said, "in fact, this is the first time in years I've known where Ron is." The priest had quoted this in his address, and Ron's mates had all laughed, knowing how true this comment was.

Doris's grandmother

For a time there were five generations in Doris's family: her mother and grandmother; her daughter Laraine (who had been telephonist in the office while I was there) and Laraine's children and Doris's son Paul's children.

Sometime after leaving FWA, I was driving past Myddelton Square, having just given a lecture at the Royal Naval College, Greenwich (at my brother's request), so I called in to see Doris. I found her very busy on the phone: "Lovely to see you, but I can't chat now. I'm having to gather the clan as Gran is dying."

I later heard that Doris had gathered the family, getting a number of them to meet in Bart's Hospital beside her grandmother's bed. A doctor was attending to the grandmother when Laraine arrived: "You are too late," he said before departing. "She's just died."

At this point a family argument broke out, all backs turned to the body on the bed, with different members of the family arguing about a bureau they each claimed their Gran had promised to leave to *them*.

While this argument was going on, a faint voice was heard from behind them: "Don't be in such a hurry. I'm not gone yet." So their Gran was still alive even though the doctor had just declared her dead, and he would have been writing out her death certificate had they not been there to stop this.

Note

1. In 1977, when I'd just qualified as a psychoanalyst, I wrote to Nick Stacey who was by that time director of social services in Kent. I told him I'd trained as a psychoanalyst, having followed his advice, and I was now a qualified *people* person. He replied with congratulations.

CHAPTER SIXTEEN

We finally settle

"Where is that rope going?" I meet up with someone who owes me a lot of money

Mansfield Road

When we moved from Coleridge Walk, where we had two rooms upstairs and one down, we moved to a house that was huge by comparison.

Trying to make this new house feel less strange for Hanna and Bella, I went out (on New Year's Eve) to buy *another* Christmas tree that I set up in what was to be our sitting room. I decorated this with the twinkling lights that I'd made especially for this. There being no such thing in those days, I had made a set of lights that did what we can now readily buy in shops. It made our tree unique in those days, all the lights twinkling. I also prepared the girls' bedroom, with their bunk beds and toys, just as it had been for them in their previous room.

These preparations certainly helped them to settle them in, but for a long time after that Hanna referred to our sitting room as she'd first seen it. She would call out for Margaret: "Mum, where are you?" Margaret, who might be on any one of the four floors of this unfamiliar house, would call back: "I'm here." But Hanna couldn't make out where "here" was. She'd call back: "Are you in the Christmas tree room?"

243

Hot pitta bread

When Bella was just three, she was invited out to a restaurant for lunch with her friend Catherine Kenyatta (granddaughter of President Kenyatta) and her mother Carol. She came back from this adventure with her eyes wide with excitement: "You'll never guess what we had to eat. We had *hot gloves!*" She'd discovered that she could open up the half pitta breads, turning them into something just like her mittens, which she could fit over her hands. She was thrilled with this discovery.

Putting in a dormer window

While we had builders working in the house, after we'd first arrived at Mansfield Road, they asked me if I would like them to put in a dormer window into the attic bedroom. It would cost £500, as money was then. It seemed a good idea and it certainly made a huge difference to the room, extending the floor space considerably.

Some time after that I received an alarming letter from my NatWest bank. We had our account at their head office (21 Lombard Street) and we may have been among the first customers to be using the head office rather than a local bank. Our account number was really quite low, then being *57088*.

Just before seeing a patient, I'd opened a letter from the bank which stated that my account was hugely overdrawn (in today's money it would have been at least £15,000), this being due to an amount of £570.88 having been drawn from the bank that day. They said that they *didn't have the details to hand* but that would be sent to me as soon as they became available.

I went into a flat spin, unable to imagine how this had happened. Then I remembered the estimate for the dormer window. Perhaps the builder had been late in sending in my payment for that. I would have to check that as soon as I had a moment free from seeing patients. In the meantime I was barely able to listen to my next two patients as I was still worrying about this, and wondering how on earth I was going to get out of this unexpected debt.

However, it suddenly struck me. It looked as if my account number may have been debited in error! I rang the bank as soon as I could and it seemed that this may indeed have been what had happened. The bank had only recently gone over to using computers and someone may have been interrupted when entering something in my account, perhaps entering the account number a second time. I could barely believe that a bank could do such a thing, and this was by no means the first time that I'd been thrown into a state of alarm through errors made at the bank. I therefore decided to write to Esther Rantzen, who was then exposing just this sort of muddle in her weekly TV programme *That's Life*. I also sent a copy to the bank:

THAT'S LIFE,
BBC,
Wood Lane, W12

Dear Esther Rantzen,

I am wondering whether I am receiving special treatment from my bank. In the past year there have been four major failures to follow written instructions relating to transactions between deposit account and current account, each time creating a false overdraft when the money said to have been deposited in one place turned out to be somewhere else instead. The most recent error, this week, was a cheque which was temporarily credited at £100 but subsequently withdrawn and referred to sender. The debt adjustment for this was entered as £700, bringing about another apparent overdraft. Those errors are just in this past year.

On previous occasions, credits have been confused between my brother's account and mine, though we have quite different initials and different addresses. On one occasion my monthly statement, then in a most unhealthy state, was sent to my brother, to his great interest and my embarrassment.

However, my favourite error so far was on 1.11.73 when I was informed: "We regret that the following item listed on your statement sheet is missing. We will forward this as soon as possible," the debit item being for £570.88. My account was then said to be about £500 in overdraft, hence the premature statement.

It later transpired that the bank had debited my account number, which is 57088, presumably for good measure! I suppose I could change my bank, but not only has my family banked with the National Westminster Bank (their head office actually) for years, but my wife's previous bank wasn't much better. Is it becoming a general practice for banks to pay only cursory attention to detail, and is it for the creating and undoing of these muddles that we pay our bank charges?

Yours sincerely,
Patrick Casement
Copy to Chairman, Nat. Westminster Bank Ltd.,
21 Lombard Street, EC3

I didn't get a reply from Esther Rantzen, but I did from NatWest. I received a letter of apology and concern from the chairman, inviting me to have luncheon in the directors' suite when they would be glad to discuss these problems with me. Margaret quickly pointed out that the errors in question were on our *joint* account, so she would expect to be included. I replied, saying that my wife and I would be glad to accept the invitation to discuss the problems relating to our account over luncheon.

We had at least two pink gins before lunch, and very fine wine with the soup and more fine wine with the meat, followed by coffee and liqueurs. We'd arrived at midday and left around 3 pm, rather unsteady on our feet—but we had certainly had a very good meal.

As I was being helped into my coat, one of the managers who had been present said that I should call on him at any time we might need special treatment, for instance if requiring finance for the purchase of a car. I thanked him for this and for the meal, and I added that I should, perhaps, also let Esther Rantzen know that my letter to her had provided us with an excellent meal at the head office of NatWest. "Oh, please don't do that," was the immediate reply.

Margaret and I then weaved our way to Bank Underground station, feeling that we'd had a most successful meeting at the head office of NatWest. Indeed we had.

"The Sandman can't come"

When Hanna was still at school she took a message from a patient of mine, a Mr. Sandman. He said: "Please tell Mr. Casement that *Sandman can't come tonight*." Hanna left me this message adding: "So you will just have to count sheep!" She was clearly familiar with the children's lullaby about the sandman who will come to send children to sleep!

246

"Where is that rope going?"

While Hanna and Bella were still at primary school, I was driving them up Pond Street on the way to a birthday party. As we approached the junction with Haverstock Hill, they noticed two children pulling on a very long rope, which disappeared round the corner. One of them said: "Where is that rope going, Dad?"

Once we had turned the corner I was delighted to see where the rope did go. On a seat, just round the corner, was someone I recognised. He'd been firmly tied to this seat by his two boys, clearly as part of some game. I said to Hanna and Bella: "I can now see where that rope goes. It goes straight to a man who owes me a lot of money."

It so happened that this man had been seeing me previously as a patient, and I'd mistakenly allowed him to build up a debt to me rather than have his therapy end prematurely. He'd been due to receive a significant sum of money, but when he had ended his therapy he'd not paid any of his debt; nor had he replied to any of my letters. So, after I'd delivered Hanna and Bella to their party, I went back to this man who was still tied up. Having parked my car I went up to him, saying: "It seems most timely, finding you here," I said. "Perhaps we can now come to some arrangement about the money you still owe me." He agreed to this and paid me within the week.

Going on holidays

We never seemed to be able to stop Hanna and Bella getting into squabbles in the back of the car, when on holiday, these often being about who was said to have most room on the back seat. We later tried having an armrest in the middle of the seat, choosing our next car with this in mind. But the problem then seemed to be who had *most of the armrest*, this being measured (by eye) to the nearest millimetre. Nothing seemed to work until we had the inspired idea of putting a friend in the back seat. So, for the following times that we went on holiday by car, we would take one of their friends, sitting between them to keep them apart, and this worked really well.

Trying to shield three adolescent beauties from Italian boys

On one holiday we went to Florence. There we were followed by a pack of boys who were trying to flirt with our two girls and the friend who'd come too. One boy managed to get up close enough to whisper in Bella's

247

ear: *"Bella."* She looked up, wide-eyed with pleasure, and said: "They even know my name!"

Bella's trip round South America

Bella quickly asserted her independence from us, planning to go round most of South America with two friends. We were terrified, knowing of the dangers they might encounter there, but we fully supported Bella's decision to go.

To help me with the anxiety of this trip I programmed my computer to display the date and to state beside this *days still to go*. I was counting every day until Bella returned.

"It's all right now, Dad"

About ten days into this trip I was sitting in my consulting room, during a ten minute break between patients, when the phone went. It was Bella ringing from South America, our first call since she left. She then told me that, the day before, they'd set off in the lorry they travelled in (there were about twenty of them) to go south from Bogota. But, as they'd approached a corner in the road, a jeep had driven very fast round this, in reverse, someone waving at them and shouting for them to get out. They'd returned to Bogota for the night, hearing that there had been guerrillas firing at traffic on the road.

The next day, they'd driven back to the same spot, having heard that it might be all right then. Round the corner, from where they had been stopped the day before, they found a bus and an ambulance that had both been burned out.

I had just a few minutes in which to recover from this shocking news, knowing that Bella still had some three more months of her trip ahead of her. I needed to get some of this off my chest before seeing my next patient; I therefore tried to ring my wife Margaret where she was working, but she was engaged.

I then rang my mother, knowing she was always sitting by the 'phone hoping it would ring. She "saved the day" as she just didn't understand what I'd told her. Having repeated to her what Bella had said, she replied: "But isn't that interesting. *How did the gorillas get hold of matches*?" This misunderstanding was just magnificent, and it did the trick. From being nearly in tears about the dangers on Bella's trip, my eyes were then wet with laughter. I was entirely recovered by the time my next patient arrived.

Bella learning to use a camera

One of Bella's boyfriends had let her use his very fine camera, he planning to teach her how to make the best use of it. One part of this education was for her to learn how to use a telephoto lens. For this, the boyfriend suggested they went down to Glastonbury: "It might be possible to get some interesting shots of people down there."

When in Glastonbury, this boyfriend had noticed, from a distance, a couple of hippies sitting on a bench. "That should make a good photo," he'd suggested, so he lined Bella up to take a telephoto shot of them. "Just zoom in until you get what you want, and then shoot." Bella began to do as she'd been told, but then she shouted out: "Good heavens, one of those hippies is *my sister*!" And so it was.

A visit to Hungary

Because of my first book (*On Learning from the Patient*) in 1987 I was invited to speak to the *Sándor Ferenczi* Society in Budapest. The day before going I was faxed by the person who had invited me, asking me if I thought the Hungarian Psychoanalytical Society should also be invited to my lecture. Clearly he had not told them I was coming, so I asked him to let them know.

Margaret came with me on this trip, which was most fortunate as I needed her company, especially when we were kept waiting for an hour at the airport before being met there. Then, when we were taken to the auditorium (for 200 people) where I was to read my paper, we found that there were only *four people* there apart from Margaret and me. Someone immediately ran to the library where he was able to persuade three other people to attend. I then had a total audience of eight people, including Margaret.

Before this lecture I had been presented with a fee of £25, paid for by the university in Budapest, for which I had to sign four copies of receipt. Then, after the lecture we took our hosts out to dinner at a restaurant of their choosing. I had been told, in London, that this was the custom when being invited to speak in a Soviet country, and Hungary was then still under communism. When the bill was presented to me after the meal I found that it came to exactly the fee I had just received. The trip so far had not cost me anything except for our air fares.

It had been made clear to me, when I was invited, that I would have to come at my own expense. However, my hosts would provide us with accommodation. What they did not explain was that this accommodation would be far outside the city. I thought they could have helped us to find a hotel in Budapest itself, at our own expense, but they had simply told us that our accommodation had been arranged.

After being driven for some miles outside Budapest, far beyond the lighted streets, we were taken up an unmarked side road until we came to a large redbrick building with a notice outside in Hungarian and English. This stated that we had come to a "Psychiatric Hospital for the Rehabilitation of Psycho-Neurotics". This was where we were to stay! We were then shown to a four-bedded ward, adjacent to an antiquated shower with very old slippery boards on a stone floor. We were to eat alongside the staff and patients.

It was immediately clear to us that, if we took a taxi next day into Budapest, we might never find our way back to this "hotel" and our luggage. So, after a rather hurried breakfast we "discharged ourselves" from this hospital and fled by taxi back to Budapest, where we signed into a rather swish hotel.

The next day we went across the river into Buda, which overlooks Pest, where we saw a very large crowd outside the main church. Suspecting that something significant was about to be happen there, we waited to see what was going on. We then saw a wedding couple enter the church followed by some very important person, to whom many of the crowd bowed low as he passed. We later learned, back in the hotel, that this had been none other than Archduke Otto von Hapsburg, the head of the House of Hapsburg.

When I gave to my accountant the details of this visit I entered the fee I had received, £25, and the expenses (travel and hotel) which came to £800. He said that this might be allowed just this once, but I should not make a regular habit of this kind of thing.

Visiting the Austen Riggs Center

In 2006 I was invited to give a paper at the Austen Riggs Center in Massachusetts. For this I had to fly to New York where I changed planes to get to Boston. I was then met and driven for two hours to my hotel.

This hotel boasted of being either the oldest hotel in America or the oldest hotel in that state, and so it might well have been. But there were problems with this from the outset.

When I went to check in I was told that I'd already been checked in, which had been a mistake. This meant they had already allocated my room to someone else, so they would have to sort this out. "Perhaps you would accept a drink on the house at the bar," they suggested. I was happy to oblige.

At the bar, being tired from my long journey, I asked for a large whisky. Large it certainly was, especially as I'd asked for it to be without ice so the barman seemed to have no idea of how much whisky to pour into my glass.

After I'd enjoyed my whisky I went to collect the keys to the replacement room, which by that time had been found for me. But when I got to this new room I found that the bathroom was completely out of action. Pipes were hanging loose from the walls, all being disconnected. So I had to return to the reception desk to ask for yet another room to be found for me.

By this time there was someone new on the desk so, as an apology for the inconvenience, I was invited (as before) to "have a drink on the house" at the bar. I returned to find the same barman serving. "The same again, please," I asked, and I was handed another huge glass of whisky. I was beginning to enjoy this inconvenience.

Eventually I was given keys to the new room that they'd found for me, where I decided I would have a hot bath before going to supper. But, as soon as I made to lie back in the bath, the overhead rails holding up the shower curtain fell on my head. But I was much more amused than injured by this.

Later, on my way to the dining room, I reported the latest problem with my search for a serviceable room; and I almost had to beg them not to send me back to the bar yet again!

CHAPTER SEVENTEEN

The passing of an era

Four funerals (for two parents) and a birthday party

Our parents' golden wedding

In 1981 our parents had their golden wedding, which was held at Mills Farm House (the house they moved to after Terwick). A highlight of this was when Emma (Elisabeth's daughter), along with Hanna and Bella, put on the goatherd's song from *The Sound of Music*, which had always been a great hit with father.

The day after this golden wedding, mother was found to be very ill. She had been trying to conceal from us how ill she was, in order not to spoil the golden wedding day. She then had to be rushed into King Edward's Hospital, near Midhurst, where she remained for quite a long time.

Margaret and I visited nearly every weekend until there was one time when mother could not even lift her head from the pillow. She seemed so much weaker than she had been when we'd seen her the weekend before. I therefore telephoned Michael in America and said that, if he wanted to see mother again, he might need to come straight away.

While this was going on father was into arranging for mother's funeral. He had everything worked out; the hymns, the caterers, and what he would then do with his life.

Michael duly arrived and his presence seemed to shock mother into realising he was only there because she could be dying. She wasn't having that. She turned a corner and didn't die, and those funeral arrangements became redundant.

Father's death

Father died (10th March 1987) exactly as he would have wished. He died fishing. He'd long had a copy of what was known as *The fisherman's prayer*, which was hung in the *gents* downstairs. This began "May God grant that I may fish until my dying day," and his wish was granted. Michael (by this time a licensed lay reader) gave a fine address at the funeral, as he did also when mother died.

Wistaria Cottage

It seemed necessary to move mother from Mills Farm House, then too big for her, to something smaller and more central in Rogate. Michael was able to find the ideal house, Wistaria (sic) Cottage and he worked hard to persuade mother to accept this move. She was very reluctant but finally, after much indecision and oscillating between "Yes" and "No", she said that she needed to sleep on it. Then, whatever she decided the next day it would be her final decision.

The next day mother had decided "Yes", she would move. Michael wasted no time, getting the solicitors to do all that was necessary to make this an irrevocable decision. By lunchtime mother had again changed her mind, but it was too late. It was, however, a good move even though it was very difficult for her, this being so soon after father had died.

A broken hip

In her later years mother broke a hip, trying to do something "helpful" in her bedroom, which meant she had to be in a hospital in Chichester for quite some time.

In the bed opposite her there was a woman who could be very difficult. She would argue with the nurses and complain when they didn't immediately do whatever she was asking for, or demanding. One day, in exasperation, this woman was heard to say: "But you don't seem to realise *who I was!*"

Backgammon

A regular event, every Friday, was for Michael's mother-in-law (Mrs. Maclean) to come round to play backgammon with mother.

I want to record here a conversation overheard by one of the carers, sometime in 2000, over this weekly game of backgammon. Mrs. Maclean was by then ninety-nine and very deaf and mother was ninety-two.

Mrs. Maclean	"What day is it?"
Mother	"I think it's Wednesday"
Mrs. Maclean	"Did you say 'Monday'?"
Mother	"No, WEDNESDAY"

At this point the carer came in and said to mother, "Actually, it's Friday."

Mrs. Maclean	"What did she say?"
Mother	"I think she said Wednesday"
Mrs. Maclean	"MONDAY? I thought it was Monday."

Once that had been settled they got on with their game of backgammon, playing with extraordinary speed, as always, but not always remembering who was playing which colour or which way round the board they were meant to be going!

"I think that mother may be dying"

Margaret and I were in Scotland visiting a friend and visiting Hanna. We then received a message from Michael to say that he thought mother was dying. This, now, for the second time. He told us not to kill ourselves trying to get back, but could we come as quickly as possible?

We collected Hanna and set off south. When we got to Wistaria Cottage, we each had a few minutes with mother. When it was my turn to be with her she'd been trying to get her words out. And I, leaning over her, had been trying to hear what might be her last words. Very slowly, and with a gasp for breath between each word, she had managed to say "I ... think ... I ... have ... lost ... my ... *teeth*!" She was clearly very weak but these were not to be her last words.

Michael spelled out to us that the doctor had visited and he'd said that mother might go any moment, possibly while we were there. At least it was unlikely she would survive the night, so Michael had made all the necessary arrangements.

Obviously, this being a Wednesday, it would be rather rushing things to have the funeral on the Saturday of the same week. But it would work out well if we went for the following Saturday. He'd therefore checked with the vicar, and he would be able to take the funeral on that following Saturday. Michael had also booked the village hall, for afterwards, and he had the caterers all lined up to provide whatever was necessary. Waiting for that later Saturday would also allow time for two of Michael's children to get back from their holidays, so that they could also be present.

However, at this point Sue said it wouldn't work for *her* children. Couldn't we have the body put on ice so that the funeral could be another week later, which would allow two of her children to get back to England for it too?

Michael, who'd been through no end of hassle over the past months—and years, needed us to stay with his arrangements. He didn't want any of us to be complicating things.

The next morning, however, mother sat up in bed and made it clear she wanted to be dressed and allowed to be in the garden. She then sat there, waving to her friends as they passed by the gate. Those funeral arrangements also became redundant. She lived for another two years.

Four funerals (for two parents) and a birthday party

As it turned out we had four funerals arranged for our parents, almost echoing the film *Four Weddings and a Funeral*. One was for father and three were for mother. Fortunately, she was not ready for either of the first two.

100th birthday party

Hanna had the brilliant idea that, as we no longer had occasions to meet as a large family, now that both of our parents were dead, it might be a good idea to have a party to celebrate her grandfather's 100th birthday. And so it was that we had this splendid party at Little Hidden Farm, with Sue and Bill providing a specially cleaned-out barn for this. It really was a great event, made all the more special in that Bella was able to be there with her husband (Duncan) and her first two children who were over from Australia in time for this.

Hanna, in my opinion, crowned the day with her comment:

> What a very strange family we must be, arranging funerals for someone who hadn't yet died and now a birthday party for someone who is no longer alive.

Such was our family, and so it has been for as long as I have been a member of it. But I have much enjoyed all of that strangeness.

* * *

So, where have I got to on my journey? As I think that we start to die when we stop growing, I hope it will still be some time before I finally become "grown-up" and begin to feel bored. At least my first eighty years, so far, have never been boring.